A Rhombus

J U N G

O N   A C T I V E   I M A G I N A T I O N

Pg 32·33 → what to do w/ the unconscious fantasies
how to answer to the images, fantasies
that occur.

feeling/critical — parallel process — displacement!!
Share
anxiety in session?

p 86 psychotherapeutic successes and failures
- can go along w/ inadequate theory, but not w/ inadequate
therapeutic techniques

DM Ap 02 — wandering into a shallow sea
where Ro schools of fish differentiate from a
massed shoals into black rotating circles

ENCOUNTERING

JUNG

JUNG ON ALCHEMY

JUNG ON EVIL

JUNG ON ACTIVE IMAGINATION

JUNG ON MYTHOLOGY

ENCOUNTERING

JUNG

ON ACTIVE IMAGINATION

EDITED AND WITH AN INTRODUCTION BY JOAN CHODOROW

PRINCETON UNIVERSITY PRESS · PRINCETON, NEW JERSEY

Published by Princeton University Press, 41 William Street,
Princeton, New Jersey 08540
In the United Kingdom by Routledge, 11 New Fetter Lane, London EC4P 4EE

Typeset in Times by Ponting–Green Publishing Services, Chesham, Buckinghamshire

Library of Congress Cataloging-in-Publication Data

Jung, C. G. (Carl Gustav), 1875–1961.
[Essays. English. Selections]
Jung on active imagination / edited and with an introduction by Joan Chodorow.
p. cm. — (Encountering Jung)
Includes bibliographical references and index.
ISBN 0-691-01576-7 (pbk. : alk. paper)
1. Imagination. 2. Subconsciousness. 3. Psychoanalysis. 4. Jungian psychology.
5. Jung, C. G. (Carl Gustav), 1875–1961.
I. Chodorow, Joan, 1937– . II. Title. III. Series: Jung, C. G. (Carl Gustav), 1875–1961.
Selections. English. 1995.
BF173.J6623 1997
153.3—dc21 97-9422

Contents

List of illustrations   vii
List of abbreviations used in notes   viii
Acknowledgements   ix

Introduction   1

1 Confrontation with the unconscious   21

2 The transcendent function   42

3 'The technique of differentiation between the ego and the
   figures of the unconscious'   61

4 Commentary on *The Secret of the Golden Flower*   73

5 The aims of psychotherapy   84

6 A study in the process of individuation   97

7 The Tavistock lectures   143

8 The psychological aspects of the Kore   154

9 On the nature of the psyche   158

10 Three letters to Mr O. (1947)   163

11 *Mysterium Coniunctionis*   166

12 Foreword to van Helsdingen: *Beelden uit het Onbewuste*   175

Afterword: Post-Jungian contributions   177

Bibliography   180

List of fantasies and visions   186

Subject index   188
Name index   197

My most fundamental views and ideas derive from these experiences. First I made the observations and only then did I hammer out my views. And so it is with the hand that guides the crayon or brush, the foot that executes the dance-step, with the eye and the ear, with the word and the thought: a dark impulse is the ultimate arbiter of the pattern, an unconscious *a priori* precipitates itself into plastic form.

(C. G. Jung 1947, par. 402)

Illustrations

FROM *The Archetypes and the Collective Unconscious*
Picture 1   99
Picture 2   101
Picture 3   105
Picture 4   109
[*Figure 6.1*]   Sketch of a drawing by a young woman patient with
                 psychogenic depression from the beginning of the
                 treatment   110
Picture 5   113
Picture 6   115
Picture 7   116
Picture 8   119
Picture 9   121
Picture 10   124
Picture 11   126
Picture 12   128
Picture 13   128
Picture 14   129
Picture 15   129
Picture 16   130
Picture 17   131
Picture 18   131
Picture 19   132

FROM *The Tavistock Lectures*
[*Figure 7.1*]   Painting by a patient   149
[*Figure 7.2*]   Painting by a patient   151

List of abbreviations used in notes

Numbered notes at the end of the chapters are mainly previously published notes by Jung. Additional notes are from Aniela Jaffé [A.J.], Cary F. Baynes [C.F.B.], Joan Chodorow [J.C.], the editors of the *Collected Works* [EDITORS] and *Letters*. Works by Jung cited in the endnotes are identified by the following abbreviations.

MDR   *Memories, Dreams, Reflections* by C. G. Jung. Recorded and edited by Aniela Jaffé; translated by Richard and Clara Winston. See Jung 1961 in Bibliography.

CW   *The Collected Works of C. G. Jung*. Edited by Gerhard Adler, Michael Fordham, and Herbert Read; William McGuire, Executive Editor; translated primarily by R. F. C. Hull. New York and Princeton (Bollingen Series XX) and London (Routledge), 1953–83. 21 volumes.

Letters   *C. G. Jung: Letters*. Selected and edited by Gerhard Adler in collaboration with Aniela Jaffé; translations by R. F. C. Hull. Princeton (Bollingen Series XCV) and London (Routledge), 1973, 1975. 2 volumes.

Works by other authors cited in the endnotes are identified by title, author, or both. For more information on Jung's sources, see bibliographies at the end of CW volumes 7, 8, 9.I, 13, 14, 16, 18. Further abbreviations used in the notes include:

Cf.   confer, or compare

DV   *Deo volente*. God willing

f.   and the following page

ff.   and the following pages

fig.   figure

Ibid.   *ibidem*, in the same place (refers to a single work cited in the note immediately preceding)

n.d.   no date

ms.   manuscript

s.v.   *sub verbo*, under the word

viz.   *videlicet*, namely

Acknowledgements

When I first met Ruth Thacker Fry, she invited me into her office to see a notebook that contained everything she could find of Jung's writings on active imagination. This was many years ago, long before the time of desk computers, scanners or copy machines. Jung's papers had been typed on an old-fashioned typewriter, including scholarly footnotes and annotations. In a playful way she told me that it was not her idea, but her animus led her to do it. We both laughed, because I too know what it is to be seized by the spirit. As we looked through her notebook together, I asked if she planned to submit it for publication and she said no, there wasn't enough interest yet – but someday, a volume of Jung's papers on active imagination would be published. That unique collection was for her own use. Her passion for active imagination impressed me deeply. Dr. Fry, Founding Director of the C. G. Jung Educational Center of Houston passed away some years ago, but I trust she would be pleased that the time has come for *Jung on Active Imagination*. The early collection she compiled and edited is a source of inspiration for this work.

I am happy to say that *Jung on Active Imagination* will now be simultaneously published on both sides of the Atlantic. David Stonestreet initiated the project from London when he invited me to submit a proposal. For many years now I have been impressed with his vision of Jung and the depth of understanding he brings to his work. I am grateful also to Edwina Welham for her patience and skill in moving it all toward publication; to Patricia Stankiewicz for her fine desk editing; I owe a debt of gratitude to Jo Thurm and Judith Reading, all at Routledge in England. My appreciation to Deborah Tegarden at Princeton University Press in the United States, and to many others who work their magic as they transform a manuscript into a book.

My heartfelt thanks to Andrew Samuels for his interest, encouragement, and good ideas at many stages along the way. As advisor in Analytical Psychology to Routledge, and as colleague and friend, his contribution has been invaluable.

Renate Oppikofer's beautiful translation of a passage by Tina Keller has restored a long-lost piece of history about dance as a form of active imagination. Who would have believed that Toni Wolff was not only an early

Jungian analyst, but also perhaps the first dance therapist? (See my Introduction on p. 16.)

For me, the great gift of this study has been to immerse once again in Jung's writings on active imagination. I have been inspired and informed also by the contribution of many colleagues whose works are cited in the bibliography and text. As I extracted my questions and explored this rich material, many individuals offered support and feedback. Others brought to my attention resources from the literature that I did not know. Thomas Kirsch was generous with his knowledge and interest in historical questions. Reference librarians Marianne Morgan and Alison Leavens of the C.G. Jung Institute of San Francisco, Ann Miyoko Hotta of the Graduate Theological Union in Berkeley, Lore Zeller of the C.G. Jung Institute of Los Angeles, and Jan Perry of the C.G. Jung Educational Center of Houston helped me locate essential papers and passages that are not easy to come by. My appreciation also to Janet Adler, Antonella Adorisio, Shira Barnett, Eugene Chodorow, Lillian Chodorow, Claire Douglas, Ainsley Faust, Carolyn Fay, Neala Haze, Carol McRae, Renate Oppikofer, Karen Signell, Daniel Stewart, Tina Stromsted, Howard Teich, and Marta Tibaldi.

It is a special pleasure to thank my beloved husband and colleague Louis H. Stewart for his differentiated understanding of the emotions as sources of the imagination. Every aspect of my work has the benefit of his wisdom and playfulness.

The book cover shows part of a painting by Jung from his *Red Book*: A small figure bows low close to the ground in homage to an enormous fire spout; as it erupts the air is filled with intricately formed red, orange and yellow flames. The original work refers to the *Satapatha Brâhmana 2, 2, 4,* a particular section of an ancient sacred text of India. The passage begins with a description of Pragâpati (the creator) and Agni (the fire he created). When Agni turns toward Pragâpati with open mouth, the creator is terrified that he might be devoured by his creation. But then, through a series of ritual offerings, Pragâpati reproduces himself, new gods are born, trees spring forth, songs are sung, and Agni too is reborn. The painting seems to express Jung's fears and passions, as well as his attitude of reverence toward the creative activity of the psyche. Many years later he wrote: 'I hit upon this stream of lava, and the heat of its fires reshaped my life' (see p. 41, below).

In closing, I want to acknowledge the heirs of C. G. Jung and their representative Leo La Rosa for permission to publish this anthology and for useful remarks that helped clarify certain aspects of the work. Finally, I express profound gratitude to the memory and spirit of C. G. Jung for his magnificent contribution.

J.C.

Introduction

It is a great pleasure to introduce this volume of Jung's writings on active imagination. For many years, people have had to search throughout the *Collected Works* and elsewhere, to identify and then read and read again these marvelous papers. Now for the first time they are gathered together for publication.

My task is to present Jung's ideas about active imagination as clearly as possible and set them in context. Jung's analytic method is based on the natural healing function of the imagination, so there are obviously many ways to express it. All the creative art psychotherapies (art, dance, music, drama, poetry) as well as Sandplay can trace their roots to Jung's early contribution. I begin with Jung's discovery of active imagination and then go into his ideas. An in-depth review of the post-Jungian literature on active imagination is beyond the scope of this work, but my discussion of Jung is interwoven with some wonderful contributions from Jungian authors and others. In closing, I say something about each of Jung's essays and then it is time to tell the story of the Rainmaker.

CONFRONTATION WITH THE UNCONSCIOUS

Jung discovered active imagination during the years 1913–16. Following the break with Freud in 1912–13, he was disorientated and experienced a time of intense inner turmoil. He was able to carry on his practice, but for three years he couldn't get himself to read a professional book and he published relatively little. He suffered from lethargy and fears; his moods threatened to overwhelm him. He had to find a way, a method to heal himself from within. Since he didn't know what to do, he decided to engage with the impulses and images of the unconscious. In a 1925 seminar and again in his memoirs, he tells the remarkable story of his experiments that led to self-healing. It all began with his rediscovery of the symbolic play of childhood. As a middle-aged man in crisis, Jung had lost touch with the creative spirit. A memory floated up of a time when he was a 10- or 11-year-old boy, deeply engrossed in building games. The memory was filled with a rush of emotion and he realized the child was alive. His task became clear: He had to develop an ongoing relationship to this lively spirit within himself. But how was he to bridge the distance? He decided to return in his imagination to that time and enact the fantasies that came to him. And so he began to play, exactly as he had when he was a boy. The process of symbolic play led him, inevitably, to one of his deepest complexes and he remembered a terrifying dream from his childhood. This startling moment came in the midst of the building game. Just as he placed a tiny altar-stone inside a miniature church, he remembered his childhood nightmare about an altar. The connection impressed him deeply. We know from his memoirs that his religious attitude was shattered when as a young child he came to associate the Lord Jesus with death. Instead of the comfort he used to feel from saying his prayers, he began to feel distrustful and uneasy. Surrounded by grown-ups who spoke only of a light, bright, loving God, he could not tell anyone about his ruminations (1961, pp. 9–14). He spent all his life re-creating what he had lost as he developed a way to approach the psyche with a religious attitude. His early nightmare both expressed the problem and pointed toward the solution. Along with retrieving the fearful, long-buried dream, he gained a more mature understanding of it. His energy began to return and his thoughts clarified. He could sense now many more fantasies stirring within. As he continued his building game, the fantasies came in an incessant stream.

Around the same time he began to experiment with specific meditative procedures, various 'rites of entry' to engage with his fantasies. For example, he was sitting at his desk one day thinking over his fears when he made the conscious decision to 'drop down' into the depths. He landed on his feet and began to explore the strange inner landscape where he met the first of a long series of inner figures. These fantasies seemed to personify his fears and other powerful emotions. Over time, he realized that when he managed to translate his emotions into images, he was inwardly calmed and reassured. He came to see that his task was to find the images that are concealed in the emotions. He continued his experiments, trying out different ways to enter into his fantasies voluntarily: sometimes he imagined climbing down a steep descent; other times he imagined digging a hole, one shovel-full of dirt at a time. With each descent, he explored the landscape and got better acquainted with the inner figures. He used a number of expressive techniques (mainly writing, drawing, painting) to give symbolic form to his experience. Here it is important to differentiate between symbolic expression and a state of unconscious merging or identification. For Jung, the great benefit of active imagination is to 'distinguish ourselves from the unconscious contents' (1928b, par. 373). Even as he opened to the unconscious and engaged with the fantasies that arose, he made every effort to maintain a self-reflective, conscious point of view. Another way of saying this: He turned his curiosity toward the inner world of the imagination. His scientific interest kept him alert and attentive. The process led to an enormous release of energy as well as insights that gave him a new orientation. The fantasy experiences ultimately reshaped his life. When he emerged from the years of preoccupation with inner images (around 1919), he was ready to take on the leadership of his own school of psychology.

Many fundamental concepts of Jung's analytical psychology come from his experiences with active imagination. For example, the Shadow, the Syzygy (Anima and Animus), the Persona, the Ego, and the Self are concepts, but they are at the same time personifications of different structures and functions of the psyche. Affect, archetype, complex, libido – all of these terms are based on real, human experiences.

In a similar way he reminds us that active imagination is a natural, inborn process. Although it can be taught, it is not so much a technique as it is an inner necessity: 'I write about things which actually happen, and am not propounding methods of treatment' (1928b, par. 369).

JUNG'S IDEAS

It is not a simple thing to present Jung's ideas on active imagination. In his writings it is almost as if he invites different inner voices to speak. As the scientist, he presents his ideas in a clear understandable way. But then he turns to explore another perspective that may seem to contradict the first. Sometimes he is the poet, weaving word images of haunting beauty. Other times ancient prophets and mystics seem to speak through him. When the Trickster appears, his writings may seem deliberately ambiguous, even vague. Just when you want to hear more, he says something like: I must content myself with these hints. The reader may be left in a state of questioning and wondering, turned back to his or her own imagination. Dr Tina Keller, a member of Jung's early circle in the years 1915–29 wrote a wonderful memoir that describes the beginnings of active imagination. Here she sheds light on Jung's multi-faceted approach to important ideas:

> I feel privileged that I met C. G. Jung in the times where he was searching and had no definite formulations. I remember how I said: 'But what you say today is just the contrary of what you said last week,' and he answered: 'That may be so, but this is true, and the other was also true; life is paradox.' It was a most stimulating experience.
>
> (Keller 1982, p. 282)

Jung's therapeutic method had many different names before he settled on the term active imagination. At first it was the 'transcendent function.' Later he called it the 'picture method.' Other names were 'active fantasy' and 'active phantasying.' Sometimes the process was referred to as 'trancing,' 'visioning,' 'exercises,' 'dialectical method,' 'technique of differentiation,' 'technique of introversion,' 'introspection,' and 'technique of the descent.' When he delivered the Tavistock Lectures in London in 1935 he used the term 'active imagination' for the first time in public .

It seems natural to wonder why it took him so long to find the right name. Since there are many forms of active imagination, perhaps he was open to the idea of having many names to describe it. Some of the terms suggest a specific meditative procedure and concentration on inner voices or images. The term 'picture method' points to the use of art materials to create symbolic paintings and drawings. We don't know whether Jung ever considered the terms 'sculpting method,' 'bodily movement method,' 'music method,' 'dialectic method,' 'dramatic method,' 'symbolic play method,' or 'writing method.' The individuation process itself 'subordinates the many to the One' (Jung 1933/50, par. 626). Active imagination is a single method, but it is expressed through many different forms.

Ruth Fry reports a conversation with Jung when she was studying in Zurich sometime in the 1950s. He told her he always tested his theories for a period of fourteen years before he shared them with the public. He did the same thing with active imagination, that is, he tested it empirically and scientifically for fourteen years (Fry 1974, p. 11). As we know, Jung's confrontation with the unconscious was driven by inner necessity, but at the same time he conceived of it as a scientific experiment. When he realized his experiment in self-healing was successful, he began to teach the method to some of his patients. He also wrote about his findings.

His first professional paper on active imagination, entitled 'The Transcendent Function', was written in 1916, but it remained unpublished for many years. At the time he wrote it his energy had returned, but material from the personal, cultural and primordial unconscious was still pouring in on him. It doesn't seem surprising that he put the paper aside for publication at a later time. 'The Transcendent Function' (1916/58) sets forth both his new psychotherapeutic method and the deeper understanding he gained about the nature of the psyche. In this early attempt to present his ideas, Jung not only describes the stages of active imagination and some of its many forms, he also links active imagination to work with dreams and the transference relationship.

Jung views emotional dysfunction as most often a problem of psychological one-sidedness, usually initiated by an over-valuing of the conscious ego viewpoint. As a natural compensation to such a one-sided position, an equally strong counterposition automatically forms in the unconscious. The likely result is an inner condition of tension, conflict and discord. Jung used the term 'emotionally toned complex' to describe the unconscious counterposition: 'Everyone knows nowadays that people "have complexes." What is not so well known, though far more important theoretically, is that complexes can *have us*' (Jung 1934, par. 200).

His early concept of the transcendent function arose out of his attempt to understand how to come to terms with the unconscious. He found that there is an inborn dynamic process that unites opposite positions within the psyche. It draws polarized energies into a common channel, resulting in a new symbolic position which contains both perspectives. 'Either/or' choices become 'both/and,' but in a new and unexpected way. The transcendent function facilitates the transition from one attitude to another. Jung described it as 'a movement out of the suspension between two opposites, a living birth that leads to a new level of being, a new situation' (Jung 1916/58, par. 189). Another time he defined it simply as 'the function of mediation between the opposites' (1921, par. 184).

The term 'transcendent function' encompasses both a *method* and an inborn *function* of the psyche. In contrast, the term 'active imagination' refers to the method alone. But, obviously, the *method* (active imagination) is based on the image-producing *function* of the psyche, that is, the imagination. Both the transcendent function and the dynamic function of the imagination are complex psychic functions made up of other functions. Both combine conscious and unconscious elements. Both are creative, integrative functions that shape and transform the living symbol. Jung's close associate Barbara Hannah (1953) understands the transcendent function as one of Jung's early ideas that was incorporated into his later concept of the archetype of unity, the Self.

Play, fantasy and the imagination

In reflecting on the nature of the imagination, Jung recognized its inestimable value – not only to the development of the individual but to human culture as well:

> Every good idea and all creative work are the offspring of the imagination, and have their source in what one is pleased to call infantile fantasy. Not the artist alone, but every creative individual whatsoever owes all that is greatest in his life to fantasy. The dynamic principle of fantasy is *play*, a characteristic also of the child, and as such it appears inconsistent with the principle of serious work. But without this playing with fantasy no creative work has ever yet come to birth. The debt we owe to the play of imagination is incalculable.
>
> (Jung 1921, par. 93)

When he speaks of play, fantasy and the imagination, his spirit seems to soar. He cites Schiller, who said that people are completely human only when they are at play. From his experiments with the building game, he knew the creative, healing power of symbolic play. Subsequent studies have confirmed Jung's ideas: Allan (1988), Erikson (1963), Roberts and Sutton-Smith (1970), C.T. Stewart (1981), L.H. Stewart (1982), and Winnicott (1971) are among those who recognize the healing function of play and the imagination. As with so many of his ideas, Jung's early understanding of play anticipated later developments in the therapeutic mainstream (Samuels 1985, pp. 9–11). The great joy of play, fantasy and the imagination is that for a time we are utterly spontaneous, free to imagine anything. In such a state of pure being, no thought is 'unthinkable.' Nothing is 'unimaginable.' That is why play and the imagination tend to put us in touch with material that is ordinarily repressed. In the spontaneous dramatic play of childhood, upsetting life situations are enacted symbolically, but this time the child is in control. The child gains a sense of mastery by playing out little dramas voluntarily with a doll, a stuffed animal, or perhaps an imaginary companion, or a pet, sibling, or friend. Unlike the original experience that may have been overwhelming, in play the child gets to imagine all kinds of variations and creative resolutions; for example, an imaginary companion may bring courage, strength, magical powers – whatever is needed. Sometimes role reversal helps. The key to the transformative healing process is – play is fun. In a seemingly magical way the life-enhancing emotions (joy and interest) modulate and transform the emotions of crisis (Stewart 1987a, 1987b). It seems clear that symbolic play is based on an inborn psychological process that heals emotional pain.

For Jung, the imagination is 'the reproductive or creative activity of the mind in general . . . . Fantasy as imaginative activity is identical with the flow of psychic energy' (1921, par. 722). Whether we are children or adults and whether we are conscious of it or not, imaginative activity goes on all the time. It is expressed in many ways including play, dreams, fantasy, creative imagination and active imagination.

Active and passive fantasy

Jung distinguishes between active and passive *attitudes* toward one's fantasies (1921, pars. 712–14). An active fantasy may be evoked when we turn our attention toward the unconscious with an attitude of expectation; something definite is about to happen. Such a state of readiness brings new energy and consciousness to the raw material emerging from the unconscious; themes are elaborated through association with parallel elements. Through this process, the unconscious affects and images are clarified and brought closer to consciousness. Such an active, positive participation of conscious and unconscious corresponds to the method of active imagination.

By contrast, a passive attitude toward fantasy does nothing at all. With a passive attitude, fantasy is not evoked, rather it drifts around unnoticed, or it erupts into consciousness uninvited. Lacking the active participation of consciousness there is the danger of identifying with a mood or dream or fantasy. For example, a person might assume that just because he or she is thinking or feeling something: 'It must be true.' A more constructive response to a compelling idea or mood might be to consider the question: 'Is that true?' Then: 'How is it true – and how is it not true?' People may then discover thoughts in their mind they don't even agree with. Passive fantasy is always in need of self-reflective, critical evaluation from the conscious everyday standpoint. Active fantasy does not require criticism: rather, the symbolic material needs to be understood (Jung 1921, par. 714).

Starting points

The raw material of the unconscious is mainly emotions, impulses and images. Everyone gets at it in their own way. Some begin with a vague mood, or it may be an irrational emotional outburst. Jung suggests concentrating on the emotionally disturbed state until a visual image appears, a visualized mood.

> He must make the emotional state the basis or starting point of the procedure. He must make himself as conscious as possible of the mood he is in, sinking himself in it without reserve and noting down on paper all the fantasies and other associations that come up. Fantasy must be allowed the freest possible play, yet not in such a manner that it leaves the orbit of its object, namely the affect.
>
> (Jung 1916/58, par. 167)

Another way to begin is to choose an image from a dream, vision or fantasy and concentrate on it. It might be a visual image, an inner voice, even a psychosomatic symptom. You can also choose a photo, picture or other object and concentrate on it until it comes alive. In German there is a word *betrachten* that means making something pregnant by giving it your attention. This special way of looking is reminiscent of a child's experience when absorbed in symbolic play:

> *looking*, psychologically, brings about the activation of the object; it is as if something were emanating from one's spiritual eye that evokes or activates the object of one's vision.
>
> The English verb, 'to look at,' does not convey this meaning, but the German *betrachten*, which is an equivalent, means also to make pregnant. . . . And if it is pregnant, then something is due to come out of it; it is alive, it produces, it multiplies. That is the case with any fantasy image; one concentrates upon it, and then finds that one has great difficulty in keeping the thing quiet, it gets restless, it shifts, something is added, or it multiplies itself; one fills it with living power and it becomes pregnant.
>
> (Jung 1930–4a, Vol. 6, Lecture I, May 4, 1932, p. 3)

Giving it form

Sometimes active imagination takes place mainly inside the mind. Other times, the imagination is given form through painting, drawing, sculpting, dancing, writing, or in other ways. The following narrative describes the experience of a 45-year-old woman patient as she created her first sculpture:

> The depression of recent days has still not passed, but it has gotten better. I feel as though I am in a cobweb. I had the intention of making something in clay and it took a huge effort to overcome my resistance to doing it, although I did sense that it would help me. I didn't know how to begin. At first I thought of the black man that had occupied my fantasies so very much lately, but he didn't want to come out. So I squeezed and kneaded the clay for half an hour between my fingers and observed the forms that arose. I saw heads of animals; I felt the cold clay and gradually stopped

thinking. And then I saw how finally the figure of a child emerged out of the clay as if from the very earth. This child had a toothache and ran to its mother to lay its head between her breasts. Thus the figure of a mother with her child gradually arose.

(Dieckmann 1979, pp. 185–6)

She says it so beautifully. Sometimes an image or idea appears first in the mind's eye, but it may or may not want to come out. More often than not, images arise in a completely spontaneous way as we work with an expressive medium. Sooner or later, the imagination is given physical form. Jung describes a wide variety of forms that include writing, drawing, painting, sculpting, weaving, music, dancing, as well as the creation of rituals and dramatic enactments. Marie-Louis von Franz reports that Jung once told her symbolic enactment with the body is more efficient than 'ordinary active imagination' but he could not say why (von Franz 1980, p. 126).

Sandplay too is a form of active imagination; Jung was the first to prove its extraordinary effectiveness. Jung's experience with symbolic play had the most powerful therapeutic effect, yet the only time he speaks of it directly is in a 1925 seminar and again in his memoirs. Perhaps when he refers to active imagination as ritual, or dramatic enactment, he is thinking about his building game. Many years after the time he played like a child – building a miniature town with houses of stone, fantastic castles and a church – he encouraged his student and colleague Dora Kalff to develop a method of symbolic play. She developed a therapeutic technique based on the sandbox and floor games that children have played throughout history, in every culture. She brought hundreds of miniature figures, cultural symbols and natural objects into the consulting room and arranged them on shelves. There they wait, until it is time for them to enter a shallow tray filled with sand as someone chooses or is chosen by them. Dora Kalff (1980) coined the term 'Sandplay,' one of the most delightful, insightful ways to elaborate and develop themes from the unconscious.

When Jung writes about active imagination, he seems to describe it from many overlapping perspectives. Sometimes he names the expressive medium, for example bodily movement, painting, drawing, sculpting, weaving, writing. Sometimes he uses words like 'dramatic,' 'dialectic,' or 'ritual,' as if to describe the quality of an inner event. Then there are times when he seems to describe a typology of the senses, for example, 'visual types' may expect to see fantasy pictures; 'audio-verbal types' tend to hear an inner voice (1916/58, par. 170). Those with a 'motor imagination' can take a mandala (or other motif) and make it into a beautiful dance (1928–30, p. 474).

One mode often leads to another. Some of Jung's fantasies began as brief visual impressions and then developed toward stories that had a dramatic structure. Finally the elements of sound and language emerged and he and the inner figures began to speak with each other. The dialogues were sometimes 'whispered' (1961, p. 178) and perhaps also spoken out loud.

There was a critical moment when Jung realized his anima did not have the speech centers he had, so he suggested that she use his (1961, p. 186).

Some people begin with a non-verbal medium such as clay, painting, Sandplay, or movement, then write about the process and reflect on its meaning. Others begin with writing. For example, after her analytic hour with Jung, Christiana Morgan used to go back to the hotel and write a summary of the session in her journal. Then she closed her eyes, attended inwardly, waited for a vision and wrote it down. Finally she turned to art materials and painted the vision or made a drawing of it. This was the rhythm of her life in Zurich while she was in analysis with Jung (Douglas 1993, 1995).

Expressive movement sometimes leads in a natural way to Sandplay, drawings, clay modeling or writing. It may also happen the other way around. Mahlendorf (1973) reports on the spontaneous interweaving of movement and sculpting. Themes that emerged first in movement were elaborated further in clay. By forming the images in clay, she could sustain a particular expression over a longer time than was possible in movement. There were also times when the work in clay led back to movement, as she would assume the bodily position of the figure she was working on. Over time, a non-verbal dialectic developed between the experience of her own body in motion and the figure she was sculpting in clay. This dialectic furthered the creative process and led to a deeper understanding of its meaning.

> There were times when I could not fully explore expression in clay and needed to transform the incomplete feeling back into motion. . . . A clay figure stretched out was expressive enough, but I felt uneasy about its discomfort. . . . As I stretched myself into the position of the figure, I felt an almost intolerable tension, as if I wanted to snap shut. I realized I was stretching against resistance toward being open; for stretching means to stretch only toward one goal, to be open to it and unguarded toward the total environment. I was tense with discomfort because I feared such total commitment and its attendant unguardedness.
>
> When I wanted to explore one posture and its emotion more fully, clay became less and less satisfactory as a medium. I wanted a medium which would not break as easily, would be more resilient and allow for more flexibility in motion. I also wanted to prolong the actual process of working on a figure to fully feel its emotional significance. Wood seemed the right choice. My basic ideas for a figure come from emotions that occupy me, but which I do not feel through and through. I try out different movements in dance to experience what feels right. I look at blocks of wood to visualize if they are right for the kind of motion I have in mind. When I settle on a piece of wood the rough shape is there.
>
> (Mahlendorf 1973, pp. 323–4)

This remarkable narrative illustrates how one form may lead to another. It also shows how getting interested in the imagination fosters the development of a self-reflective, psychological attitude. As she used her own body to 'try on,' or imagine the experience of her clay figure, she entered more deeply into the fantasy, yet at the same time maintained an active, curious, self-reflective point of view. This ability to bear the tension between conscious and unconscious is the essence of active imagination. As Jung put it: 'A product is created which is influenced by both conscious and unconscious, embodying the striving of the unconscious for the light and the striving of the conscious for substance' (1916/58, par. 168).

Stages of active imagination

Active imagination has two parts or stages: First, *letting the unconscious come up*; and second, *coming to terms with the unconscious*. As I understand Jung, it is a natural sequence that may go on over many years. Sometimes it takes a long time to assimilate the material. Jung spent the last fifty years of his life coming to terms with the emotions and fantasies that at first overwhelmed him. Yet there are also times when a single experience of active imagination includes both stages and it feels complete. There are times when the two parts interweave back and forth, or they may occur simultaneously. When he speaks of what it is 'to struggle for hours with refractory brush and colors' (Jung 1931, par. 106), he is both letting the unconscious come up and beginning to shape it actively. The example by Mahlendorf (above) shows how insight emerges from self-reflective physical action. It seems clear that symbolic expression (giving it form) can be part of either stage, or both.

In his discussion of the first step, Jung speaks of the need for systematic exercises to eliminate critical attention and produce a vacuum in consciousness. This part of the experience is familiar to many psychological approaches and forms of meditation. It involves a suspension of our rational, critical faculties in order to give free rein to fantasy. The special way of looking that brings things alive (*betrachten*) would be related to this phase of active imagination. In his 'Commentary on *The Secret of the Golden Flower*' (1929) Jung speaks of the first step in terms of *wu wei*, that is, the Taoist idea of letting things happen. There are many ways to approach active imagination. At first, the unconscious takes the lead while the conscious ego serves as a kind of attentive inner witness and perhaps scribe or recorder. The task is to gain access to the contents of the unconscious.

In the second part of active imagination, consciousness takes the lead. As the affects and images of the unconscious flow into awareness, the ego enters actively into the experience. This part might begin with a spontaneous string of insights; the larger task of evaluation and integration remains. Insight must be converted into an ethical obligation – to live it in life. For Jung, the second stage is the more important part because it involves questions of meaning and moral demands. In the German language, this is the *auseinandersetzung*, an almost untranslatable word that has to do with a differentiating process, a real dialectic. All the parts of an issue are laid out so that differences can be seen and resolved. In Jung's writings *auseinandersetzung* is usually translated as 'coming to terms' with the unconscious.

The poet Rilke describes the quality of such an inner dialogue. In the following extract he advises a young poet who is oppressed by self-critical tendencies. His young colleague is filled with doubt. It is obvious that Rilke knows from his own experience the value of deep, differentiated engagement with a troublesome mood or emotion. In the most natural way, he personifies the mood and relates to it. In time it will be transformed and destructive attack will become constructive criticism. Rilke had no knowledge of a psychological method called active imagination, yet his 1904 letter to a young poet is one of the best descriptions I know of an *auseinandersetzung* between the ego and a figure from the unconscious.

And your doubt can become a good quality if you 'train' it. It must become 'knowing,' it must become criticism. Ask it, whenever it wants to spoil something for you, 'why' something is ugly, demand proofs from it, test it, and you will find it perhaps bewildered and embarrassed, perhaps also protesting. But don't give in, insist on arguments, and act in this way, attentive and persistent, every single time, and the day will come when instead of being a destroyer, it will become one of your best workers – perhaps the most intelligent of all the ones that are building your life.

(Rilke 1903–8/1984, p. 102)

Jung had great admiration for Rilke. He recognized that the poet was deeply psychological: 'Rilke drew from the same deep springs as I did – the collective unconscious. He as poet and visionary. I as a psychologist and empiricist' (Jung 1951–61, pp. 381–2).

Building on Jung's idea that active imagination has two parts or stages, a number of Jungian authors have proposed a subdivision of active imagination into four or five different stages. Marie-Louise von Franz (1980) was the first. She proposed: (1) Empty the 'mad mind' of the ego; (2) Let an unconscious fantasy image arise; (3) Give it some form of expression; and (4) Ethical confrontation. Later on she adds: Apply it to ordinary life. Janet Dallett (1982) and Robert Johnson (1986) built on von Franz, making certain changes. For Dallett the steps are: (1) Opening to the unconscious; (2) Giving it form; (3) Reaction by the ego; and (4) Living it. She points out that it is useful to divide the process into smaller parts in order to look at it more closely, but 'It is unlikely that anyone ever actually does active imagination in such an orderly fashion' (Dallett 1982, p. 177). Johnson proposes: (1) The invitation (invite the unconscious); (2) The dialogue (dialogue and experience); (3) The values (add the ethical element); and (4) The rituals (make it concrete with physical ritual). Each author both reflects and extends Jung's two-part outline. Looking at them together reminds me that there are many ways to approach active imagination. Perhaps in the deepest sense, each of us has to find our own way.

Creative formulation versus understanding

As the inner experience is given tangible form, it may help to be aware of two tendencies that arise: the aesthetic way of formulation and the scientific way of understanding. Each tendency seems to be the regulating principle of the other. For active imagination, a balance of both is needed. If the first tendency predominates, a person may lose the goal of psychological development and instead get fascinated with the artistic elaboration of a theme. If the second tendency predominates, there is the danger of so much analysis and interpretation that the transformative power of the symbol is lost. The important thing is to develop a self-reflective, psychological attitude (Henderson 1984) that draws from both the aesthetic passion for beauty and the scientific passion to understand. The task is to express both, yet not be consumed by either.

Reductive and constructive: two ways to understand

It may be helpful to remember that Jung was a Freudian analyst before he established his own school. He knew the therapeutic value of recollecting, reconstructing, and working through personal history, with special attention to childhood memories. But even before the break with Freud, he questioned whether every symbol should be interpreted in a literal, concrete, reductive way. To balance such a one-sided emphasis on the past, Jung developed a more imaginative, synthetic, constructive treatment of the unconscious, based on the scholarly imaginative process of symbolic amplification. The dream or fantasy images of an individual are mirrored by association to similar themes that have appeared throughout the history of humankind. Whereas the Reductive method seeks to understand a problem through its origins in childhood, the Constructive method points toward the larger picture and what it might mean for the future. Problems are approached through questions of meaning and purpose. The personal pain of an individual is not denied, but in addition to reconstructing early origins, it is beneficial to recognize the cultural and universal aspects of a symbol. It seems obvious that both approaches are useful and necessary.

Dangers of active imagination

The major danger of the method involves being overwhelmed by the powerful affects, impulses and images of the unconscious. It should be attempted only by psychologically mature individuals who are capable of withstanding a powerful confrontation with the unconscious. A well-developed ego standpoint is needed so that conscious and unconscious may encounter each other as equals. Lesser dangers described by Jung include the patient getting 'caught in the sterile circle of his own complexes' or 'remaining stuck in an all-enveloping phantasmagoria' (1916/58, p. 68) so that nothing is gained.

Liberation from the analyst

An important benefit of the method is to liberate patients through their own efforts rather than remaining dependent on the analyst. Jung even spoke of it as a touchstone of psychological maturity. Active imagination is a way to gain independence by doing your own inner work, yet for many it is also an intrinsic part of analysis. All of this leads to questions about the role of the analyst in active imagination.

The role of the analyst

Jung's papers on active imagination include certain reflections on the role of the analyst. In the following paragraph he describes an important shift in his way of working. After the break with Freud, he began simply to listen and to ask open-ended questions.

> I felt it necessary to develop a new attitude toward my patients. I resolved for the present not to bring any theoretical premises to bear upon them, but to wait and see what they would tell of their own accord. My aim became to leave things to chance. The result was that the patients would spontaneously report their dreams and fantasies to me, and I would merely ask, 'What occurs to you in connection with that?' or, 'How do you mean that, where does that come from, what do you think about it?' The interpretations seemed to follow of their own accord from the patients' replies and associations.
>
> (Jung 1961, p. 170)

From this passage we see the early beginnings of non-directive psychotherapy. Jung often points out that active imagination is not so much a technique as it is a natural process. Some of his patients discovered it entirely on their own. Others had a dream or fantasy with a particular theme that led them to it in the course of analysis. There were times also when Jung suggested to certain patients that they should paint an image from a dream or fantasy, or elaborate a theme, or develop it in any number of ways. So Jung was non-directive and at times he was a mentor as well.

Sometimes he gave general advice about the creative process, for example: Don't be afraid of color; vivid colors seem to attract the unconscious. Also, use fantasy to circumvent technical limitations. Sometimes his advice was more specific. For example, in a 1933 paper he reports on his work with Miss X, who had discovered active imagination on her own and brought a painting she made to their first analytic hour. This first painting showed a single image from a longer fantasy. She painted the figure of a woman (herself) in a helpless, imprisoned state, stuck in a block of rock. She had not painted the conclusion of her fantasy: A medieval sorcerer (Jung) responded to her cries for help, touched the rock with his wand, the rock burst open and she was free. After Miss X showed him her painting of the woman who was stuck, she told him about the rest of her fantasy. Jung advised her 'not to let it go at a mere fantasy image of the act of liberation, but to try to make a picture of it' (1933/50, par. 530). When she tried to paint the act of liberation, her efforts were at first unsuccessful. At some point Jung offered the idea: If a human figure doesn't work, use some kind of hieroglyph. 'It then suddenly struck her that the sphere was a suitable symbol for the individual human being' (1933/50, par. 538). By painting the part of her fantasy she had not painted before, and exploring the realm of abstract images, she was led to a completely new style. From that point on, her paintings all explore the theme of the mandala. Many questions arise. For example, would she have discovered the mandala if Jung had not suggested the idea of using a hieroglyph? Or, would she have painted the act of liberation if he had not drawn her attention to it? In Jung's view, suggestions are effective only when they mirror something within a patient that is ready to emerge.

After an unconscious affect or image is given form, Jung generally encouraged his patients to live with it, relate to it, be with it. The image has everything it needs; allow the meaning to emerge from it. When pushed to give an interpretation, he tried to make it as provisional as possible, never going beyond the bounds of the picture in front of him. He says he 'took good care to let the interpretation of each image tail off into a question whose answer was left to the free fantasy-activity of the patient' (Jung 1947, par. 400).

Although he preferred not to interpret the images of active imagination, he was fascinated by their meaning. In his writings, he amplifies the symbols by linking them to the images of archeology, myth and the world's religions. His vast knowledge of cultural symbols surely filled the analytic atmosphere with an attitude of respect for the images and curiosity about them. Sometimes he spoke, reflecting with his patients on the meaning and purpose of the symbols. Sometimes he did not speak, or he said very little. Sometimes he amplified a symbol not so much with words, but by showing his patient a corresponding image from a picture in his collection. In this non-verbal way he could mirror and enlarge his patient's perspective on a theme that might otherwise be understood only as subjective and strange.

For Jung, paintings and other products of the unconscious were useful for both diagnosis and prognosis. 'You can tell right away from such a picture where the patient stands, whether he has a schizophrenic disposition or is merely neurotic' (1935, par. 414). But even though Jung was skilled in the diagnostic use of symbols, his greatest interest in active imagination seemed to be in the natural healing. The therapeutic effect is almost magical, both during the creative process and again when the person looks at it afterwards.

Another facet of the analyst's role is to 'mediate the transcendent function' (1916/58, par. 146) – that is, maintain an open channel between conscious and unconscious. As mediator, he recognized that the doctor cannot cure without using himself and his own reactions, both conscious and unconscious. This inner-directed way of working has enormous power. When the analyst is able to hold the opposites within, the patient is free to do the same. Jung describes this self-reflective experience:

> The therapist must at all times keep watch over himself, over the way he is reacting to his patient. For we do not react only with our consciousness. Also we must always be asking ourselves: How is our unconscious experiencing this situation? We must therefore observe our dreams, pay the closest attention and study ourselves just as carefully as we do the patient. Otherwise the entire treatment may go off the rails.
>
> (Jung 1961, p. 133)

Jung doesn't write much about it, but his work with certain patients included spontaneous songs, dances and dramatic enactments in the analytic hour. Laurens van der Post describes Jung's seemingly miraculous treatment of a simple country girl who had lost her incentive and spirit. As she talked with him about the things she loved when she was a child, he sensed with great excitement a quickening of her spirit and 'he joined in the singing of her nursery songs and her renderings of simple mountain ballads. He even danced with her' (van der Post 1975, p. 57). Van der Post reports that this deep empathy expressed through rhythmic harmony had a lasting therapeutic effect.

I am reminded also of those curious moments when analyst and patient experience themselves at opposite poles. A state of inner tension or conflict may be expressed in many ways. For some, intrapsychic conflict can be contained and expressed symbolically through a series of inner dialogues or other forms of active imagination. For others, the tension between conscious and unconscious (ego and shadow) is more likely to come to consciousness through outer dialogues, interactions with another human. In Jung's view, the inner dialogue 'could just as well take place between patient and analyst, the role of the devil's advocate easily falling to the latter' (1916/58, par. 186). The essential thing is to develop a symbolic perspective. Certain tensions and conflicts in analysis may take on the quality of dramatic enactment, as if analyst and patient are embroiled in the opera, while at the same time watching it with great interest to see what they can learn. Is this not also active imagination? In her important paper 'Transference as a Form of Active Imagination' (1966), Dorothy Davidson says:

> During analysis a hitherto unconscious drama . . . is enacted in the here and now; . . . repeating the same type of relationship, or non-relationship, like 'a stuck gramophone record', as one patient put it. The record can become unstuck if the enacting of the drama has been, so to speak, realized by being lived through and worked through within the transference. The patient is then freed to possess and use his own emotions and imagery instead of being compulsively driven by the unconscious drama within him. It is in this sense that I think a successful analysis can be thought of as a lived-through active imagination.
>
> (Davidson 1966, p. 135)

In his seminar on dream analysis, Jung refers to a woman patient who danced a mandala from a drawing she made. He often mentions dance as a form of active imagination, but this is the only passage I know that describes how it was part of an analytic hour with Jung:

> A patient once brought me a drawing of a mandala, telling me that it was a sketch for certain movements along lines in space. She danced it for me, but most of us are too self-conscious and not brave enough to do it. It was a conjuration or incantation to the sacred pool or flame in the middle, the final goal, to be approached not directly but by the stations of the cardinal points.
>
> (Jung 1928–30, p. 304)

Then there is the wonderful narrative by Tina Keller about the beginnings of active imagination. She brings alive an analytic hour sometime in the mid-1920s when she first discovered dance as a way to express the imagination. Toni Wolff was the analyst-witness.

> When I was in analysis with Miss Toni Wolff, I often had the feeling that something in me hidden deep inside wanted to express itself; but I also knew that this 'something' had no words. As we were looking for another means of expression, I suddenly had the idea: 'I could dance it.' Miss Wolff encouraged me to try. The body sensation I felt was oppression, the image came that I was inside a stone and had to release myself from it to emerge as a separate, self standing individual. The movements that grew out of the body sensations had the goal of my liberation from the stone just as the image had. It took a good deal of the hour. After a painful effort I stood there, liberated. This very freeing event was much more potent than the hours in which we only talked. This was a 'psychodrama' of an inner happening or that which Jung had named 'active imagination.' Only here it was the body that took the active part.
>
> (Keller 1972, p. 22, translation by R. Oppikofer)

Tina Keller gives us a privileged insight into the deep, self-directed process that led her to dance her inner experience. There is also much to learn from the attentive, non-intrusive woman analyst who encouraged her to try and then watched quietly for a good part of the hour. Keller writes of Toni Wolff: 'Her presence was conducive to the acting-out of the drama' (Keller 1982, p. 288).

The analyst's role in active imagination has many aspects. We have seen how Jung was non-directive, yet he served also as mentor, scholar, mediator and participant-witness. As mentor in the creative process and scholar of individual and cultural history, Jung mirrored two tendencies that arise in the process of active imagination: the aesthetic passion for beauty and the scientific passion to understand. As mediator of the transcendent function he worked on an intrapsychic level; as participant-witness, he worked also on an interpersonal level. Above all, he turned his rich cultural resources toward a central goal: The psychological development of an individual.

In approaching Jung's ideas about the role of the analyst, I gathered together many pages of quotes – everything he wrote about active imagination and the therapeutic relationship. As I pause now to reflect, it is extraordinary to see that Jung as analyst drew from all the symbolic cultural attitudes described by Henderson (1984). As creative mentor, he drew from and mirrored the aesthetic attitude. As scholar, he drew from and mirrored the philosophic/scientific attitude. As mediator, he drew from and mirrored the religious attitude (dialogue with the god within). As participant-witness, he drew from and mirrored the social attitude. The central, self-reflective psychological attitude functions as a kind of quintessence. As Stewart (1992) points out, active imagination and creative imagination are basically the same process. The difference is that creative imagination is turned to the creation of the age-old cultural forms (art, religion, philosophy, society), while active imagination is turned to the creation of the personality ('Know Thyself').

Active imagination is most often done alone, away from the analyst. But some forms, particularly Sandplay and Movement usually include the analyst as witness. For some, liberation requires learning to be oneself in the presence of another. For others it is essential to work alone. Everyone is unique. As I understand Jung, he distrusted dogmatic rules and presented his important ideas with much room for variation and creative possibilities.

JUNG ON ACTIVE IMAGINATION – KEY SELECTIONS

Jung's understanding of active imagination developed over time. In his earlier works, active imagination is an adjunctive technique, and he speaks of active imagination and dream interpretation as two distinct psychotherapeutic methods. In his later years he says that his dream interpretation method is based on active imagination (1947, par. 404) and he describes active imagination as his 'analytical method of psychotherapy' (1955, p. 222). In his final great work, *Mysterium Coniunctionis*, he shows how active imagination is the way to self-knowledge ('Know Thyself'), and the process of individuation. From this mature perspective, he is describing much more than a specific meditative procedure or expressive technique. In the deepest sense, active imagination is the essential, inner-directed symbolic attitude that is at the core of psychological development.

Some of Jung's early works were revised in later years. I have tried to list the date of original composition or publication, and when indicated the date of revision, for example, 1916/58. I begin with Jung's memoirs and then present his writings more or less in sequence.

'Confrontation with the Unconscious', from Jung's memoirs (1961) is a vivid narrative of his inner development during the years 1913–19 when he discovered active imagination.

'The Transcendent Function' (1916/58) is the first major paper Jung wrote about the method he later came to call active imagination. This early paper concentrates on the forms of active imagination and its possibilities. He points out that a task for the future will be to give an account of the meaning and purpose of the symbolic contents.

'The Technique of Differentiation between the Ego and the Figures of the Unconscious' (1928b) is a section from his longer work, *The Relations Between the Ego and the Unconscious*. For Jung, direct experience of the unconscious and active engagement with it is the way gradually to transform and dissolve a troublesome complex. Two case examples are presented to show the difference between passive fantasy and an attitude of active participation.

An excerpt from Jung's 'Commentary on *The Secret of the Golden Flower*' (1929) includes important material on both his method and the meaning of the symbolic contents that emerge. He discusses the Chinese term *wu wei*, the concept of the *Tao*, and the mandala as it appears in drawings and dance. Extraordinary visions of light reported by Edward Maitland and Hildegard of Bingen include the same symbols described in the ancient Chinese text.

'The Aims of Psychotherapy' (1931) begins with the contributions of Freud and Adler; Jung then tells how he developed his own point of view. He regards his method as a direct extension of Freud's free association. Active imagination is described in pars. 100–6, but I include the entire paper for the larger perspective.

'A Study in the Process of Individuation' (1933/50) describes the case of Miss X, whose analysis with Jung is made visible through a marvelous series of paintings. This paper is mainly an example of Jung's method of symbolic amplification. Due to its length, I have cut about thirty pages of highly specialized material that seems to take the reader far from the paintings of Miss X. Also in an effort to keep *Jung on Active Imagination* affordable, the pictures are reproduced in black and white, so you may want to use Jung's description of the colors, your imagination and perhaps some colored pencils. The original uncut version with beautiful color plates can be seen in *CW* 9.1.

Excerpts from 'The Tavistock Lectures' (1935) in London begin with a brief overview of the material. The major portion is from the closing discussion when Dr Hadfield asks Jung to describe active imagination. Jung covers a lot of material in a short time. He describes the healing power of active imagination and gives a number of examples. His comparative work with the symbols offers insight into the structure of the unconscious. At the end, he looks at two drawings by a patient of Dr Bennet and they discuss questions of diagnosis and prognosis.

An excerpt from 'The Psychological Aspects of the Kore' (1940) includes a series of spontaneous visual impressions that came to a gifted woman patient who wrote them down and painted them. Jung presents this material to illustrate the theme of the Kore (daughter) in relation to Demeter (mother). The complete series is discussed in *The Visions Seminars*.

'On the Nature of the Psyche' (1947) includes a beautiful, deeply moving passage on active imagination.

Three letters 'To Mr O' (1947) contain simple, direct descriptions of what active imagination is about, and straightforward advice about how to do it.

I have selected two excerpts on active imagination from the concluding section of *Mysterium Coniunctionis* (1955). Here, Jung presents a psychological interpretation of the alchemical procedure. In my view, the key to the images of alchemy is in the emotions, particularly the mixtures, modulations and transmutations of the emotions of life-enhancement and the emotions of crisis (Stewart 1987a; 1987b; 1992, pp. 92–100). Just as the alchemical *caleum* represents the sweetness of life, so the illumination of joy and interest make it all possible.

In his brief 'Foreword to van Helsdingen: *Pictures from the Unconscious*' (1957), Jung comments on the series of paintings that were made available for publication by a former patient.

For further readings on active imagination, I include a postscript as well as an extensive bibliography. In addition to the works of Jung and the contribution of Jungian authors, there are books about the creative art therapies and the use of imagery in the cultural collective. It seems clear that Jung's active imagination is not only his analytical method of psychotherapy, but in addition it has become the source of some of the most important developments in modern psychotherapy, education and alternate approaches to healing.

THE RAINMAKER

It is time to tell the story of the rainmaker. Jung said to never give a seminar on active imagination without telling this story:

> There was a drought in a village in China. They sent for a rainmaker who was known to live in the farthest corner of the country, far away. Of course that would be so, because we never trust a prophet who lives in our region; he has to come from far away. So he arrived, and he found the village in a miserable state. The cattle were dying, the vegetation was dying, the people were affected. The people crowded around him and were very curious what he would do. He said, 'Well, just give me a little hut and leave me alone for a few days.' So he went into this little hut and people were wondering and wondering, the first day, the second day. On the third day it started pouring rain and he came out. They asked him, 'What did you do?' 'Oh,' he said, 'that is very simple. I didn't do anything.' 'But look,' they said, 'now it rains. What happened?' And he explained, 'I come from an area that is in Tao, in balance. We have rain, we have sunshine. Nothing is out of order. I come into your area and find that it is chaotic. The rhythm of life is disturbed, so when I come into it I, too, am disturbed. The whole thing affects me and I am immediately out of order. So what can I do? I

want a little hut to be by myself, to meditate, to set myself straight. And then, when I am able to get myself in order, everything around is set right. We are now in Tao, and since the rain was missing, now it rains.'

(Zeller 1982, pp. 109–10)

1   Confrontation with the unconscious

emotion (who has been) are transitory and therefore
do not count

From: *Memories, Dreams, Reflections* (1961),
ch. 6, pp. 170–99

After the parting of the ways with Freud, a period of inner uncertainty began for me. It would be no exaggeration to call it a state of disorientation. I felt totally suspended in mid-air, for I had not yet found my own footing. Above all, I felt it necessary to develop a new attitude toward my patients. I resolved for the present not to bring any theoretical premises to bear upon them, but to wait and see what they would tell of their own accord. My aim became to leave things to chance. The result was that the patients would spontaneously report their dreams and fantasies to me, and I would merely ask, 'What occurs to you in connection with that?' or, 'How do you mean that, where does that come from, what do you think about it?' The interpretations seemed to follow of their own accord from the patients' replies and associations. I avoided all theoretical points of view and simply helped the patients to understand the dream-images by themselves, without application of rules and theories.

Soon I realized that it was right to take the dreams in this way as the basis of interpretation, for that is how dreams are intended. They are the facts from which we must proceed. Naturally, the aspects resulting from this method were so multitudinous that the need for a criterion grew more and more pressing – the need, I might almost put it, for some initial orientation.

About this time I experienced a moment of unusual clarity in which I looked back over the way I had traveled so far. I thought, 'Now you possess a key to mythology and are free to unlock all the gates of the unconscious psyche.' But then something whispered within me, 'Why open all gates?' And promptly the question arose of what, after all, I had accomplished. I had explained the myths of peoples of the past; I had written a book about the hero, the myth in which man has always lived. But in what myth does man live nowadays? In the Christian myth, the answer might be, 'Do *you* live in it?' I asked myself. To be honest, the answer was no. 'For me, it is not what I live by.' 'Then do we no longer have any myth?' 'No, evidently we no longer have any myth.' 'But then what is your myth – the myth in which you do live?' At this point the dialogue with myself became uncomfortable, and I stopped thinking. I had reached a dead end.

Then, around Christmas of 1912, I had a dream. In the dream I found myself in a magnificent Italian loggia with pillars, a marble floor, and a marble balustrade. I was sitting on a gold Renaissance chair; in front of me was a table of rare beauty. It was made of green stone, like emerald. There I sat, looking out into the distance, for the loggia was set high up on the tower of a castle. My children were sitting at the table too.

Suddenly a white bird descended, a small sea gull or a dove. Gracefully, it came to rest on the table, and I signed to the children to be still so that they would not frighten away the pretty white bird. Immediately, the dove was transformed into a little girl, about eight years of age, with golden blond hair. She ran off with the children and played with them among the colonnades of the castle.

I remained lost in thought, musing about what I had just experienced. The little girl returned and tenderly placed her arms around my neck. Then she suddenly vanished; the dove was back and spoke slowly in a human voice. 'Only in the first hours of the night can I transform myself into a human being, while the male dove is busy with the twelve dead.' Then she flew off into the blue air, and I awoke.

I was greatly stirred. What business would a male dove be having with twelve dead people? In connection with the emerald table the story of the Tabula Smaragdina occurred to me, the emerald table in the alchemical legend of Hermes Trismegistos. He was said to have left behind him a table upon which the basic tenets of alchemical wisdom were engraved in Greek.

I also thought of the twelve apostles, the twelve months of the year, the signs of the zodiac, etc. But I could find no solution to the enigma. Finally I had to give it up. All I knew with any certainty was that the dream indicated an unusual activation of the unconscious. But I knew no technique whereby I might get to the bottom of my inner processes, and so there remained nothing for me to do but wait, go on with my life, and pay close attention to my fantasies.

One fantasy kept returning: there was something dead present, but it was also still alive. For example, corpses were placed in crematory ovens, but were then discovered to be still living. These fantasies came to a head and were simultaneously resolved in a dream.

I was in a region like the Alyscamps near Arles. There they have a lane of sarcophagi which go back to Merovingian times. In the dream I was coming from the city, and saw before me a similar lane with a long row of tombs. They were pedestals with stone slabs on which the dead lay. They reminded me of old church burial vaults, where knights in armor lie out-stretched. Thus the dead lay in my dream, in their antique clothes, with hands clasped, the difference being that they were not hewn out of stone, but in a curious fashion mummified. I stood still in front of the first grave and looked at the dead man, who was a person of the eighteen-thirties. I looked at his clothes with interest, whereupon he suddenly moved and came to life. He unclasped his hands; but that was only because I was looking at him. I had an extremely unpleasant feeling, but walked on and came to another body. He belonged to the eighteenth century. There exactly the same thing happened: when I looked at him, he came to life and moved his hands. So I went down the whole row, until I came to the twelfth century – that is, to a crusader in chain mail who lay there with clasped hands. His figure seemed carved out of wood. For a long time I looked at him and thought he was really dead. But suddenly I saw that a finger of his left hand was beginning to stir gently.

Of course I had originally held to Freud's view that vestiges of old experiences exist in the unconscious.[1] But dreams like this, and my actual experiences of the unconscious, taught me that such contents are not dead, outmoded forms, but belong to our living being. My work had confirmed this assumption, and in the course of years there developed from it the theory of archetypes.

The dreams, however, could not help me over my feeling of disorientation. On the contrary, I lived as if under constant inner pressure. At times this became so strong that I suspected there was some psychic disturbance in myself. Therefore I twice went over all the details of my entire life, with particular attention to childhood memories; for I thought there might be something in my past which I could not see and which might possibly be the cause of the disturbance. But this retrospection led to nothing but a fresh acknowledgement of my own ignorance. Thereupon I said to myself, 'Since I know nothing at all, I shall simply do whatever occurs to me.' Thus I consciously submitted myself to the impulses of the unconscious.

The first thing that came to the surface was a childhood memory from perhaps my tenth or eleventh year. At that time I had had a spell of playing passionately with building blocks. I distinctly recalled how I had built little houses and castles, using bottles to form the sides of gates and vaults. Somewhat later I had used ordinary stones, with mud for mortar. These structures had fascinated me for a long time. To my astonishment, this memory was accompanied by a good deal of emotion. 'Aha,' I said to myself, 'there is still life in these things. The small boy is still around, and possesses a creative life which I lack. But how can I make my way to it?' For as a grown man it seemed impossible to me that I should be able to bridge the distance from the present back to my eleventh year. Yet if I wanted to re-establish contact with that period, I had no choice but to return to it and take up once more that child's life with his childish games. This moment was a turning point in my fate, but I gave in only after endless resistances and with a sense of resignation. For it was a painfully humiliating experience to realize that there was nothing to be done except play childish games.

Nevertheless, I began accumulating suitable stones, gathering them partly from the lake shore and partly from the water. And I started building: cottages, a castle, a whole village. The church was still missing, so I made a square building with a hexagonal drum on top of it, and a dome. A church also requires an altar, but I hesitated to build that.

Preoccupied with the question of how I could approach this task, I was walking along the lake as usual one day, picking stones out of the gravel on the shore. Suddenly I caught sight of a red stone, a four-sided pyramid about an inch and a half high. It was a fragment of stone which had been polished into this shape by the action of the water – a pure product of chance. I knew at once: this was the altar! I placed it in the middle under the dome, and as I did so, I recalled the underground phallus of my childhood dream. This connection gave me a feeling of satisfaction.

I went on with my building game after the noon meal every day, whenever the weather permitted. As soon as I was through eating, I began playing, and continued to do so until the patients arrived; and if I was finished with my work early enough in the evening, I went back to building. In the course of this activity my thoughts clarified, and I was able to grasp the fantasies whose presence in myself I dimly felt.

Naturally, I thought about the significance of what I was doing, and asked myself, 'Now, really, what are you about? You are building a small town, and doing it as if it were a rite!' I had no answer to my question, only the inner certainty that I was on the way to discovering my own myth. For the building game was only a beginning. It released a stream of fantasies which I later carefully wrote down.

This sort of thing has been consistent with me, and at any time in my later life when I came up against a blank wall, I painted a picture or hewed stone. Each such experience proved to be a *rite d'entrée* for the ideas and works that followed hard upon it. Everything that I have written this year[2] and last year, 'The Undiscovered Self,' 'Flying Saucers: A Modern Myth,' 'A Psychological View of Conscience,' has grown out of the stone sculptures I did after my wife's death.[3] The close of her life, the end, and what it made me realize, wrenched me violently out of myself. It cost me a great deal to regain my footing, and contact with stone helped me.

Toward the autumn of 1913 the pressure which I had felt was in *me* seemed to be moving outward, as though there were something in the air. The atmosphere actually seemed to me darker than it had been. It was as though the sense of oppression no longer sprang exclusively from a psychic situation, but from concrete reality. This feeling grew more and more intense.

In October, while I was alone on a journey, I was suddenly seized by an overpowering vision: I saw a monstrous flood covering all the northern and low-lying lands between the North Sea and the Alps. When it came up to Switzerland I saw that the mountains grew higher and higher to protect our country. I realized that a frightful catastrophe was in progress. I saw the mighty yellow waves, the floating rubble of civilization, and the drowned bodies of uncounted thousands. Then the whole sea turned to blood. This vision lasted about one hour. I was perplexed and nauseated, and ashamed of my weakness.

Two weeks passed; then the vision recurred, under the same conditions, even more vividly than before, and the blood was more emphasized. An inner voice spoke. 'Look at it well; it is wholly real and it will be so. You cannot doubt it.' That winter someone asked me what I thought were the political prospects of the world in the near future. I replied that I had no thoughts on the matter, but that I saw rivers of blood.

I asked myself whether these visions pointed to a revolution, but could not really imagine anything of the sort. And so I drew the conclusion that they had to do with me myself, and decided that I was menaced by a psychosis. The idea of war did not occur to me at all.

Soon afterward, in the spring and early summer of 1914, I had a thrice-repeated dream that in the middle of summer an Arctic cold wave descended and froze the land to ice. I saw, for example, the whole of Lorraine and its canals frozen and the entire region totally deserted by human beings. All living green things were killed by frost. This dream came in April and May, and for the last time in June, 1914.

In the third dream frightful cold had again descended from out of the cosmos. This dream, however, had an unexpected end. There stood a leaf-bearing tree, but without fruit (my tree of life, I thought), whose leaves had been transformed by the effects of the frost into sweet grapes full of healing juices. I plucked the grapes and gave them to a large, waiting crowd.

At the end of July 1914 I was invited by the British Medical Association to deliver a lecture, 'On the Importance of the Unconscious in Psycho-pathology,' at a congress in Aberdeen. I was prepared for something to happen, for such visions and dreams are fateful. In my state of mind just then, with the fears that were pursuing me, it seemed fateful to me that I should have to talk on the importance of the unconscious at such a time!

On August 1 the world war broke out. Now my task was clear: I had to try to understand what had happened and to what extent my own experience coincided with that of mankind in general. Therefore my first obligation was to probe the depths of my own psyche. I made a beginning by writing down the fantasies which had come to me during my building game. This work took precedence over everything else.

An incessant stream of fantasies had been released, and I did my best not to lose my head but to find some way to understand these strange things. I stood helpless before an alien world; everything in it seemed difficult and in-comprehensible. I was living in a constant state of tension; often I felt as if gigantic blocks of stone were tumbling down upon me. One thunder-storm followed another. My enduring these storms was a question of brute strength. Others have been shattered by them – Nietzsche, and Hölderlin, and many others. But there was a demonic strength in me, and from the beginning there was no doubt in my mind that I must find the meaning of what I was experiencing in these fantasies. When I endured these assaults of the unconscious I had an unswerving conviction that I was obeying a higher will, and that feeling continued to uphold me until I had mastered the task.

I was frequently so wrought up that I had to do certain yoga exercises in order to hold my emotions in check. But since it was my purpose to know what was going on within myself, I would do these exercises only until I had calmed myself enough to resume my work with the unconscious. As soon as I had the feeling that I was myself again, I abandoned this restraint upon the emotions and allowed the images and inner voices to speak afresh. The Indian, on the other hand, does yoga exercises in order to obliterate completely the multitude of psychic contents and images.

To the extent that I managed to translate the emotions into images – that is to say, to find the images which were concealed in the emotions – I was inwardly calmed and reassured. Had I left those images hidden in the emotions, I might have been torn to pieces by them. There is a chance that I might have succeeded in splitting them off; but in that case I would inexorably have fallen into a neurosis and so been ultimately destroyed by them anyhow. As a result of my experiment I learned how helpful it can be, from the therapeutic point of view, to find the particular images which lie behind emotions.

I wrote down the fantasies as well as I could, and made an earnest effort to analyze the psychic conditions under which they had arisen. But I was able to do this only in clumsy language. First I formulated the things as I had observed them, usually in 'high-flown language,' for that corresponds to the style of the archetypes. Archetypes speak the language of high rhetoric, even of bombast. It is a style I find embarrassing; it grates on my nerves, as when someone draws his nails down a plaster wall, or scrapes his knife against a plate. But since I did not know what was going on, I had no choice but to write everything down in the style selected by the unconscious itself. Sometimes it was as if I were hearing it with my ears, sometimes feeling it with my mouth, as if my tongue were formulating words; now and then I heard myself whispering aloud. Below the threshold of consciousness everything was seething with life.

From the beginning I had conceived my voluntary confrontation with the unconscious as a scientific experiment which I myself was conducting and in whose outcome I was vitally interested. Today I might equally well say that it was an experiment which was being conducted on *me*. One of the greatest difficulties for me lay in dealing with my negative feelings. I was voluntarily submitting myself to emotions of which I could not really approve, and I was writing down fantasies which often struck me as nonsense, and toward which I had strong resistances. For as long as we do not understand their meaning, such fantasies are a diabolical mixture of the sublime and the ridiculous. It cost me a great deal to undergo them, but I had been challenged by fate. Only by extreme effort was I finally able to escape from the labyrinth.

In order to grasp the fantasies which were stirring in me 'underground,' I knew that I had to let myself plummet down into them, as it were. I felt not only violent resistance to this, but a distinct fear. For I was afraid of losing command of myself and becoming a prey to the fantasies – and as a psychiatrist I realized only too well what that meant. After prolonged hesitation, however, I saw that there was no other way out. I had to take the chance, had to try to gain power over them; for I realized that if I did not do so, I ran the risk of their gaining power over me. A cogent motive for my making the attempt was the conviction that I could not expect of my patients something I did not dare to do myself. The excuse that a helper stood at their side would not pass muster, for I was well aware that the so-called helper – that is, myself – could not help them unless he knew their fantasy material from his own direct experience, and that at present all he possessed were a few theoretical prejudices of dubious value. This idea – that I was committing myself to a dangerous enterprise not for myself alone, but also for the sake of my patients – helped me over several critical phases.

It was during Advent of the year 1913 – December 12, to be exact – that I resolved upon the decisive step. I was sitting at my desk once more, thinking over my fears. Then I let myself drop. Suddenly it was as though the ground literally gave way beneath my feet, and I plunged down into dark depths. I could not fend off a feeling of panic. But then, abruptly, at not too great a depth, I landed on my feet in a soft, sticky mass. I felt great relief, although I was apparently in complete darkness. After a while my eyes grew accustomed to the gloom, which was rather like a deep twilight. Before me was the entrance to a dark cave, in which stood a dwarf with a leathery skin, as if he were mummified. I squeezed past him through the narrow entrance and waded knee deep through icy water to the other end of the cave where, on a projecting rock, I saw a glowing red crystal. I grasped the stone, lifted it, and discovered a hollow underneath. At first I could make out nothing, but then I saw that there was running water. In it a corpse floated by, a youth with blond hair and a wound in the head. He was followed by a gigantic black scarab and then by a red, newborn sun, rising up out of the depths of the water. Dazzled by the light, I wanted to replace the stone upon the opening, but then a fluid welled out. It was blood. A thick jet of it leaped up, and I felt nauseated. It seemed to me that the blood continued to spurt for an unendurably long time. At last it ceased, and the vision came to an end.

I was stunned by this vision. I realized, of course, that it was a hero and solar myth, a drama of death and renewal, the rebirth symbolized by the Egyptian scarab. At the end, the dawn of the new day should have followed, but instead came that intolerable outpouring of blood – an altogether abnormal phenomenon, so it seemed to me. But then I recalled the vision of blood that I had had in the autumn of that same year, and I abandoned all further attempt to understand.

Six days later (December 18, 1913), I had the following dream. I was with an unknown, brown-skinned man, a savage, in a lonely, rocky mountain landscape. It was before dawn; the eastern sky was already bright, and the stars fading. Then I heard Siegfried's horn sounding over the mountains and I knew that we had to kill him. We were armed with rifles and lay in wait for him on a narrow path over the rocks.

Then Siegfried appeared high up on the crest of the mountain, in the first ray of the rising sun. On a chariot made of the bones of the dead he drove at furious speed down the precipitous slope. When he turned a corner, we shot at him, and he plunged down, struck dead.

Filled with disgust and remorse for having destroyed something so great and beautiful, I turned to flee, impelled by the fear that the murder might be discovered. But a tremendous downfall of rain began, and I knew that it would wipe out all traces of the dead. I had escaped the danger of discovery; life could go on, but an unbearable feeling of guilt remained.

When I awoke from the dream, I turned it over in my mind, but was unable to understand it. I tried therefore to fall asleep again, but a voice within me said, 'You *must* understand the dream, and must do so at once!' The inner urgency mounted until the terrible moment came when the voice said, 'If you do not understand the dream, you must shoot yourself!' In the drawer of my night table lay a loaded revolver, and I became frightened. Then I began pondering once again, and suddenly the meaning of the dream dawned on me. 'Why, that is the problem that is being played out in the world.' Siegfried, I thought, represents what the Germans want to achieve, heroically to impose their will, have their own way. 'Where there is a will there is a way!' I had wanted to do the same. But now that was no longer possible. The dream showed that the attitude embodied by Siegfried, the hero, no longer suited me. Therefore it had to be killed.

After the deed I felt an overpowering compassion, as though I myself had been shot: a sign of my secret identity with Siegfried, as well as of the grief a man feels when he is forced to sacrifice his ideal and his conscious attitudes. This identity and my heroic idealism had to be abandoned, for there are higher things than the ego's will, and to these one must bow.

These thoughts sufficed for the present, and I fell asleep again.

The small, brown-skinned savage who accompanied me and had actually taken the initiative in the killing was an embodiment of the primitive shadow. The rain showed that the tension between consciousness and the unconscious was being resolved. Although at the time I was not able to understand the meaning of the dream beyond these few hints, new forces were released in me which helped me to carry the experiment with the unconscious to a conclusion.

In order to seize hold of the fantasies, I frequently imagined a steep descent. I even made several attempts to get to very bottom. The first time I reached, as it were, a depth of about a thousand feet; the next time I found myself at the edge of a cosmic abyss. It was like a voyage to the moon, or a descent into empty space. First came the image of a crater, and I had the feeling that I was in the land of the dead. The atmosphere was that of the other world. Near the steep slope of a rock I caught sight of two figures, an old man with a white beard and a beautiful young girl. I summoned up my courage and approached them as though they were real people, and listened attentively to what they told me. The old man explained that he was Elijah, and that gave me a shock. But the girl staggered me even more, for she called herself

Salome! She was blind. What a strange couple: Salome and Elijah. But Elijah assured me that he and Salome had belonged together from all eternity, which completely astounded me. . . . They had a black serpent living with them which displayed an unmistakable fondness for me. I stuck close to Elijah because he seemed to be the most reasonable of the three, and to have a clear intelligence. Of Salome I was distinctly suspicious. Elijah and I had a long conversation which, however, I did not understand.

Naturally I tried to find a plausible explanation for the appearance of Biblical figures in my fantasy by reminding myself that my father had been a clergyman. But that really explained nothing at all. For what did the old man signify? What did Salome signify? Why were they together? Only many years later, when I knew a great deal more than I knew then, did the connection between the old man and the young girl appear perfectly natural to me.

In such dream wanderings one frequently encounters an old man who is accompanied by a young girl, and examples of such couples are to be found in many mythic tales. Thus, according to Gnostic tradition, Simon Magus went about with a young girl whom he had picked up in a brothel. Her name was Helen, and she was regarded as the reincarnation of the Trojan Helen. Klingsor and Kundry, Lao-tzu and the dancing girl, likewise belong to this category.

I have mentioned that there was a third figure in my fantasy besides Elijah and Salome: the large black snake. In myths the snake is a frequent counterpart of the hero. There are numerous accounts of their affinity. For example, the hero has eyes like a snake, or after his death he is changed into a snake and revered as such, or the snake is his mother, etc. In my fantasy, therefore, the presence of the snake was an indication of a hero-myth.

Salome is an anima figure. She is blind because she does not see the meaning of things. Elijah is the figure of the wise old prophet and represents the factor of intelligence and knowledge; Salome, the erotic element. One might say that the two figures are personifications of Logos and Eros. But such a definition would be excessively intellectual. It is more meaningful to let the figures be what they were for me at the time – namely, events and experiences.

Soon after this fantasy another figure rose out of the unconscious. He developed out of the Elijah figure. I called him Philemon. Philemon was a pagan and brought with him an Egypto-Hellenistic atmosphere with a Gnostic coloration. His figure first appeared to me in the following dream.

There was a blue sky, like the sea, covered not by clouds but by flat brown clods of earth. It looked as if the clods were breaking apart and the blue water of the sea were becoming visible between them. But the water was the blue sky. Suddenly there appeared from the right a winged being sailing across the sky. I saw that it was an old man with the horns of a bull. He held a bunch of four keys, one of which he clutched as if he were about to open a lock. He had the wings of the kingfisher with its characteristic colors.

Since I did not understand this dream-image, I painted it in order to impress it upon my memory. During the days when I was occupied with the painting, I found in my garden, by the lake shore, a dead kingfisher! I was thunderstruck, for kingfishers are quite rare in the vicinity of Zürich and I have never since found a dead one. The body was recently dead – at the most, two or three days – and showed no external injuries.

Philemon and other figures of my fantasies brought home to me the crucial insight that there are things in the psyche which I do not produce, but which produce themselves and have their own life. Philemon represented a force which was not myself. In my fantasies I held conversations with him, and he said things which I had not consciously thought. For I observed clearly that it was he who spoke, not I. He said I treated thoughts as if I generated them myself, but in his view thoughts were like animals in the forest, or people in a room, or birds in the air, and added, 'If you should see people in a room, you would not think that you had made those people, or that you were responsible for them.' It was he who taught me psychic objectivity, the reality of the psyche. Through him the distinction was clarified between myself and the object of my thought. He confronted me in an objective manner, and I understood that there is something in me which can say things that I do not know and do not intend, things which may even be directed against me.

Psychologically, Philemon represented superior insight. He was a mysterious figure to me. At times he seemed to me quite real, as if he were a living personality. I went walking up and down the garden with him, and to me he was what the Indians call a guru.

Whenever the outlines of a new personification appeared, I felt it almost as a personal defeat. It meant: 'Here is something else you didn't know until now!' Fear crept over me that the succession of such figures might be endless, that I might lose myself in bottomless abysses of ignorance. My ego felt devalued – although the successes I had been having in worldly affairs might have reassured me. In my darkness (*horridas nostrae mentis purga tenebras* – 'cleanse the horrible darkness of our mind' – the *Aurora Consurgens*[4] says) I could have wished for nothing better than a real, live guru, someone possessing superior knowledge and ability, who would have disentangled for me the involuntary creations of my imagination. This task was undertaken by the figure of Philemon, whom in this respect I had willy-nilly to recognize as my psychagogue. And the fact was that he conveyed to me many an illuminating idea.

More than fifteen years later a highly cultivated elderly Indian visited me, a friend of Gandhi's, and we talked about Indian education – in particular, about the relationship between guru and chela. I hesitantly asked him whether he could tell me anything about the person and character of his own guru, whereupon he replied in a matter-of-fact tone, 'Oh yes, he was Shankaracharya.'

'You don't mean the commentator on the Vedas who died centuries ago?' I asked.

'Yes, I mean him,' he said, to my amazement.

'Then you are referring to a spirit?' I asked.

'Of course it was his spirit,' he agreed.

At that moment I thought of Philemon.

'There are ghostly gurus too,' he added. 'Most people have living gurus. But there are always some who have a spirit for teacher.'

This information was both illuminating and reassuring to me. Evidently, then, I had not plummeted right out of the human world, but had only experienced the sort of thing that could happen to others who made similar efforts.

Later, Philemon became relativized by the emergence of yet another figure, whom I called Ka. In ancient Egypt the 'king's ka' was his earthly form, the embodied soul. In my fantasy the ka-soul came from below, out of the earth as if out of a deep shaft. I did a painting of him, showing him in his earth-bound form, as a herm with base of stone and upper part of bronze. High up in the painting appears a kingfisher's wing, and between it and the head of Ka floats a round, glowing nebula of stars. Ka's expression has something demonic about it – one might also say, Mephistophelian. In one hand he holds something like a colored pagoda, or a reliquary, and in the other a stylus with which he is working on the reliquary. He is saying, 'I am he who buries the gods in gold and gems.'

Philemon had a lame foot, but was a winged spirit, whereas Ka represented a kind of earth demon or metal demon. Philemon was the spiritual aspect, or 'meaning.' Ka, on the other hand, was a spirit of nature like the Anthroparion of Greek alchemy – with which at the time I was still unfamiliar.[5] Ka was he who made everything real, but who also obscured the halcyon spirit, Meaning, or replaced it by beauty, the 'eternal reflection.'

In time I was able to integrate both figures through the study of alchemy.

When I was writing down these fantasies, I once asked myself, 'What am I really doing? Certainly this has nothing to do with science. But then what is it?' Whereupon a voice within me said, 'It is art.' I was astonished. It had never entered my head that what I was writing had any connection with art. Then I thought, 'Perhaps my unconscious is forming a personality that is not me, but which is insisting on coming through to expression.' I knew for a certainty that the voice had come from a woman. I recognized it as the voice of a patient, a talented psychopath who had a strong transference to me. She had become a living figure within my mind.

Obviously what I was doing wasn't science. What then could it be but art? It was as though these were the only alternatives in the world. That is the way a woman's mind works.

I said very emphatically to this voice that my fantasies had nothing to do with art, and I felt a great inner resistance. No voices came through, however, and I kept on writing. Then came the next assault, and again the same assertion: 'That is art.' This time I caught her and said, 'No, it is not art! On the contrary, it is nature,' and prepared myself for an argument. When nothing of the sort occurred, I reflected that the 'woman within me' did not have the speech centers I had. And so I suggested that she use mine. She did so and came through with a long statement.

I was greatly intrigued by the fact that a woman should interfere with me from within. My conclusion was that she must be the 'soul,' in the primitive sense, and I began to speculate on the reasons why the name 'anima' was given to the soul. Why was it thought of as feminine? Later I came to see that this inner feminine figure plays a typical, or archetypal, role in the unconscious of a man, and I called her the 'anima.' The corresponding figure in the unconscious of woman I called the 'animus.'

At first it was the negative aspect of the anima that most impressed me. I felt a little awed by her. It was like the feeling of an invisible presence in the room. Then a new idea came to me: in putting down all this material for analysis I was in effect writing letters to the anima, that is, to a part of myself with a different viewpoint from my conscious one. I got remarks of an unusual and unexpected character. I was like a patient in analysis with a ghost and a woman! Every evening I wrote very conscientiously, for I thought if I did not write, there would be no way for the anima to get at my fantasies. Also, by writing them out I gave her no chance to twist them into intrigues. There is a tremendous difference between intending to tell something and actually telling it. In order to be as honest as possible with myself, I wrote everything down very carefully, following the old Greek maxim: 'Give away all that thou hast, then shalt thou receive.'

Often, as I was writing, I would have peculiar reactions that threw me off. Slowly I learned to distinguish between myself and the interruption. When something emotionally vulgar or banal came up, I would say to myself, 'It is perfectly true that I have thought and felt this way at some time or other, but I don't have to think and feel that way now. I need not accept this banality of mine in perpetuity; that is an unnecessary humiliation.'

The essential thing is to differentiate oneself from these unconscious contents by personifying them, and at the same time to bring them into relationship with consciousness. That is the technique for stripping them of their power. It is not too difficult to personify them, as they always possess a certain degree of autonomy, a separate identity of their own. Their autonomy is a most uncomfortable thing to reconcile oneself to, and yet the very fact that the unconscious presents itself in that way gives us the best means of handling it.

What the anima said seemed to me full of a deep cunning. If I had taken these fantasies of the unconscious as art, they would have carried no more conviction than visual perceptions, as if I were watching a movie. I would have felt no moral obligation toward them. The anima might then have easily seduced me into believing that I was a misunderstood artist, and that my so-called artistic nature gave me the right to neglect reality. If I had followed her voice, she would in all probability have said to me one day, 'Do you imagine the nonsense you're engaged in is really art? Not a bit.' Thus the insinuations of the anima, the mouthpiece of the unconscious, can utterly destroy a man. In the final analysis the decisive factor is always consciousness, which can understand the manifestations of the unconscious and take up a position toward them.

But the anima has a positive aspect as well. It is she who communicates the images of the unconscious to the conscious mind, and that is what I chiefly valued her for. For decades I always turned to the anima when I felt that my emotional behavior was disturbed, and that something had been constellated in the unconscious. I would then ask the anima: 'Now what are you up to? What do you see? I should like to know.' After some resistance she regularly produced an image. As soon as the image was there, the unrest or the sense of oppression vanished. The whole energy of these emotions was transformed into interest in and curiosity about the image. I would speak with the anima about the images she communicated to me, for I had to try to understand them as best I could, just like a dream.

Today I no longer need these conversations with the anima, for I no longer have such emotions. But if I did have them, I would deal with them in the same way. Today I am directly conscious of the anima's ideas because I have learned to accept the contents of the unconscious and to understand them. I know how I must behave toward the inner images. I can read their meaning directly from my dreams, and therefore no longer need a mediator to communicate them.

I wrote these fantasies down first in the Black Book; later, I transferred them to the Red Book, which I also embellished with drawings.[6] It contains most of my mandala drawings. In the Red Book I tried an esthetic elaboration of my fantasies, but never finished it. I became aware that I had not yet found the right language, that I still had to translate it into something else. Therefore I gave up this estheticizing tendency in good time, in favor of a rigorous process of *understanding*. I saw that so much fantasy needed firm ground underfoot, and that I must first return wholly to reality. For me, reality meant scientific comprehension. I had to draw concrete conclusions from the insights the unconscious had given me – and that task was to become a life work.

It is of course ironical that I, a psychiatrist, should at almost every step of my experiment have run into the same psychic material which is the stuff of psychosis and is found in the insane. This is the fund of unconscious images which fatally confuse the mental patient. But it is also the matrix of a mythopoeic imagination which has vanished from our rational age. Though such imagination is present everywhere, it is both tabooed and dreaded, so that it even appears to be a risky experiment or a questionable adventure to entrust oneself to the uncertain path that leads into the depths of the unconscious. It is considered the path of error, of equivocation and misunderstanding. I am reminded of Goethe's words: 'Now let me dare to open wide the gate/Past which men's steps have ever flinching trod.'[7] The second part of *Faust*, too, was more than a literary exercise. It is a link in the *Aurea Catena*[8] which has existed from the beginnings of philosophical alchemy and Gnosticism down to Nietzsche's *Zarathustra*. Unpopular, ambiguous, and dangerous, it is a voyage of discovery to the other pole of the world.

Particularly at this time, when I was working on the fantasies, I needed a point of support in 'this world,' and I may say that my family and my professional work were that to me. It was most essential for me to have a normal life in the real world as a counterpoise to that strange inner world. My family and my profession remained the base, to which I could always return, assuring me that I was an actually existing, ordinary person. The unconscious contents could have driven me out of my wits. But my family, and the knowledge: I have a medical diploma from a Swiss university, I must help my patients, I have a wife and five children, I live at 228 Seestrasse in Küsnacht – these were actualities which made demands upon me and proved to me again and again that I really existed, that I was not a blank page whirling about in the winds of the spirit, like Nietzsche. Nietzsche had lost the ground under his feet because he possessed nothing more than the inner world of his thoughts – which incidentally possessed him more than he it. He was uprooted and hovered above the earth, and therefore he succumbed to exaggeration and irreality. For me, such irreality was the quintessence of horror, for I aimed, after all, at *this* world and *this* life. No matter how deeply absorbed or how blown about I was, I always knew that everything I was experiencing was ultimately directed at this real life of mine. I meant to meet its obligations and fulfill its meanings. My watchword was: *Hic Rhodus, hic salta!*

Thus my family and my profession always remained a joyful reality and a guarantee that I also had a normal existence.

Very gradually the outlines of an inner change began making their appearance within me. In 1916 I felt an urge to give shape to something. I was compelled from within, as it were, to formulate and express what might have been said by Philemon. This was how the *Septem Sermones ad Mortuos*[9] with its peculiar language came into being.

It began with a restlessness, but I did not know what it meant or what 'they' wanted of me. There was an ominous atmosphere all around me. I had the strange feeling that the air was filled with ghostly entities. Then it was as if my house began to be haunted. My eldest daughter saw a white figure passing through the room. My second daughter, independently of her elder sister, related that twice in the night her blanket had been snatched away; and that same night my nine-year-old son had an anxiety dream. In the morning he asked his mother for crayons, and he, who ordinarily never drew, now made a picture of his dream. He called it 'The Picture of the Fisherman.' Through the middle of the picture ran a river, and a fisherman with a rod was standing on the shore. He had caught a fish. On the fisherman's head was a chimney from which flames were leaping and smoke rising. From the other side of the river the devil came flying through the air. He was cursing because his fish had been stolen. But above the fisherman hovered an angel who said, 'You cannot do anything to him; he only catches the bad fish!' My son drew this picture on a Saturday.

Around five o'clock in the afternoon on Sunday the front door-bell began ringing frantically. It was a bright summer day; the two maids were in the kitchen, from which the open square outside the front door could be seen. Everyone immediately looked to see who was there, but there was no one in sight. I was sitting near the doorbell, and not only heard it but saw it moving. We all simply stared at one another. The atmosphere was thick, believe me! Then I knew that something had to happen. The whole house was filled as if there were a crowd present, crammed full of spirits. They were packed deep right up to the door, and the air was so thick it was scarcely possible to breathe. As for myself, I was all a-quiver with the question: 'For God's sake, what in the world is this?' Then they cried out in chorus, 'We have come back from Jerusalem where we found not what we sought.' That is the beginning of the *Septem Sermones*.

Then it began to flow out of me, and in the course of three evenings the thing was written. As soon as I took up the pen, the whole ghostly assemblage evaporated. The room quieted and the atmosphere cleared. The haunting was over.

The experience has to be taken for what it was, or as it seems to have been. No doubt it was connected with the state of emotion I was in at the time, and which was favorable to parapsychological phenomena. It was an unconscious constellation whose peculiar atmosphere I recognized as the numen of an archetype. 'It walks abroad, it's in the air!'[10] The intellect, of course, would like to arrogate to itself some scientific, physical knowledge of the affair, or, preferably, to write the whole thing off as a violation of the rules. But what a dreary world it would be if the rules were not violated sometimes!

Shortly before this experience I had written down a fantasy of my soul having flown away from me. This was a significant event: the soul, the anima, establishes the relationship to the collectivity of the dead; for the unconscious corresponds to the mythic land of the dead, the land of the ancestors. If, therefore, one has a fantasy of the soul vanishing, this means that it has withdrawn into the unconscious or into the land of the dead. There it produces a mysterious animation and gives visible form to the ancestral traces, the collective contents. Like a medium, it gives the dead a chance to manifest themselves. Therefore, soon after the disappearance of my soul the 'dead' appeared to me, and the result was the *Septem Sermones*. This is an example of what is called 'loss of soul' – a phenomenon encountered quite frequently among primitives.

From that time on, the dead have become ever more distinct for me as the voices of the Unanswered, Unresolved, and Unredeemed; for since the questions and demands which my destiny required me to answer did not come to me from outside, they must have come from the inner world. These conversations with the dead formed a kind of prelude to what I had to communicate to the world about the unconscious: a kind of pattern of order and interpretation of its general contents.

When I look back upon it all today and consider what happened to me during the period of my work on the fantasies, it seems as though a message had come to me with overwhelming force. There were things in the images which concerned not only myself but many others also. It was then that I ceased to belong to myself alone, ceased to have the right to do so. From then on, my life belonged to the generality. The knowledge I was concerned with, or was seeking, still could not be found in the science of those days. I myself had to undergo the original experience, and, moreover, try to plant the results of my experience in the soil of reality; otherwise they would have remained subjective assumptions without validity. It was then that I dedicated myself to service of the psyche. I loved it and hated it, but it was my greatest wealth. My delivering myself over to it, as it were, was the only way by which I could endure my existence and live it as fully as possible.

Today I can say that I have never lost touch with my initial experiences. All my works, all my creative activity, has come from those initial fantasies and dreams which began in 1912, almost fifty years ago. Everything that I accomplished in later life was already contained in them, although at first only in the form of emotions and images.

My science was the only way I had of extricating myself from that chaos. Otherwise the material would have trapped me in its thicket, strangled me like jungle creepers. I took great care to try to understand every single image, every item of my psychic inventory, and to classify them scientifically – so far as this was possible – and, above all, to realize them in actual life. That is what we usually neglect to do. We allow the images to rise up, and maybe we wonder about them, but that is all. We do not take the trouble to understand them, let alone draw ethical conclusions from them. This stopping-short conjures up the negative effects of the unconscious.

It is equally a grave mistake to think that it is enough to gain some understanding of the images and that knowledge can here make a halt. Insight into them must be converted into an ethical obligation. Not to do so is to fall prey to the power principle, and this produces dangerous effects which are destructive not only to others but even to the knower. The images of the unconscious place a great responsibility upon a man. Failure to understand them, or a shirking of ethical responsibility, deprives him of his wholeness and imposes a painful fragmentariness on his life.

In the midst of this period when I was so preoccupied with the images of the unconscious, I came to the decision to withdraw from the university, where I had lectured for eight years as *Privatdozent* (since 1905). My experience and experiments with the unconscious had brought my intellectual activity to a standstill. After the completion of *The Psychology of the*

Unconscious[11] I found myself utterly incapable of reading a scientific book. This went on for three years. I felt I could no longer keep up with the world of the intellect, nor would I have been able to talk about what really preoccupied me. The material brought to light from the unconscious had, almost literally, struck me dumb.[12] I could neither understand it nor give it form. At the university I was in an exposed position, and felt that in order to go on giving courses there I would first have to find an entirely new and different orientation. It would be unfair to continue teaching young students when my own intellectual situation was nothing but a mass of doubts.

I therefore felt that I was confronted with the choice of either continuing my academic career, whose road lay smooth before me, or following the laws of my inner personality, of a higher reason, and forging ahead with this curious task of mine, this experiment in confrontation with the unconscious. But until it was completed I could not appear before the public.

Consciously, deliberately, then, I abandoned my academic career. For I felt that something great was happening to me, and I put my trust in the thing which I felt to be more important *sub specie aeternitatis*. I knew that it would fill my life, and for the sake of that goal I was ready to take any kind of risk.

What, after all, did it matter whether or not I became a professor? Of course it bothered me to have to give this up; in many respects I regretted that I could not confine myself to generally understandable material. I even had moments when I stormed against destiny. But emotions of this kind are transitory, and do not count. The other thing, on the contrary, is important, and if we pay heed to what the inner personality desires and says, the sting vanishes. That is something I have experienced again and again, not only when I gave up my academic career. Indeed, I had my first experiences of this sort as a child. In my youth I was hot-tempered; but whenever the emotion had reached its climax, suddenly it swung around and there followed a cosmic stillness. At such times I was remote from everything, and what had only a moment before excited me seemed to belong to a distant past.

The consequence of my resolve, and my involvement with things which neither I nor anyone else could understand, was an extreme loneliness. I was going about laden with thoughts of which I could speak to no one: they would only have been misunderstood. I felt the gulf between the external world and the interior world of images in its most painful form. I could not yet see that interaction of both worlds which I now understand. I saw only an irreconcilable contradiction between 'inner' and 'outer'.

However, it was clear to me from the start that I could find contact with the outer world and with people only if I succeeded in showing – and this would demand the most intensive effort – that the contents of psychic experience are real, and real not only as my own personal experiences, but as collective experiences which others also have. Later I tried to demonstrate this in my scientific work, and I did all in my power to convey to my intimates a new way of seeing things. I knew that if I did not succeed, I would be condemned to absolute isolation.

It was only toward the end of the First World War that I gradually began to emerge from the darkness. Two events contributed to this. The first was that I broke with the woman who was determined to convince me that my fantasies had artistic value; the second and principal event was that I began to understand mandala drawings. This happened in 1918–19. I had painted the first mandala[13] in 1916 after writing the *Septem Sermones*; naturally I had not, then, understood it.

In 1918–19 I was in Château d'Oex as Commandant de la Région Anglaise des Internés de Guerre. While I was there I sketched every morning in a notebook a small circular drawing, a mandala, which seemed to correspond to my inner situation at the time. With the help of these drawings I could observe my psychic transformations from day to day. One day, for example, I received a letter from that esthetic lady in which she again stubbornly maintained that the fantasies arising from my unconscious had artistic value and should be considered art. The letter got on my nerves. It was far from stupid, and therefore dangerously persuasive. The modern artist, after all, seeks to create art out of the unconscious. The utilitarianism and self-importance concealed behind this thesis touched a doubt in myself, namely, my uncertainty as to whether the fantasies I was producing were really spontaneous and natural, and not ultimately my own arbitrary inventions. I was by no means free from the bigotry and hubris of consciousness which wants to believe that any halfway decent inspiration is due to one's own merit, whereas inferior reactions come merely by chance, or even derive from alien sources. Out of this irritation and disharmony within myself there proceeded, the following day, a changed mandala: part of the periphery had burst open and the symmetry was destroyed.

Only gradually did I discover what the mandala really is: 'Formation, Transformation, Eternal Mind's eternal recreation.'[14] And that is the self, the wholeness of the personality, which if all goes well is harmonious, but which cannot tolerate self-deceptions.

My mandalas were cryptograms concerning the state of the self which were presented to me anew each day. In them I saw the self – that is, my whole being – actively at work. To be sure, at first I could only dimly understand them; but they seemed to me highly significant, and I guarded them like precious pearls. I had the distinct feeling that they were something central, and in time I acquired through them a living conception of the self. The self, I thought, was like the monad which I am, and which is my world. The mandala represents this monad, and corresponds to the microcosmic nature of the psyche.

I no longer know how many mandalas I drew at this time. There were a great many. While I was working on them, the question arose repeatedly: What is this process leading to? Where is its goal? From my own experience, I knew by now that I could not presume to choose a goal which would seem trustworthy to me. It had been proved to me that I had to abandon the idea of the superordinate position of the ego. After all, I had been brought up short when I had attempted to maintain it. I had wanted to go on with the scientific analysis of myths which I had begun in *Wandlungen und Symbole*. That was still my goal – but I must not think of that! I was being compelled to go through this process of the unconscious. I had to let myself be carried along by the current, without a notion of where it would lead me. When I began drawing the mandalas, however, I saw that everything, all the paths I had been following, all the steps I had taken, were leading back to a single point – namely, to the mid-point. It became increasingly plain to me that the mandala is the center. It is the exponent of all paths. It is the path to the center, to individuation.

During those years, between 1918 and 1920, I began to understand that the goal of psychic development is the self. There is no linear evolution; there is only a circumambulation of the self. Uniform development exists, at most, only at the beginning; later, everything points toward the center. This insight gave me stability, and gradually my inner peace returned. I knew that in finding the mandala as an expression of the self I had attained what was for me the ultimate. Perhaps someone else knows more, but not I.

Some years later (in 1927) I obtained confirmation of my ideas about the center and the self by way of a dream. I represented its essence in a mandala which I called 'Window on Eternity.' The picture is reproduced in *The Secret of the Golden Flower* (Fig. 3).[15] A year later I painted a second picture, like wise a mandala,[16] with a golden castle in the center. When it was finished, I asked myself, 'Why is this so Chinese?' I was impressed by the form and choice of colors, which seemed to me Chinese, although there was nothing outwardly Chinese about it. Yet that was how it affected me. It was a strange coincidence that shortly afterward I received a letter from Richard Wilhelm enclosing the manuscript of a Taoist-alchemical treatise entitled *The Secret of the Golden Flower*, with a request that I write a commentary on it. I devoured the manuscript at once, for the text gave me undreamed-of confirmation of my ideas about the mandala and the circumambulation of the center. That was the first event which broke through my isolation. I became aware of an affinity; I could establish ties with something and someone.[17]

In remembrance of this coincidence, this 'synchronicity,' I wrote underneath the picture which had made so Chinese an impression upon me: 'In 1928, when I was painting this picture, showing the golden, well-fortified castle, Richard Wilhelm in Frankfurt sent me the thousand-year-old Chinese text on the yellow castle, the germ of the immortal body.'

This is the dream I mentioned earlier: I found myself in a dirty, sooty city. It was night, and winter, and dark, and raining. I was in Liverpool. With a number of Swiss – say, half a dozen – I walked through the dark streets. I had the feeling that there we were coming from the harbor, and that the real city was actually up above, on the cliffs. We climbed up there. It reminded me of Basel, where the market is down below and then you go up through the Totengässchen ('Alley of the Dead'), which leads to a plateau above and so to the Petersplatz and the Peterskirche. When we reached the plateau, we found a broad square dimly illuminated by street lights, into which many streets converged. The various quarters of the city were arranged radially around the square. In the center was a round pool, and in the middle of it a small island. While everything round about was obscured by rain, fog, smoke, and dimly lit darkness, the little island blazed with sunlight. On it stood a single tree, a magnolia, in a shower of reddish blossoms. It was as though the tree stood in the sunlight and were at the same time the source of light. My companions commented on the abominable weather, and obviously did not see the tree. They spoke of another Swiss who was living in Liverpool, and expressed surprise that he should have settled here. I was carried away by the beauty of the flowering tree and the sunlit island, and thought, 'I know very well why he has settled here.' Then I awoke.

On one detail of the dream I must add a supplementary comment: the individual quarters of the city were themselves arranged radially around a central point. This point formed a small open square illuminated by a larger street lamp, and constituted a small replica of the island. I knew that the 'other Swiss' lived in the vicinity of one of these secondary centers.

This dream represented my situation at the time. I can still see the grayish-yellow raincoats, glistening with the wetness of the rain. Everything was extremely unpleasant, black and opaque – just as I felt then. But I had had a vision of unearthly beauty, and that was why I was able to live at all. Liverpool is the 'pool of life.' The 'liver,' according to an old view, is the seat of life – that which 'makes to live.'

This dream brought with it a sense of finality. I saw that here the goal had been revealed. One could not go beyond the center. The center is the goal, and everything is directed toward that center. Through this dream I understood that the self is the principle and archetype of orientation and meaning. Therein lies its healing function. For me, this insight signified an approach to the center and therefore to the goal. Out of it emerged a first inkling of my personal myth.

After this dream I gave up drawing or painting mandalas. The dream depicted the climax of the whole process of development of consciousness. It satisfied me completely, for it gave a total picture of my situation. I had known, to be sure, that I was occupied with something important, but I still lacked understanding, and there had been no one among my associates who could have understood. The clarification brought about by the dream made it possible for me to take an objective view of the things that filled my being.

Without such a vision I might perhaps have lost my orientation and been compelled to abandon my undertaking. But here the meaning had been made clear. When I parted from Freud, I knew that I was plunging into the unknown. Beyond Freud, after all, I knew nothing; but I had taken the step into darkness. When that happens, and then such a dream comes, one feels it as an act of grace.

It has taken me virtually forty-five years to distill within the vessel of my scientific work the things I experienced and wrote down at that time. As a young man my goal had been to accomplish something in my science. But then, I hit upon this stream of lava, and the heat of its fires reshaped my life. That was the primal stuff which compelled me to work upon it, and my works are a more or less successful endeavor to incorporate this incandescent matter into the contemporary picture of the world.

The years when I was pursuing my inner images were the most important in my life – in them everything essential was decided. It all began then; the later details are only supplements and clarifications of the material that burst forth from the unconscious, and at first swamped me. It was the *prima materia* for a lifetime's work.

NOTES

1 Freud speaks of 'archaic vestiges.'
2 1957.
3 November 27, 1955.
4 An alchemical treatise ascribed to Thomas Aquinas.
5 [The Anthroparion is a tiny man, a kind of homunculus. He is found, for example, in the visions of Zosimos of Panopolis, an important alchemist of the third century. To the group which includes the Anthroparion belong the gnomes, the Dactyls of classical antiquity, and the homunculi of the alchemists. As the spirit of quicksilver, the alchemical Mercurius was also an Anthroparion. – A.J.]
6 [The Black Book consists of six black-bound, smallish leather notebooks. The Red Book, a folio volume bound in red leather, contains the same fantasies couched in elaborately literary form and language, and set down in calligraphic Gothic script, in the manner of medieval manuscripts. – A.J.]
7 *Faust*, Part One.
8 [The Golden (or Homeric) Chain in alchemy is the series of great wise men, beginning with Hermes Trismegistos, which links earth with heaven. – A.J.]
9 Privately printed (n.d.) and pseudonymously subtitled 'The Seven Sermons to the Dead written by Basilides in Alexandria, the City where the East toucheth the West'. [Appendix V in MDR]
10 *Faust*, Part Two.
11 See Chap. V, n. 5, p. 155 in MDR.
12 [During this 'fallow period' Jung wrote very little: a handful of papers in English, and the very important first versions of the essays published in English translation as *Two Essays on Analytical Psychology* (*CW* 7). The period came to an end with the publication of *Psychologische Typen* in 1921 (English trans.: *Psychological Types*, CW 6.) – A.J.]
13 [Reproduced as the frontispiece to *The Archetypes and the Collective Unconscious* (*CW* 9, i). – A.J.]
14 *Faust*, Part Two, trans. by Philip Wayne (Harmondsworth, England, Penguin Books Ltd., 1959), p. 79.
15 Cf. 'Concerning Mandala Symbolism,' in *The Archetypes and the Collective Unconscious* (*CW* 9, i,), fig. 6 and pars 654–5.
16 *The Secret of the Golden Flower*, fig. 10 in CW13. See also 'Concerning Mandala Symbolism,' fig. 36 and par. 691 in CW 9, i.
17 On Richard Wilhelm, see Appendix IV, pp. 373–77 in MDR.

2   The transcendent function[1]

From: *The Structure and Dynamics of the Psyche* (1916/58) (*CW* 8), pars. 131–93

Prefatory note

This essay was written in 1916. Recently it was discovered by students of the C. G. Jung Institute, Zurich, and was brought out in a private edition in its first, provisional form, in an English translation. In order to prepare it for publication, I have worked over the manuscript, while preserving the main trend of thought and the unavoidable limitedness of its horizon. After forty-two years, the problem has lost nothing of its topicality, though its presentation is still in need of extensive improvement, as anyone can see who knows the material. The essay may therefore stand, with all its imperfections, as an historical document. It may give the reader some idea of the efforts of understanding which were needed for the first attempts at a synthetic view of the psychic process in analytical treatment. As its basic argument is still valid today, it may stimulate the reader to a broader and deeper understanding of the problem. This problem is identical with the universal question: How does one come to terms with the unconscious?

This is the question posed by the philosophy of India, and particularly by Buddhism and Zen. Indirectly, it is the fundamental question, in practice, of all religions and all philosophies. For the unconscious is not this thing or that; it is the Unknown as it immediately affects us.

The method of 'active imagination,' hereinafter described, is the most important auxiliary for the production of those contents of the unconscious which lie, as it were, immediately below the threshold of consciousness and, when intensified, are the most likely to irrupt spontaneously into the conscious mind. The method, therefore, is not without its dangers and should, if possible, not be employed except under expert supervision. One of the lesser dangers is that the procedure may not lead to any positive result, since it easily passes over into the so-called 'free association' of Freud, whereupon the patient gets caught in the sterile circle of his own complexes, from which he is in any case unable to escape. A further danger, in itself harmless, is that, though authentic contents may be produced, the patient evinces an exclusively aesthetic interest in them and consequently remains stuck in an all-enveloping phantasmagoria, so that once more nothing is gained. The meaning and value of these fantasies are revealed only through their integration into the personality as a whole – that is to say, at the moment when one is confronted not only with what they mean but also with their moral demands.

Finally, a third danger – and this may in certain circumstances be a very serious matter – is that the subliminal contents already possess such a high energy charge that, when afforded an outlet by active imagination, they may overpower the conscious mind and take possession of the personality. This gives rise to a condition which – temporarily, at least – cannot easily be distinguished from schizophrenia, and may even lead to a genuine 'psychotic interval.' The method of active imagination, therefore, is not a plaything for children. The prevailing undervaluation of the unconscious adds considerably to the dangers of this method. On the other hand, there can be no doubt that it is an invaluable auxiliary for the psychotherapist.

C.G.J.

Küsnacht, July 1958 / September 1959

131 There is nothing mysterious or metaphysical about the term 'transcendent function.' It means a psychological function comparable in its way to a mathematical function of the same name, which is a function of real and imaginary numbers. The psychological 'transcendent function' arises from the union of conscious and unconscious contents.

132 Experience in analytical psychology has amply shown that the conscious and the unconscious seldom agree as to their contents and their tendencies. This lack of parallelism is not just accidental or purposeless, but is due to the fact that the unconscious behaves in a compensatory or complementary manner towards the conscious. We can also put it the other way round and say that the conscious behaves in a complementary manner towards the unconscious. The reasons for this relationship are:

(1) Consciousness possesses a threshold intensity which its contents must have attained, so that all elements that are too weak remain in the unconscious.

(2) Consciousness, because of its directed functions, exercises an inhibition (which Freud calls censorship) on all incompatible material, with the result that it sinks into the unconscious.

(3) Consciousness constitutes the momentary process of adaptation, whereas the unconscious contains not only all the forgotten material of the individual's own past, but all the inherited behaviour traces constituting the structure of the mind.

(4) The unconscious contains all the fantasy combinations which have not yet attained the threshold intensity, but which in the course of time and under suitable conditions will enter the light of consciousness.

133 This readily explains the complementary attitude of the unconscious towards the conscious.

134 The definiteness and directedness of the conscious mind are qualities that have been acquired relatively late in the history of the human race,

and are for instance largely lacking among primitives today. These qualities are often impaired in the neurotic patient, who differs from the normal person in that his threshold of consciousness gets shifted more easily; in other words, the partition between conscious and unconscious is much more permeable. The psychotic, on the other hand, is under the direct influence of the unconscious.

135   The definiteness and directedness of the conscious mind are extremely important acquisitions which humanity has bought at a very heavy sacrifice, and which in turn have rendered humanity the highest service. Without them science, technology, and civilization would be impossible, for they all presuppose the reliable continuity and directedness of the conscious process. For the statesman, doctor, and engineer as well as for the simplest labourer, these qualities are absolutely indispensable. We may say in general that social worthlessness increases to the degree that these qualities are impaired by the unconscious. Great artists and others distinguished by creative gifts are, of course, exceptions to this rule. The very advantage that such individuals enjoy consists precisely in the permeability of the partition separating the conscious and the unconscious. But, for those professions and social activities which require just this continuity and reliability, these exceptional human beings are as a rule of little value.

136   It is therefore understandable, and even necessary, that in each individual the psychic process should be as stable and definite as possible, since the exigencies of life demand it. But this involves a certain disadvantage: the quality of directedness makes for the inhibition or exclusion of all those psychic elements which appear to be, or really are, incompatible with it, i.e., likely to bias the intended direction to suit their purpose and so lead to an undesired goal. But how do we know that the concurrent psychic material is 'incompatible'? We know it by an act of judgment which determines the direction of the path that is chosen and desired. This judgment is partial and prejudiced, since it chooses one particular possibility at the cost of all the others. The judgment in its turn is always based on experience, i.e., on what is already known. As a rule it is never based on what is new, what is still unknown, and what under certain conditions might considerably enrich the directed process. It is evident that it cannot be, for the very reason that the unconscious contents are excluded from consciousness.

137   Through such acts of judgment the directed process necessarily becomes one-sided, even though the rational judgment may appear many-sided and unprejudiced. The very rationality of the judgment may even be the worst prejudice, since we call reasonable what appears reasonable to us. What appears to us unreasonable is therefore doomed to be excluded because of its irrational character. It may really be irrational, but may equally well merely appear irrational without actually being so when seen from another standpoint.

138   One-sidedness is an unavoidable and necessary characteristic of the directed process, for direction implies one-sidedness. It is an advantage and a drawback at the same time. Even when no outwardly visible drawback seems to be present, there is always an equally pronounced counter-position in the unconscious, unless it happens to be the ideal case where all the psychic components are tending in one and the same direction. This possibility cannot be disputed in theory, but in practice it very rarely happens. The counter-position in the unconscious is not dangerous so long as it does not possess any high energy-value. But if the tension increases as a result of too great one-sidedness, the counter-tendency breaks through into consciousness, usually just at the moment when it is most important to maintain the conscious direction. Thus the speaker makes a slip of the tongue just when he particularly wishes not to say anything stupid. This moment is critical because it possesses a high energy tension which, when the unconscious is already charged, may easily 'spark' and release the unconscious content.

139   Civilized life today demands concentrated, directed conscious functioning, and this entails the risk of a considerable dissociation from the unconscious. The further we are able to remove ourselves from the unconscious through directed functioning, the more readily a powerful counter-position can build up in the unconscious, and when this breaks out it may have disagreeable consequences.

140   Analysis has given us a profound insight into the importance of unconscious influences, and we have learnt so much from this for our practical life that we deem it unwise to expect an elimination or standstill of the unconscious after the so-called completion of the treatment. Many patients, obscurely recognizing this state of affairs, have great difficulty in deciding to give up the analysis, although both they and the analyst find the feeling of dependency irksome. Often they are afraid to risk standing on their own feet, because they know from experience that the unconscious can intervene again and again in their lives in a disturbing and apparently unpredictable manner.

141   It was formerly assumed that patients were ready to cope with normal life as soon as they had acquired enough practical self-knowledge to understand their own dreams. Experience has shown, however, that even professional analysts, who might be expected to have mastered the art of dream interpretation, often capitulate before their own dreams and have to call in the help of a colleague. If even one who purports to be an expert in the method proves unable to interpret his own dreams satisfactorily, how much less can this be expected of the patient. Freud's hope that the unconscious could be 'exhausted' has not been fulfilled. Dream-life and intrusions from the unconscious continue – *mutatis mutandis* – unimpeded.

142   There is a widespread prejudice that analysis is something like a 'cure,' to which one submits for a time and is then discharged healed. That is a layman's error left over from the early days of psychoanalysis. Analytical

treatment could be described as a readjustment of psychological attitude achieved with the help of the doctor. Naturally this newly won attitude, which is better suited to the inner and outer conditions, can last a considerable time, but there are very few cases where a single 'cure' is permanently successful. It is true that medical optimism has never stinted itself of publicity and has always been able to report definitive cures. We must, however, not let ourselves be deceived by the all-too-human attitude of the practitioner, but should always remember that the life of the unconscious goes on and continually produces problematical situations. There is no need for pessimism; we have seen too many excellent results achieved with good luck and honest work for that. But this need not prevent us from recognizing that analysis is no once-and-for-all 'cure'; it is no more, at first, than a more or less thorough readjustment. There is no change that is unconditionally valid over a long period of time. Life has always to be tackled anew. There are, of course, extremely durable collective attitudes which permit the solution of typical conflicts. A collective attitude enables the individual to fit into society without friction, since it acts upon him like any other condition of life. But the patient's difficulty consists precisely in the fact that his individual problem cannot be fitted without friction into a collective norm; it requires the solution of an individual conflict if the whole of his personality is to remain viable. No rational solution can do justice to this task, and there is absolutely no collective norm that could replace an individual solution without loss.

143   The new attitude gained in the course of analysis tends sooner or later to become inadequate in one way or another, and necessarily so, because the constant flow of life again and again demands fresh adaptation. Adaptation is never achieved once and for all. One might certainly demand of analysis that it should enable the patient to gain new orientations in later life, too, without undue difficulty. And experience shows that this is true up to a point. We often find that patients who have gone through a thorough analysis have considerably less difficulty with new adjustments later on. Nevertheless, these difficulties prove to be fairly frequent and may at times be really troublesome. That is why even patients who have had a thorough analysis often turn to their old analyst for help at some later period. In the light of medical practice in general there is nothing very unusual about this, but it does contradict a certain misplaced enthusiasm on the part of the therapist as well as the view that analysis constitutes a unique 'cure.' In the last resort it is highly improbable that there could ever be a therapy that got rid of all difficulties. Man needs difficulties; they are necessary for health. What concerns us here is only an excessive amount of them.

144   The basic question for the therapist is not how to get rid of the momentary difficulty, but how future difficulties may be successfully countered. The question is: what kind of mental and moral attitude is it necessary to have towards the disturbing influences of the unconscious, and how can it be conveyed to the patient?

145   The answer obviously consists in getting rid of the separation between conscious and unconscious. This cannot be done by condemning the contents of the unconscious in a one-sided way, but rather by recognizing their significance in compensating the one-sidedness of consciousness and by taking this significance into account. The tendencies of the conscious and the unconscious are the two factors that together make up the transcendent function. It is called 'transcendent' because it makes the transition from one attitude to another organically possible, without loss of the unconscious. The constructive or synthetic method of treatment presupposes insights which are at least potentially present in the patient and can therefore be made conscious. If the analyst knows nothing of these potentialities he cannot help the patient to develop them either, unless analyst and patient together devote proper scientific study to this problem, which as a rule is out of the question.

146   In actual practice, therefore, the suitably trained analyst mediates the transcendent function for the patient, i.e., helps him to bring conscious and unconscious together and so arrive at a new attitude. In this function of the analyst lies one of the many important meanings of the *transference*. The patient clings by means of the transference to the person who seems to promise him a renewal of attitude; through it he seeks this change, which it vital to him, even though he may not be conscious of doing so. For the patient, therefore, the analyst has the character of an indispensable figure absolutely necessary for life. However infantile this dependence may appear to be, it expresses an extremely important demand which, if disappointed, often turns to bitter hatred of the analyst. It is therefore important to know what this demand concealed in the transference is really aiming at; there is a tendency to understand it in the reductive sense only, as an erotic fantasy. But that would mean taking this fantasy, which is usually concerned with the parents, literally, as though the patient, or rather his unconscious, still had the expectations the child once had towards the parents. Outwardly it still is the same expectation of the child for the help and protection of the parents, but in the meantime the child has become an adult, and what was normal for a child is improper in an adult. It has become a metaphorical expression of the not consciously realized need for help in a crisis. Historically it is correct to explain the erotic character of the transference in terms of the infantile *eros*. But in that way the meaning and purpose of the transference are not understood, and its interpretation as an infantile sexual fantasy leads away from the real problem. The understanding of the transference is to be sought not in its historical antecedents but in its purpose. The one-sided, reductive explanation becomes in the end nonsensical, especially when absolutely nothing new comes out of it except the increased resistances of the patient. The sense of boredom which then appears in the analysis is simply an expression of the monotony and poverty of ideas – not of the unconscious, as is sometimes supposed, but of the analyst, who does not understand that

these fantasies should not be taken merely in a concretistic-reductive sense, but rather in a constructive one. When this is realized, the standstill is often overcome at a single stroke.

147   Constructive treatment of the unconscious, that is, the question of meaning and purpose, paves the way for the patient's insight into that process which I call the transcendent function.

148   It may not be superfluous, at this point, to say a few words about the frequently heard objection that the constructive method is simply 'suggestion.' The method is based, rather, on evaluating the symbol (i.e., dream-image or fantasy) not *semiotically*, as a sign for elementary instinctual processes, but symbolically in the true sense, the word 'symbol' being taken to mean the best possible expression for a complex fact not yet clearly apprehended by consciousness. Through reductive analysis of this expression nothing is gained but a clearer view of the elements originally composing it, and though I would not deny that increased insight into these elements may have its advantages, it nevertheless bypasses the question of purpose. Dissolution of the symbol at this stage of analysis is therefore a mistake. To begin with, however, the method for working out the complex meanings suggested by the symbol is the same as in reductive analysis. The associations of the patient are obtained, and as a rule they are plentiful enough to be used in the synthetic method. Here again they are evaluated not semiotically but symbolically. The question we must ask is: to what meaning do the individual associations A, B, C point, when taken in conjunction with the manifest dream-content?

149   An unmarried woman patient dreamt that *someone gave her a wonderful, richly ornamented, antique sword dug up out of a tumulus.* [For interpretation, see table opposite]

150   In this case there was no need of any supplementary analogies on the part of the analyst. The patient's associations provided all that was necessary. It might be objected that this treatment of the dream involves suggestion. But this ignores the fact that a suggestion is never accepted without an inner readiness for it, or if after great insistence it is accepted, it is immediately lost again. A suggestion that is accepted for any length of time always presupposes a marked psychological readiness which is merely brought into play by the so-called suggestion. This objection is therefore thoughtless and credits suggestion with a magical power it in no way possesses, otherwise suggestion therapy would have an enormous effect and would render analytical procedures quite superfluous. But this is far from being the case. Furthermore, the charge of suggestion does not take account of the fact that the patient's own associations point to the cultural significance of the sword.

151   After this digression, let us return to the question of the transcendent function. We have seen that during treatment the transcendent function is, in a sense, an 'artificial' product because it is largely supported by the analyst. But if the patient is to stand on his own feet he must not depend

ASSOCIATIONS	ANALYTICAL INTERPRETATION	CONSTRUCTIVE INTERPRETATION
Her *father's* dagger, which he once flashed in the sun in front of her. It made a great impression on her. Her father was in every respect an energetic, strong-willed man, with an impetuous temperament, and adventurous in love affairs. A *Celtic* bronze sword: Patient is proud of her Celtic ancestry. The Celts are full of temperament, impetuous, passionate. The ornamentation has a mysterious look about it, ancient tradition, runes, signs of ancient wisdom, ancient civilizations, heritage of mankind, brought to light again out of the grave.	Patient has a prounounced father complex and a rich tissue of sexual fantasies about her father, whom she lost early. She always put herself in her mother's place, although with strong resistances towards her father. She has never been able to accept a man like her father and has therefore chosen weakly, neurotic men against her will. Also in the analysis violent resistance towards the physician-father. The dream digs up her wish for her father's 'weapon.' The rest is clear. In theory, this would immediately point to a phallic fantasy.	It is as if the patient needed such a weapon. Her father had the weapon. He was energetic, lived accordingly, and also took upon himself the difficulties inherent in his temperament. Therefore, though living a passionate, exciting life he was not neurotic. This weapon is a very ancient heritage of mankind, which lay buried in the patient and was brought to light through excavation (analysis). The weapon has to do with in-sight, with wisdom. It is a means of attack and defence. Her father's weapon was a passionate, unbending will, with which he made his way

through life. Up till now the patient has been the opposite in every respect. She is just on the point of realizing that a person can also will something and need not merely be driven, as she had always believed. The will based on a knowledge of life and on insight is an ancient heritage of the human race, which also is in her, but till now lay buried, for in this respect, too, she is her father's daughter. But she had not appreciated this till now, because her character had been that of a perpetually whining, pampered, spoilt child. She was extremely passive and completely given to sexual fantasies.

Interpretation of dream (see par. 149)

permanently on outside help. The interpretation of dreams would be an ideal method for synthesizing the conscious and unconscious data, but in practice the difficulties of analyzing one's own dreams are too great.

152   We must now make clear what is required to produce the transcendent function. First and foremost, we need the unconscious material. The most readily accessible expression of unconscious processes is undoubtedly dreams. The dream is, so to speak, a pure product of the unconscious. The alterations which the dream undergoes in the process of reaching consciousness, although undeniable, can be considered irrelevant, since they too derive from the unconscious and are not intentional distortions. Possible modifications of the original dream-image derive from a more superficial layer of the unconscious and therefore contain valuable material too. They are further fantasy-products following the general trend of the dream. The same applies to the subsequent images and ideas which frequently occur while dozing or rise up spontaneously on waking. Since the dream originates in sleep, it bears all the characteristics of an 'abaissement du niveau mental' (Janet), or of low energy-tension: logical discontinuity, fragmentary character, analogy formations, superficial associations of the verbal, clang, or visual type, condensations, irrational expressions, confusion, etc. With an increase of energy-tension, the

dreams acquire a more ordered character; they become dramatically composed and reveal clear sense-connections, and the valency of the associations increases.

153　Since the energy-tension in sleep is usually very low, dreams, compared with conscious material, are inferior expressions of unconscious contents and are very difficult to understand from a constructive point of view, but are usually easier to understand reductively. In general, dreams are unsuitable or difficult to make use of in developing the transcendent function, because they make too great demands on the subject.

154　We must therefore look to other sources for the unconscious material. There are, for instance, the unconscious interferences in the waking state, ideas 'out of the blue,' slips, deceptions and lapses of memory, symptomatic actions, etc. This material is generally more useful for the reductive method than for the constructive one; it is too fragmentary and lacks continuity, which is indispensable for a meaningful synthesis.

155　Another source is spontaneous fantasies. They usually have a more composed and coherent character and often contain much that is obviously significant. Some patients are able to produce fantasies at any time, allowing them to rise up freely simply by eliminating critical attention. Such fantasies can be used, though this particular talent is none too common. The capacity to produce free fantasies can, however, be developed with practice. The training consists first of all in systematic exercises for eliminating critical attention, thus producing a vacuum in consciousness. This encourages the emergence of any fantasies that are lying in readiness. A prerequisite, of course, is that fantasies with a high libido-charge are actually lying ready. This is naturally not always the case. Where this is not so, special measures are required.

156　Before entering upon a discussion of these, I must yield to an uncomfortable feeling which tells me that the reader may be asking dubiously, what really is the point of all this? And why is it so absolutely necessary to bring up the unconscious contents? Is it not sufficient if from time to time they come up of their own accord and make themselves unpleasantly felt? Does one have to drag the unconscious to the surface by force? On the contrary, should it not be the job of analysis to empty the unconscious of fantasies and in this way render it ineffective?

157　It may be as well to consider these misgivings in somewhat more detail, since the methods for bringing the unconscious to consciousness may strike the reader as novel, unusual, and perhaps even rather weird. We must therefore first discuss these natural objections, so that they shall not hold us up when we begin demonstrating the methods in question.

158　As we have seen, we need the unconscious contents to supplement the conscious attitude. If the conscious attitude were only to a slight degree 'directed,' the unconscious could flow in quite of its own accord. This is what does in fact happen with all those people who have a low level of conscious tension, as for instance primitives. Among primitives, no special measures are required to bring up the unconscious. Nowhere, really, are special measures required for this, because those people who are least aware of their unconscious side are the most influenced by it. But they are unconscious of what is happening. The secret participation of the unconscious is everywhere present without our having to search for it, but as it remains unconscious we never really know what is going on or what to expect. What we are searching for is a way to make conscious those contents which are about to influence our actions, so that the secret interference of the unconscious and its unpleasant consequences can be avoided.

159   The reader will no doubt ask: why cannot the unconscious be left to its own devices? Those who have not already had a few bad experiences in this respect will naturally see no reason to control the unconscious. But anyone with sufficiently bad experience will eagerly welcome the bare possibility of doing so. Directedness is absolutely necessary for the conscious process, but as we have seen it entails an unavoidable one-sidedness. Since the psyche is a self-regulating system, just as the body is, the regulating counteraction will always develop in the unconscious. Were it not for the directedness of the conscious function, the counteracting influences of the unconscious could set in unhindered. It is just this directedness that excludes them. This, of course, does not inhibit the counteraction, which goes on in spite of everything. Its regulating influence, however, is eliminated by critical attention and the directed will, because the counteraction as such seems incompatible with the conscious direction. To this extent the psyche of civilized man is no longer a self-regulating system but could rather be compared to a machine whose speed-regulation is so insensitive that it can continue to function to the point of self-injury, while on the other hand it is subject to the arbitrary manipulations of a one-sided will.

160   Now it is a peculiarity of psychic functioning that when the unconscious counteraction is suppressed it loses its regulating influence. It then begins to have an accelerating and intensifying effect on the conscious process. It is as though the counteraction had lost its regulating influence, and hence its energy, altogether, for a condition then arises in which not only no inhibiting counteraction takes place, but in which its energy seems to add itself to that of the conscious direction. To begin with, this naturally facilitates the execution of the conscious intentions, but because they are unchecked, they may easily assert themselves at the cost of the whole. For instance, when someone makes a rather bold assertion and suppresses the counteraction, namely a well-placed doubt, he will insist on it all the more, to his own detriment.

161   The ease with which the counteraction can be eliminated is proportional to the degree of dissociability of the psyche and leads to loss of instinct. This is characteristic of, as well as very necessary for, civilized man, since instincts in their original strength can render social adaptation almost impossible. It is not a real atrophy of instinct but, in most cases, only a

relatively lasting product of education, and would never have struck such deep roots had it not served the interests of the individual.

162   Apart from the everyday cases met with in practice, a good example of the suppression of the unconscious regulating influence can be found in Nietzsche's *Zarathustra*. The discovery of the 'higher' man, and also of the 'ugliest' man, expresses the regulating influence, for the 'higher' men want to drag Zarathustra down to the collective sphere of average humanity as it always has been, while the 'ugliest' man is actually the personification of the counteraction. But the roaring lion of Zarathustra's moral conviction forces all these influences, above all the feeling of pity, back again into the cave of the unconscious. Thus the regulating influence is suppressed, but not the secret counteraction of the unconscious, which from now on becomes clearly noticeable in Nietzsche's writings. First he seeks his adversary in Wagner, whom he cannot forgive for *Parsifal*, but soon his whole wrath turns against Christianity and in particular against St. Paul, who in some ways suffered a fate similar to Nietzsche's. As is well known, Nietzsche's psychosis first produced an identification with the 'Crucified Christ' and then with the dismembered Dionysus. With this catastrophe the counteraction at last broke through to the surface.

163   Another example is the classic case of megalomania preserved for us in the fourth chapter of the Book of Daniel. Nebuchadnezzar at the height of his power had a dream which foretold disaster if he did not humble himself. Daniel interpreted the dream quite expertly, but without getting a hearing. Subsequent events showed that his interpretation was correct, for Nebuchadnezzar, after suppressing the unconscious regulating influence, fell victim to a psychosis that contained the very counteraction he had sought to escape: he, the lord of the earth, was degraded to an animal.

164   An acquaintance of mine once told me a dream in which he *stepped out into space from the top of a mountain.* I explained to him something of the influence of the unconscious and warned him against dangerous mountaineering expeditions, for which he had a regular passion. But he laughed at such ideas. A few months later while climbing a mountain he actually did step off into space and was killed.

165   Anyone who has seen things happen over and over again in every conceivable shade of dramatic intensity is bound to ponder. He becomes aware how easy it is to overlook the regulating influences, and that he should endeavour to pay attention to the unconscious regulation which is so necessary for our mental and physical health. Accordingly he will try to help himself by practising self-observation and self-criticism. But mere self-observation and intellectual self-analysis are entirely inadequate as a means to establishing contact with the unconscious. Although no human being can be spared bad experiences, everyone shrinks from risking them, especially if he sees any way by which they might be circumvented. Knowledge of the regulating influences of the unconscious offers just such a possibility and actually does render much bad experience unnecessary.

We can avoid a great many detours that are distinguished by no particular attraction but only by tiresome conflicts. It is bad enough to make detours and painful mistakes in unknown and unexplored territory, but to get lost in inhabited country on broad highways is merely exasperating. What, then, are the means at our disposal of obtaining knowledge of the regulating factors?

166 If there is no capacity to produce fantasies freely, we have to resort to artificial aid. The reason for invoking such aid is generally a depressed or disturbed state of mind for which no adequate cause can be found. Naturally the patient can give any number of rationalistic reasons – the bad weather alone suffices as a reason. But none of them is really satisfying as an explanation, for a causal explanation of these states is usually satisfying only to an outsider, and then only up to a point. The outsider is content if his causal requirements are more or less satisfied; it is sufficient for him to know where the thing comes from; he does not feel the challenge which, for the patient, lies in the depression. The patient would like to know what it is all for and how to gain relief. *In the intensity of the emotional disturbance itself lies the value, the energy which he should have at his disposal in order to remedy the state of reduced adaptation.* Nothing is achieved by repressing this state or devaluing it rationally.

167 In order, therefore, to gain possession of the energy that is in the wrong place, he must make the emotional state the basis or starting point of the procedure. He must make himself as conscious as possible of the mood he is in, sinking himself in it without reserve and noting down on paper all the fantasies and other associations that come up. Fantasy must be allowed the freest possible play, yet not in such a manner that it leaves the orbit of its object, namely the affect, by setting off a kind of 'chain-reaction' association process. This 'free association,' as Freud called it, leads away from the object to all sorts of complexes, and one can never be sure that they relate to the affect and are not displacements which have appeared in its stead. Out of this preoccupation with the object there comes a more or less complete expression of the mood, which reproduces the content of the depression in some way, either concretely or symbolically. Since the depression was not manufactured by the conscious mind but is an unwelcome intrusion from the unconscious, the elaboration of the mood is, as it were, a picture of the contents and tendencies of the unconscious that were massed together in the depression. The whole procedure is a kind of enrichment and clarification of the affect, whereby the affect and its contents are brought nearer to consciousness, becoming at the same time more impressive and more understandable. This work by itself can have a favourable and vitalizing influence. At all events, it creates a new situation, since the previously unrelated affect has become a more or less clear and articulate idea, thanks to the assistance and co-operation of the conscious mind. This is the beginning of the transcendent function, i.e., of the collaboration of conscious and unconscious data.

168   The emotional disturbance can also be dealt with in another way, not by clarifying it intellectually but by giving it visible shape. Patients who possess some talent for drawing or painting can give expression to their mood by means of a picture. It is not important for the picture to be technically or aesthetically satisfying, but merely for the fantasy to have free play and for the whole thing to be done as well as possible. In principle this procedure agrees with the one first described. Here too a product is created which is influenced by both conscious and unconscious, embodying the striving of the unconscious for the light and the striving of the conscious for substance.

169   Often, however, we find cases where there is no tangible mood or depression at all, but just a general, dull discontent, a feeling of resistance to everything, a sort of boredom or vague disgust, an indefinable but excruciating emptiness. In these cases no definite starting point exists – it would first have to be created. Here a special introversion of libido is necessary, supported perhaps by favourable external conditions, such as complete rest, especially at night, when the libido has in any case a tendency to introversion. (''Tis night: now do all fountains speak louder. And my soul also is a bubbling fountain.'[2])

170   Critical attention must be eliminated. Visual types should concentrate on the expectation that an inner image will be produced. As a rule such a fantasy-picture will actually appear – perhaps hypnagogically – and should be carefully observed and noted down in writing. Audio-verbal types usually hear inner words, perhaps mere fragments of apparently meaningless sentences to begin with, which however should be carefully noted down too. Others at such times simply hear their 'other' voice. There are, indeed, not a few people who are well aware that they possess a sort of inner critic or judge who immediately comments on everything they say or do. Insane people hear this voice directly as auditory hallucinations. But normal people too, if their inner life is fairly well developed, are able to reproduce this inaudible voice without difficulty, though as it is notoriously irritating and refactory it is almost always repressed. Such persons have little difficulty in procuring the unconscious material and thus laying the foundation of the transcendent function.

171   There are others, again, who neither see nor hear anything inside themselves, but whose hands have the knack of giving expression to the contents of the unconscious. Such people can profitably work with plastic materials. Those who are able to express the unconscious by means of bodily movements are rather rare. The disadvantage that movements cannot easily be fixed in the mind must be met by making careful drawings of the movements afterwards, so that they shall not be lost to the memory. Still rarer, but equally valuable, is automatic writing, direct or with the planchette. This, too, yields useful results.

172   We now come to the next question: what is to be done with the material obtained in one of the manners described. To this question there is no *a*

priori answer; it is only when the conscious mind confronts the products of the unconscious that a provisional reaction will ensue which determines the subsequent procedure. Practical experience alone can give us a clue. So far as my experience goes, there appear to be two main tendencies. One is the way of *creative formulation*, the other the way of *understanding*.

173   Where the principle of creative formulation predominates, the material is continually varied and increased until a kind of condensation of motifs into more or less stereotyped symbols takes place. These stimulate the creative fantasy and serve chiefly as aesthetic motifs. This tendency leads to the aesthetic problem of artistic formulation.

174   Where, on the other hand, the principle of understanding predominates, the aesthetic aspect is of relatively little interest and may occasionally even be felt as a hindrance. Instead, there is an intensive struggle to understand the *meaning* of the unconscious product.

175   Where aesthetic formulation tends to concentrate on the formal aspect of the motif, an intuitive understanding often tries to catch the meaning from barely adequate hints in the material, without considering those elements which would come to light in a more careful formulation.

176   Neither of these tendencies can be brought about by an arbitrary effort of will; they are far more the result of the peculiar make-up of the individual personality. Both have their typical dangers and may lead one astray. The danger of the aesthetic tendency is overvaluation of the formal or 'artistic' worth of the fantasy-productions; the libido is diverted from the real goal of the transcendent function and sidetracked into purely aesthetic problems of artistic expression. The danger of wanting to understand the meaning is overvaluation of the content, which is subjected to intellectual analysis and interpretation, so that the essentially symbolic character of the product is lost. Up to a point these bypaths must be followed in order to satisfy aesthetic or intellectual requirements, which-ever predominate in the individual case. But the danger of both these bypaths is worth stressing, for, after a certain point of psychic development has been reached, the products of the unconscious are greatly overvalued precisely because they were boundlessly undervalued before. This under-valuation is one of the greatest obstacles in formulating the unconscious material. It reveals the collective standards by which anything individual is judged: nothing is considered good or beautiful that does not fit into the collective schema, though it is true that contemporary art is beginning to make compensatory efforts in this respect. What is lacking is not the collective recognition of the individual product but its subjective appreci-ation, the understanding of its meaning and value for the *subject*. This feeling of inferiority for one's own product is of course not the rule everywhere. Sometimes we find the exact opposite: a naïve and uncritical overvaluation coupled with the demand for collective recognition once the initial feeling of inferiority has been overcome. Conversely, an initial overvaluation can easily turn into depreciatory scepticism. These erroneous

judgments are due to the individual's unconsciousness and lack of self-reliance: either he is able to judge only by collective standards, or else, owing to ego-inflation, he loses his capacity for judgment altogether.

177   *One tendency seems to be the regulating principle of the other*; both are bound together in a compensatory relationship. Experience bears out this formula. So far as it is possible at this stage to draw more general conclusions, we could say that aesthetic formulation needs understanding of the meaning, and understanding needs aesthetic formulation. The two supplement each other to form the transcendent function.

178   The first steps along both paths follow the same principle: consciousness puts its media of expression at the disposal of the unconscious content. It must not do more than this at first, so as not to exert undue influence. In giving the content form, the lead must be left as far as possible to the chance ideas and associations thrown up by the unconscious. This is naturally something of a setback for the conscious standpoint and is often felt as painful. It is not difficult to understand this when we remember how the contents of the unconscious usually present themselves: as things which are too weak by nature to cross the threshold, or as incompatible elements that were repressed for a variety of reasons. Mostly they are unwelcome, unexpected, irrational contents, disregard or repression of which seems altogether understandable. Only a small part of them has any unusual value, either from the collective or from the subjective standpoint. But contents that are collectively valueless may be exceedingly valuable when seen from the standpoint of the individual. This fact expresses itself in their affective tone, no matter whether the subject feels it as negative or positive. Society, too, is divided in its acceptance of new and unknown ideas which obtrude their emotionality. The purpose of the initial procedure is to discover the feeling-toned contents, for in these cases we are always dealing with situations where the onesidedness of consciousness meets with the resistance of the instinctual sphere.

179   The two ways do not divide until the aesthetic problem becomes decisive for the one type of person and the intellectual-moral problem for the other. The ideal case would be if these two aspects could exist side by side or rhythmically succeed each other; that is, if there were an alternation of creation and understanding. It hardly seems possible for the one to exist without the other, though it sometimes does happen in practice: the creative urge seizes possession of the object at the cost of its meaning, or the urge to understand overrides the necessity of giving it form. The unconscious contents want first of all to be seen clearly, which can only be done by giving them shape, and to be judged only when everything they have to say is tangibly present. It was for this reason that Freud got the dream-contents, as it were, to express themselves in the form of 'free associations' before he began interpreting them.

180   It does not suffice in all cases to elucidate only the conceptual context of a dream-content. Often it is necessary to clarify a vague content by

giving it a visible form. This can be done by drawing, painting, or modelling. Often the hands know how to solve a riddle with which the intellect has wrestled in vain. By shaping it, one goes on dreaming the dream in greater detail in the waking state, and the initially incomprehensible, isolated event is integrated into the sphere of the total personality, even though it remains at first unconscious to the subject. Aesthetic formulation leaves it at that and gives up any idea of discovering a meaning. This sometimes leads patients to fancy themselves artists – misunderstood ones, naturally. The desire to understand, if it dispenses with careful formulation, starts with the chance idea or association and therefore lacks an adequate basis. It has better prospects of success if it begins only with the formulated product. The less the initial material is shaped and developed, the greater is the danger that understanding will be governed not by the empirical facts but by theoretical and moral considerations. The kind of understanding with which we are concerned at this stage consists in a reconstruction of the meaning that seems to be immanent in the original 'chance' idea.

181   It is evident that such a procedure can legitimately take place only when there is a sufficient motive for it. Equally, the lead can be left to the unconscious only if it already contains the will to lead. This naturally happens only when the conscious mind finds itself in a critical situation. Once the unconscious content has been given form and the meaning of the formulation is understood, the question arises as to how the ego will relate to this position, and how the ego and the unconscious are to come to terms. This is the second and more important stage of the procedure, the bringing together of opposites for the production of a third: the transcendent function. At this stage it is no longer the unconscious that takes the lead, but the ego.

182   We shall not define the individual ego here, but shall leave it in its banal reality as that continuous centre of consciousness whose presence has made itself felt since the days of childhood. It is confronted with a psychic product that owes its existence mainly to an unconscious process and is therefore in some degree opposed to the ego and its tendencies.

183   This standpoint is essential in coming to terms with the unconscious. The position of the ego must be maintained as being of equal value to the counter-position of the unconscious, and vice versa. This amounts to a very necessary warning: for just as the conscious mind of civilized man has a restrictive effect on the unconscious, so the rediscovered unconscious often has a really dangerous effect on the ego. In the same way that the ego suppressed the unconscious before, a liberated unconscious can thrust the ego aside and overwhelm it. There is a danger of the ego losing its head, so to speak, that it will not be able to defend itself against the pressure of affective factors – a situation often encountered at the beginning of schizophrenia. This danger would not exist, or would not be so acute, if the process of having it out with the unconscious could somehow divest the affects of their dynamism. And this is what does in

fact happen when the counter-position is aestheticized or intellectualized. But the confrontation with the unconscious must be a many-sided one, for the transcendent function is not a partial process running a conditioned course; it is a total and integral event in which all aspects are, or should be, included. The affect must therefore be deployed in its full strength. Aestheticization and intellectualization are excellent weapons against dangerous affects, but they should be used only when there is a vital threat, and not for the purpose of avoiding a necessary task.

184   Thanks to the fundamental insight of Freud, we know that emotional factors must be given full consideration in the treatment of the neuroses. The personality *as a whole* must be taken seriously into account, and this applies to both parties, the patient as well as the analyst. How far the latter may hide behind the shield of theory remains a delicate question, to be left to his discretion. At all events, the treatment of neurosis is not a kind of psychological water-cure but a renewal of the personality, working in every direction and penetrating every sphere of life. Coming to terms with the counter-position is a serious matter on which sometimes a very great deal depends. Taking the other side seriously is an essential prerequisite of the process, for only in that way can the regulating factors exert an influence on our actions. Taking it seriously does not mean taking it literally, but it does mean giving the unconscious credit, so that it has a chance to co-operate with consciousness instead of automatically disturbing it.

185   Thus, in coming to terms with the unconscious, not only is the standpoint of the ego justified, but the unconscious is granted the same authority. The ego takes the lead, but the unconscious must be allowed to have its say too – *audiatur et altera pars*.

186   The way this can be done is best shown by those cases in which the 'other' voice is more or less distinctly heard. For such people it is technically very simple to note down the 'other' voice in writing and to answer its statements from the standpoint of the ego. It is exactly as if a dialogue were taking place between two human beings with equal rights, each of whom gives the other credit for a valid argument and considers it worth while to modify the conflicting standpoints by means of thorough comparison and discussion or else to distinguish them clearly from one another. Since the way to agreement seldom stands open, in most cases a long conflict will have to be borne, demanding sacrifices from both sides. Such a rapprochement could just as well take place between patient and analyst, the role of devil's advocate falling to the latter.

187   The present day shows with appalling clarity how little able people are to let the other man's argument count, although this capacity is a funda-mental and indispensable condition for any human community. Everyone who proposes to come to terms with himself must reckon with this basic problem. For, to the degree that he does not admit the validity of the other person, he denies the 'other' within himself the right to exist – and vice versa. The capacity for inner dialogue is a touchstone for outer objectivity.

188   Simple as the process of coming to terms may be in the case of the inner dialogue, it is undoubtedly more complicated in other cases where only visual products are available, speaking a language which is eloquent enough for one who understands it, but which seems like deaf-and-dumb language to one who does not. Faced with such products, the ego must seize the initiative and ask: 'How am I affected by this sign?'[3] This Faustian question can call forth an illuminating answer. The more direct and natural the answer is, the more valuable it will be, for directness and naturalness guarantee a more or less total reaction. It is not absolutely necessary for the process of confrontation itself to become conscious in every detail. Very often a total reaction does not have at its disposal those theoretical assumptions, views, and concepts which would make clear apprehension possible. In such cases one must be content with the wordless but suggestive feelings which appear in their stead and are more valuable than clever talk.

189   The shuttling to and fro of arguments and affects represents the transcendent function of opposites. The confrontation of the two positions generates a tension charged with energy and creates a living, third thing – not a logical stillbirth in accordance with the principle *tertium non datur* but a movement out of the suspension between opposites, a living birth that leads to a new level of being, a new situation. The transcendent function manifests itself as a quality of conjoined opposites. So long as these are kept apart – naturally for the purpose of avoiding conflict – they do not function and remain inert.

190   In whatever form the opposites appear in the individual, at bottom it is always a matter of consciousness lost and obstinately stuck in one-sidedness, confronted with the image of instinctive wholeness and freedom. This presents a picture of the anthropoid and archaic man with, on the one hand, his supposedly uninhibited world of instinct and, on the other, his often misunderstood world of spiritual ideas, who, compensating and correcting our one-sidedness, emerges from the darkness and shows us how and where we have deviated from the basic pattern and crippled ourselves psychically.

191   I must content myself here with a description of the outward forms and possibilities of the transcendent function. Another task of greater importance would be the description of its *contents*. There is already a mass of material on this subject, but not all the difficulties in the way of exposition have yet been overcome. A number of preparatory studies are still needed before the conceptual foundation is laid which would enable us to give a clear and intelligible account of the contents of the transcendent function. I have unfortunately had the experience that the scientific public are not everywhere in a position to follow a purely psychological argument, since they either take it too personally or are bedevilled by philosophical or intellectual prejudices. This renders any meaningful appreciation of the psychological factors quite impossible. If people take it personally their

judgment is always subjective, and they declare everything to be impossible which seems not to apply in their case or which they prefer not to
acknowledge. They are quite incapable of realizing that what is valid for
them may not be valid for another person with a different psychology. We
are still very far from possessing a general valid scheme of explanation in
all cases.

192   One of the greatest obstacles to psychological understanding is the
inquisitive desire to know whether the psychological factor adduced is
'true' or 'correct.' If the description of it is not erroneous or false, then
the factor is valid in itself and proves its validity by its very existence.
One might just as well ask if the duck-billed platypus is a 'true' or 'correct'
invention of the Creator's will. Equally childish is the prejudice against
the role which mythological assumptions play in the life of the psyche.
Since they are not 'true,' it is argued, they have no place in a scientific
explanation. But mythologems *exist*, even though their statements do not
coincide with our incommensurable idea of 'truth.'

193   As the process of coming to terms with the counter-position has a total
character, nothing is excluded. Everything takes part in the discussion,
even if only fragments become conscious. Consciousness is continually
widened through the confrontation with previously unconscious contents,
or – to be more accurate – could be widened if it took the trouble to
integrate them. That is naturally not always the case. Even if there is
sufficient intelligence to understand the procedure, there may yet be a lack
of courage and self-confidence, or one is too lazy, mentally and morally,
or too cowardly, to make an effort. But where the necessary premises exist,
the transcendent function not only forms a valuable addition to psychotherapeutic treatment, but gives the patient the inestimable advantage of
assisting the analyst on his own resources, and of breaking a dependence
which is often felt as humiliating. It is a way of attaining liberation by
one's own efforts and of finding the courage to be oneself.

NOTES

1 [Written in 1916 under the title 'Die Transzendente Funktion,' the ms. lay in
   Professor Jung's files until 1953. First published in 1957 by the Students
   Association, C. G. Jung Institute, Zurich, in an English translation by A. R. Pope.
   The German original, considerably revised by the author, was published in *Geist
   und Werk . . . zum 75. Geburtstag von Dr. Daniel Brody* (Zurich, 1958), together
   with a prefatory note of more general import specially written for that volume.
   The author has partially rewritten the note for publication here. The present
   translation is based on the revised German version, and Mr Pope's translation has
   been consulted. – EDITORS.]
2 [Nietzsche, *Thus Spake Zarathustra*, XXXI; Common trans., p. 156. – EDITORS.]
3 [Cf. *Faust: Part I*, Wayne trans., p. 46.]

3 'The technique of differentiation between the ego and the figures of the unconscious'

From: 'The relations between the ego and the unconscious', in *Two Essays on Analytical Psychology* (1928) (*CW* 7), pars. 341–73

341   I owe it to the reader to give him a detailed example of the specific activity of animus and anima. Unfortunately this material is so enormous and demands so much explanation of symbols that I cannot include such an account within the compass of this essay. I have, however, published some of these products with all their symbolical associations in a separate work,[1] and to this I must refer the reader. In that book I said nothing about the animus, because at that time this function was still unknown to me. Nevertheless, if I advise a woman patient to associate her unconscious contents, she will always produce the same kind of fantasy. The masculine hero figure who almost unfailingly appears is the animus, and the succession of fantasy-experiences demonstrates the gradual transformation and dissolution of the autonomous complex.

342   This transformation is the aim of the analysis of the unconscious. If there is no transformation, it means that the determining influence of the unconscious is unabated, and that it will in some cases persist in maintaining neurotic symptoms in spite of all our analysis and all our understanding. Alternatively, a compulsive transference will take hold, which is just as bad as a neurosis. Obviously in such cases no amount of suggestion, good will, and purely reductive understanding has helped to break the power of the unconscious. This is not to say – once again I would like to emphasize this point very clearly – that all psychotherapeutic methods are, by and large, useless. I merely want to stress the fact that there are not a few cases where the doctor has to make up his mind to deal fundamentally with the unconscious, to come to a real settlement with it. This is of course something very different from interpretation. In the latter case it is taken for granted that the doctor *knows* beforehand, so as to be able to interpret. But in the case of a real settlement it is not a question of interpretation: it is a question of releasing unconscious processes and letting them come into the conscious mind in the form of fantasies. We can try our hand at interpreting these fantasies if we like. In many cases it may be quite important for the patient to have some idea of the meaning of the fantasies produced. But it is of vital importance that he should experience them to the full and, in so far as intellectual understanding

belongs to the totality of experience, also understand them. Yet I would not give priority to understanding. Naturally the doctor must be able to assist the patient in his understanding, but, since he will not and indeed cannot understand everything, the doctor should assiduously guard against clever feats of interpretation. For the important thing is not to interpret and understand the fantasies, but primarily to experience them. Alfred Kubin has given a very good description of the unconscious in his book *Die andere Seite*; that is, he has described what he, as an artist, experienced of the unconscious. It is an artistic experience which, in the deeper meaning of human experience, is incomplete. I would like to recommend an attentive reading of this book to everybody who is interested in these questions. He will then discover the incompleteness I speak of: the vision is experienced artistically, but not humanly. By 'human' experience I mean that the person of the author should not just be included passively in the vision, but that he should face the figures of the vision actively and reactively, with full consciousness. I would level the same criticism at the authoress of the fantasies dealt with in the book mentioned above; she, too, merely stands opposite the fantasies forming themselves out of the unconscious, perceiving them, or at best passively enduring them. But a real settlement with the unconscious demands a firmly opposed conscious standpoint.

343   I will try to explain what I mean by an example. One of my patients had the following fantasy: *He sees his fiancée running down the road towards the river. It is winter, and the river is frozen. She runs out on the ice, and he follows her. She goes right out, and then the ice breaks, a dark fissure appears, and he is afraid she is going to jump in. And that is what happens: she jumps into the crack, and he watches her sadly.*

344   This fragment, although torn out of its context, clearly shows the attitude of the conscious mind: it perceives and passively endures, the fantasy-image is merely seen and felt, it is two-dimensional, as it were, because the patient is not sufficiently involved. Therefore the fantasy remains a flat image, concrete and agitating perhaps, but unreal, like a dream. This unreality comes from the fact that he himself is not playing an active part. If the fantasy happened in reality, he would not be at a loss for some means to prevent his fiancée from committing suicide. He could, for instance, easily overtake her and restrain her bodily from jumping into the crack. Were he to act in reality as he acted in the fantasy, he would obviously be paralysed, either with horror, or because of the unconscious thought that he really has no objection to her committing suicide. The fact that he remains passive in the fantasy merely expresses his attitude to the activity of the unconscious in general: he is fascinated and stupefied by it. In reality he suffers from all sorts of depressive ideas and convictions; he thinks he is no good, that he has some hopeless hereditary taint, that his brain is degenerating, etc. These negative feelings are so many auto-suggestions which he accepts without argument. Intellectually, he can

understand them perfectly and recognize them as untrue, but nevertheless the feelings persist. They cannot be attacked by the intellect because they have no intellectual or rational basis; they are rooted in an unconscious, irrational fantasy-life which is not amenable to conscious criticism. In these cases the unconscious must be given an opportunity to produce its fantasies, and the above fragment is just such a product of unconscious fantasy activity. Since the case was one of psychogenic depression, the depression itself was due to fantasies of whose existence the patient was totally unconscious. In genuine melancholia, extreme exhaustion, poisoning, etc., the situation would be reversed: the patient has such fantasies because he is in a depressed condition. But in a case of psychogenic depression he is depressed because he has such fantasies. My patient was a very clever young man who had been intellectually enlightened as to the cause of his neurosis by a lengthy analysis. However, intellectual understanding made no difference to his depression. In cases of this sort the doctor should spare himself the useless trouble of delving still further into the causality; for, when a more or less exhaustive understanding is of no avail, the discovery of yet another little bit of causality will be of no avail either. The unconscious has simply gained an unassailable ascendency; it wields an attractive force that can invalidate all conscious contents – in other words, it can withdraw libido from the conscious world and thereby produce a 'depression,' an *abaissement du niveau mental* (Janet). But as a result of this we must, according to the law of energy, expect an accumulation of value – i.e., libido – in the unconscious.

345   Libido can never be apprehended except in a definite form; that is to say, it is identical with fantasy-images. And we can only release it from the grip of the unconscious by bringing up the corresponding fantasy-images. That is why, in a case like this, we give the unconscious a chance to bring its fantasies to the surface. This is how the foregoing fragment was produced. It is a single episode from a long and very intricate series of fantasy-images, corresponding to the quota of energy that was lost to the conscious mind and its contents. The patient's conscious world has become cold, empty, and grey; but his unconscious is activated, powerful, and rich. It is characteristic of the nature of the unconscious psyche that it is sufficient unto itself and knows no human considerations. Once a thing has fallen into the unconscious it is retained there, regardless of whether the conscious mind suffers or not. The latter can hunger and freeze, while everything in the unconscious becomes verdant and blossoms.

346   So at least it appears at first. But when we look deeper, we find that this unconcern of the unconscious has a meaning, indeed a purpose and a goal. There are psychic goals that lie beyond the conscious goals; in fact, they may even be inimical to them. But we find that the unconscious has an inimical or ruthless bearing towards the conscious only when the latter adopts a false or pretentious attitude.

347   The conscious attitude of my patient is so one-sidedly intellectual and

rational that nature herself rises up against him and annihilates his whole world of conscious values. But he cannot de-intellectualize himself and make himself dependent on another function, e.g., feeling, for the very simple reason that he has not got it. The unconscious has it. Therefore we have no alternative but to hand over the leadership to the unconscious and give it the opportunity of becoming a conscious content in the form of fantasies. If, formerly, my patient clung to his intellectual world and defended himself with rationalizations against what he regarded as his illness, he must now yield himself up to it entirely, and when a fit of depression comes upon him, he must no longer force himself to some kind of work in order to forget, but must accept his depression and give it a hearing.

348   Now this is the direct opposite of succumbing to a mood, which is so typical of neurosis. It is no weakness, no spineless surrender, but a hard achievement, the essence of which consists in keeping your objectivity despite the temptations of the mood, and in making the mood your object, instead of allowing it to become in you the dominating subject. So the patient must try to get his mood to speak to him; his mood must tell him all about itself and show him through what kind of fantastic analogies it is expressing itself.

349   The foregoing fragment is a bit of visualized mood. If he had not succeeded in keeping his objectivity in relation to his mood, he would have had, in place of the fantasy-image, only a crippling sense that everything was going to the devil, that he was incurable, etc. But because he gave his mood a chance to express itself in an image, he succeeded in converting at least a small sum of libido, of unconscious creative energy in eidetic form, into a conscious content and thus withdrawing it from the sphere of the unconscious.

350   But this effort is not enough, for the fantasy, to be completely experienced, demands not just perception and passivity, but active participation. The patient would comply with this demand if he conducted himself in the fantasy as he would doubtless conduct himself in reality. He would never remain an idle spectator while his fiancée tried to drown herself; he would leap up and stop her. This should also happen in the fantasy. If he succeeds in behaving in the fantasy as he would behave in a similar situation in reality, he would prove that he was taking the fantasy seriously, i.e., assigning absolute reality value to the unconscious. In this way he would have won a victory over his one-sided intellectualism and, indirectly, would have asserted the validity of the irrational standpoint of the unconscious.

351   That would be the complete experience of the unconscious demanded of him. But one must not underestimate what that actually means: your whole world is menaced by fantastic irreality. It is almost insuperably difficult to forget, even for a moment, that all this is only fantasy, a figment

of the imagination that must strike one as altogether arbitrary and artificial. How can one assert that anything of this kind is 'real' and take it seriously?

352   We can hardly be expected to believe in a sort of double life, in which we conduct ourselves on one plane as modest average citizens, while on another we have unbelievable adventures and perform heroic deeds. In other words, we must not concretize our fantasies. But there is in man a strange propensity to do just this, and all his aversion to fantasy and his critical depreciation of the unconscious come solely from the deep-rooted fear of this tendency. Concretization and the fear of it are both primitive superstitions, but they still survive in the liveliest form among so-called enlightened people. In his civic life a man may follow the trade of a shoemaker, but as the member of a sect he puts on the dignity of an archangel. To all appearances he is a small tradesman, but among the freemasons he is a mysterious grandee. Another sits all day in his office; at evening, in his circle, he is a reincarnation of Julius Caesar, fallible as a man, but in his official capacity infallible. These are all unintentional concretizations.

353   As against this, the scientific credo of our time has developed a superstitious phobia about fantasy. But the real is what works. And the fantasies of the unconscious work, there can be no doubt about that. Even the cleverest philosopher can be the victim of a thoroughly idiotic agoraphobia. Our famous scientific reality does not afford us the slightest protection against the so-called irreality of the unconscious. Something works behind the veil of fantastic images, whether we give this something a good name or a bad. It is something real, and for this reason its manifestations must be taken seriously. But first the tendency to con-cretization must be overcome; in other words, we must not take the fantasies literally when we approach the question of interpreting them. While we are in the grip of the actual experience, the fantasies cannot be taken literally enough. But when it comes to understanding them, we must on no account mistake the semblance, the fantasy-image as such, for the operative process underlying it. The semblance is not the thing itself, but only its expression.

354   Thus my patient is not experiencing the suicide scene 'on another plane' (though in every other respect it is just as concrete as a real suicide); he experiences something real which looks like a suicide. The two opposing 'realities,' the world of the conscious and the world of the unconscious, do not quarrel for supremacy, but each makes the other relative. That the reality of the unconscious is very relative indeed will presumably arouse no violent contradiction; but that the reality of the conscious world could be doubted will be accepted with less alacrity. And yet both 'realities' are psychic experience, psychic semblances painted on an inscrutably dark back-cloth. To the critical intelligence, nothing is left of *absolute* reality.

355   Of the essence of things, of absolute being, we know nothing. But we experience various effects: from 'outside' by way of the senses, from

'inside' by way of fantasy. We would never think of asserting that the colour 'green' had an independent existence; similarly we ought never to imagine that a fantasy-experience exists in and for itself, and is therefore to be taken quite literally. It is an expression, an appearance standing for something unknown but real. The fantasy-fragment I have mentioned coincides in time with a wave of depression and desperation, and this event finds expression in the fantasy. The patient really does have a fiancée; for him she represents the one emotional link with the world. Snap that link, and it would be the end of his relation to the world. This would be an altogether hopeless aspect. But his fiancée is also a symbol for his anima, that is, for his relation to the unconscious. Hence the fantasy simultaneously expresses the fact that, without any hindrance on his part, his anima is disappearing again into the unconscious. This aspect shows that once again his mood is stronger than he is. It throws everything to the winds, while he looks on without lifting a hand. But he could easily step in and arrest the anima.

356   I give preference to this latter aspect, because the patient is an introvert whose life-relationship is ruled by inner facts. Were he an extravert, I would have to give preference to the first aspect, because for the extravert life is governed primarily by his relation to human beings. He might in the trough of a mood do away with his fiancée and himself too, whereas the introvert harms himself most when he casts off his relation to the anima, i.e., to the object within.

357   So my patient's fantasy clearly reveals the negative movement of the unconscious, a tendency to recoil from the conscious world so energetically that it sucks away the libido from consciousness and leaves the latter empty. But, by making the fantasy conscious, we stop this process from happening unconsciously. If the patient were himself to participate actively in the way described above, he would possess himself of the libido invested in the fantasy, and would thus gain added influence over the unconscious.

358   Continual conscious realization of unconscious fantasies, together with active participation in the fantastic events, has, as I have witnessed in a very large number of cases, the effect firstly of extending the conscious horizon by the inclusion of numerous unconscious contents; secondly of gradually diminishing the dominant influence of the unconscious; and thirdly of bringing about a change of personality.

359   This change of personality is naturally not an alteration of the original hereditary disposition, but rather a transformation of the general attitude. Those sharp cleavages and antagonisms between conscious and unconscious, such as we see so clearly in the endless conflicts of neurotic natures, nearly always rest on a noticeable one-sidedness of the conscious attitude, which gives absolute precedence to one or two functions, while the others are unjustly thrust into the background. Conscious realization

and experience of fantasies assimilates the unconscious inferior functions to the conscious mind – a process which is naturally not without far-reaching effects on the conscious attitude.

360 For the moment I will refrain from discussing the nature of this change of personality, since I only want to emphasize the fact that an important change does take place. I have called this change, which is the aim of our analysis of the unconscious, the transcendent function. This remarkable capacity of the human psyche for change, expressed in the transcendent function, is the principal object of late medieval alchemical philosophy, where it was expressed in terms of alchemical symbolism. Herbert Silberer, in his very able book *Problems of Mysticism and Its Symbolism*, has already pointed out the psychological content of alchemy. It would be an unpardonable error to accept the current view and reduce these 'alchymical' strivings to a mere matter of alembics and melting-pots. This side certainly existed; it represented the tentative beginnings of exact chemistry. But alchemy also had a spiritual side which must not be underestimated and whose psychological value has not yet been sufficiently appreciated: there was an 'alchymical' philosophy, the groping precursor of the most modern psychology. The secret of alchemy was in fact the transcendent function, the transformation of personality through the blending and fusion of the noble with the base components, of the differentiated with the inferior functions, of the conscious with the unconscious.

361 But, just as the beginnings of scientific chemistry were hopelessly distorted and confused by fantastic conceits and whimsicalities, so alchemical philosophy, hampered by the inevitable concretizations of the still crude and undifferentiated intellect, never advanced to any clear psychological formulation, despite the fact that the liveliest intuition of profound truths kept the medieval thinker passionately attached to the problems of alchemy. No one who has undergone the process of assimilating the unconscious will deny that it gripped his very vitals and changed him.

362 I would not blame my reader at all if he shakes his head dubiously at this point, being quite unable to imagine how such a *quantité négligeable* as the footling fantasy given above could ever have the slightest influence on anybody. I admit at once that in considering the transcendent function and the extraordinary influence attributed to it, the fragment we have quoted is anything but illuminating. But it is – and here I must appeal to the benevolent understanding of my reader – exceedingly difficult to give any examples, because every example has the unfortunate characteristic of being impressive and significant only to the individual concerned. Therefore I always advise my patients not to cherish the naïve belief that what is of the greatest significance to them personally also has objective significance.

363 The vast majority of people are quite incapable of putting themselves

individually into the mind of another. This is indeed a singularly rare art, and, truth to tell, it does not take us very far. Even the man whom we think we know best and who assures us himself that we understand him through and through is at bottom a stranger to us. He is *different*. The most we can do, and the best, is to have at least some inkling of his otherness, to respect it, and to guard against the outrageous stupidity of wishing to interpret it.

364   I can, therefore, produce nothing convincing, nothing that would convince the reader as it convinces the man whose deepest experience it is. We must simply believe it by reason of its analogy with our own experience. Ultimately, when all else fails, the end-result is plain beyond a doubt: the perceptible change of personality. With these reservations in mind, I would like to present the reader with another fantasy-fragment, this time from a woman. The difference from the previous example leaps to the eye: here the experience is total, the observer takes an active part and thus makes the process her own. The material in this case is very extensive, culminating in a profound transformation of personality. The fragment comes from a late phase of personal development and is an organic part of a long and continuous series of transformations which have as their goal the attainment of the mid-point of the personality.

365   It may not be immediately apparent what is meant by a 'mid-point of the personality.' I will therefore try to outline this problem in a few words. If we picture the conscious mind, with the ego as its centre, as being opposed to the unconscious, and if we now add to our mental picture the process of assimilating the unconscious, we can think of this assimilation as a kind of approximation of conscious and unconscious, where the centre of the total personality no longer coincides with the ego, but with a point midway between the conscious and the unconscious. This would be the point of new equilibrium, a new centering of the total personality, a virtual centre which, on account of its focal position between conscious and unconscious, ensures for the personality a new and more solid foundation. I freely admit that visualizations of this kind are no more than the clumsy attempts of the unskilled mind to give expression to inexpressible, and well-nigh indescribable, psychological facts. I could say the same thing in the words of St. Paul: 'Yet not I live, but Christ liveth in me.' Or I might invoke Lao-tzu and appropriate his concept of Tao, the Middle Way and creative centre of all things. In all these the same thing is meant. Speaking as a psychologist with a scientific conscience, I must say at once that these things are psychic factors of undeniable power; they are not the inventions of an idle mind, but definite psychic events obeying definite laws and having their legitimate causes and effects, which can be found among the most widely differing peoples and races today, as thousands of years ago. I have no theory as to what constitutes the nature of these processes. One would first have to know what constitutes the nature of the psyche. I am content simply to state the facts.

366   Coming now to our example: it concerns a fantasy of intensely visual character, something which in the language of the ancients would be called a 'vision.' Not a 'vision seen in a dream,' but a vision perceived by intense concentration on the background of consciousness, a technique that is perfected only after long practice.[2] Told in her own words, this is what the patient saw:

'I climbed the mountain and came to a place where I saw seven red stones in front of me, seven on either side, and seven behind me. I stood in the middle of this quadrangle. The stones were flat like steps. I tried to lift the four stones nearest me. In doing so I discovered that these stones were the pedestals of four statues of gods buried upside down in the earth. I dug them up and arranged them about me so that I was standing in the middle of them. Suddenly they leaned towards one another until their heads touched, forming something like a tent over me. I myself fell to the ground and said, 'Fall upon me if you must! I am tired.' Then I saw that beyond, encircling the four gods, a ring of flame had formed. After a time I got up from the ground and overthrew the statues of the gods. Where they fell, four trees shot up. At that blue flames leapt up from the ring of fire and began to burn the foliage of the trees. Seeing this I said, 'This must stop. I must go into the fire myself so that the leaves shall not be burned.' Then I stepped into the fire. The trees vanished and the fiery ring drew together to one immense blue flame that carried me up from the earth.'

367   Here the vision ended. Unfortunately I cannot see how I can make conclusively clear to the reader the extraordinarily interesting meaning of this vision. The fragment is an excerpt from a long sequence, and one would have to explain everything that happened before and afterwards, in order to grasp the significance of the picture. At all events the unprejudiced reader will recognize at once the idea of a 'mid-point' that is reached by a kind of climb (mountaineering, effort, struggle, etc.). He will also recognize without difficulty the famous medieval conundrum of the squaring of the circle, which belongs to the field of alchemy. Here it takes its rightful place as a symbol of individuation. The total personality is indicated by the four cardinal points, the four gods, i.e., the four functions which give bearings in psychic space, and also by the circle enclosing the whole. Overcoming the four gods who threaten to smother the individual signifies liberation from identification with the four functions, a fourfold *nirdvandva* ('free from opposites') followed by an approximation to the circle, to undivided wholeness. This in its turn leads to further exaltation.

368   I must content myself with these hints. Anyone who takes the trouble to reflect upon the matter will be able to form a rough idea of how the transformation of personality proceeds. Through her active participation the patient merges herself in the unconscious processes, and she gains possession of them by allowing them to possess her. In this way she joins the conscious to the unconscious. The result is ascension in the flame,

transmutation in the alchemical heat, the genesis of the 'subtle spirit.' That is the transcendent function born of the union of opposites.

369   I must recall at this point a serious misunderstanding to which my readers often succumb, and doctors most commonly. They invariably assume, for reasons unknown, that I never write about anything except my method of treatment. This is far from being the case. I write about *psychology*. I must therefore expressly emphasize that my method of treatment does not consist in causing my patients to indulge in strange fantasies for the purpose of changing their personality, and other nonsense of that kind. I merely put it on record that there are certain cases where such a development occurs, not because I force anyone to it, but because it springs from inner necessity. For many of my patients these things are and must remain double Dutch. Indeed, even if it were possible for them to tread this path, it would be a disastrously wrong turning, and I would be the first to hold them back. The way of the transcendent function is an individual destiny. But on no account should one imagine that this way is equivalent to the life of a psychic anchorite, to alienation from the world. Quite the contrary, for such a way is possible and profitable only when the specific worldly tasks which these individuals set themselves are carried out in reality. Fantasies are no substitute for living; they are fruits of the spirit which fall to him who pays his tribute to life. The shirker experiences nothing but his own morbid fear, and it yields him no meaning. Nor will this way ever be known to the man who has found his way back to Mother Church. There is no doubt that the *mysterium magnum* is hidden in her forms, and in these he can live his life sensibly. Finally, the normal man will never be burdened, either, with this knowledge, for he is everlastingly content with the little that lies within his reach. Wherefore I entreat my reader to understand that I write about things which actually happen, and am not propounding methods of treatment.

370   These two examples of fantasy represent the positive activity of anima and animus. To the degree that the patient takes an active part, the personified figure of anima or animus will disappear. It becomes the function of relationship between conscious and unconscious. But when the unconscious contents – these same fantasies – are not 'realized,' they give rise to a negative activity and personification, i.e., to the autonomy of animus and anima. Psychic abnormalities then develop, states of possession ranging in degree from ordinary moods and 'ideas' to psychoses. All these states are characterized by one and the same fact that an unknown 'something' has taken possession of a smaller or greater portion of the psyche and asserts its hateful and harmful existence undeterred by all our insight, reason, and energy, thereby proclaiming the power of the unconscious over the conscious mind, the sovereign power of possession. In this state the possessed part of the psyche generally develops an animus or anima psychology. The woman's incubus consists of a host of masculine demons; the man's succubus is a vampire.

371   This particular concept of a soul which, according to the conscious attitude, either exists by itself or disappears in a function, has, as anyone can see, not the remotest connection with the Christian concept of the soul.

372   The second fantasy is a typical example of the kind of content produced by the collective unconscious. Although the form is entirely subjective and individual, the substance is none the less collective, being composed of universal images and ideas common to the generality of men, components, therefore, by which the individual is assimilated to the rest of mankind. If these contents remain unconscious, the individual is, in them, unconsciously commingled with other individuals – in other words, he is not differentiated, not individuated.

373   Here one may ask, perhaps, why it is so desirable that a man should be individuated. Not only is it desirable, it is absolutely indispensable because, through his contamination with others, he falls into situations and commits actions which bring him into disharmony with himself. From all states of unconscious contamination and non-differentiation there is begotten a compulsion to be and to act in a way contrary to one's own nature. Accordingly a man can neither be at one with himself nor accept responsibility for himself. He feels himself to be in a degrading, unfree, unethical condition. But the disharmony with himself is precisely the neurotic and intolerable condition from which he seeks to be delivered, and deliverance from this condition will come only when he can be and act as he feels is conformable with his true self. People have a feeling for these things, dim and uncertain at first, but growing ever stronger and clearer with progressive development. When a man can say of his states and actions, 'As I am, so I act,' he can be at one with himself, even though it be difficult, and he can accept responsibility for himself even though he struggle against it. We must recognize that nothing is more difficult to bear with than oneself. ('You sought the heaviest burden, and found yourself,' says Nietzsche.) Yet even this most difficult of achievements becomes possible if we can distinguish ourselves from the unconscious contents. The introvert discovers these contents in himself, the extravert finds them projected upon human objects. In both cases the unconscious contents are the cause of blinding illusions which falsify ourselves and our relations to our fellow men, making both unreal. For these reasons individuation is indispensable for certain people, not only as a therapeutic necessity, but as a high ideal, an idea of the best we can do. Nor should I omit to remark that it is at the same time the primitive Christian ideal of the Kingdom of Heaven which 'is within you.' The idea at the bottom of this ideal is that right action comes from right thinking, and that there is no cure and no improving of the world that does not begin with the individual himself. To put the matter drastically: the man who is a pauper or parasite will never solve the social question.

NOTES

1 *Symbols of Transformation* (CW5).
2 [This technique is elsewhere called 'active imagination.' Cf. 'The Transcendent Function,' pars. 166ff., and *Mysterium Coniunctionis*, pars. 706 and 749ff. – Editors.]

4   Commentary on *The Secret of the Golden Flower*

Excerpt from: *Alchemical Studies* (1929) (*CW* 13), pars. 17–45

[. . .]

17 As I have said, the essential reason which prompted me to look for a new way was the fact that the fundamental problem of the patient seemed to me insoluble unless violence was done to one or the other side of his nature. I had always worked with the temperamental conviction that at bottom there are no insoluble problems, and experience justified me in so far as I have often seen patients simply outgrow a problem that had destroyed others. This 'outgrowing,' as I formerly called it, proved on further investigation to be a new level of consciousness. Some higher or wider interest appeared on the patient's horizon, and through this broadening of his outlook the insoluble problem lost its urgency. It was not solved logically in its own terms, but faded out when confronted with a new and stronger life urge. It was not repressed and made unconscious, but merely appeared in a different light, and so really did become different. What, on a lower level, had led to the wildest conflicts and to panicky outbursts of emotion, from the higher level of personality now looked like a storm in the valley seen from the mountain top. This does not mean that the storm is robbed of its reality, but instead of being in it one is above it. But since, in a psychic sense, we are both valley and mountain, it might seem a vain illusion to deem oneself beyond what is human. One certainly does feel the affect and is shaken and tormented by it, yet at the same time one is aware of a higher consciousness looking on which prevents one from becoming identical with the affect, a consciousness which regards the affect as an object, and can say, 'I *know* that I suffer.' What our text says of indolence, 'Indolence of which a man is conscious, and indolence of which he is unconscious, are a thousand miles apart,'[1] holds true in the highest degree of affect.

18 Now and then it happened in my practice that a patient grew beyond himself because of unknown potentialities, and this became an experience of prime importance to me. In the meantime, I had learned that all the greatest and most important problems of life are fundamentally insoluble. They must be so, for they express the necessary polarity inherent in every self-regulating system. They can never be solved, but only outgrown. I therefore asked myself whether this outgrowing, this possibility of further

psychic development, was not the normal thing, and whether getting stuck in a conflict was pathological. Everyone must possess that higher level, at least in embryonic form, and must under favourable circumstances be able to develop this potentiality. When I examined the course of development in patients who quietly, and as if unconsciously, outgrew themselves, I saw that their fates had something in common. The new thing came to them from obscure possibilities either outside or inside themselves; they accepted it and grew with its help. It seemed to me typical that some took the new thing from outside themselves, others from inside; or rather, that it grew into some persons from without, and into others from within. But the new thing never came exclusively either from within or from without. If it came from outside, it became a profound inner experience; if it came from inside, it became an outer happening. In no case was it conjured into existence intentionally or by conscious willing, but rather seemed to be borne along on the stream of time.

19   We are so greatly tempted to turn everything into a purpose and a method that I deliberately express myself in very abstract terms in order to avoid prejudicing the reader in one way or the other. The new thing must not be pigeon-holed under any heading, for then it becomes a recipe to be used mechanically, and it would again be a case of the 'right means in the hands of the wrong man.' I have been deeply impressed by the fact that the new thing prepared by fate seldom or never comes up to conscious expectations. And still more remarkable, though the new thing goes against deeply rooted instincts as we have known them, it is a strangely appropriate expression of the total personality, an expression which one could not imagine in a more complete form.

20   What did these people do in order to bring about the development that set them free? As far as I could see they did nothing (*wu wei*[2]) but let things happen. As Master Lü-tsu teaches in our text, the light circulates according to its own law if one does not give up one's ordinary occupation. The art of letting things happen, action through non-action, letting go of oneself as taught by Meister Eckhart, became for me the key that opens the door to the way. We must be able to let things happen in the psyche. For us, this is an art of which most people know nothing. Consciousness is forever interfering, helping, correcting, and negating, never leaving the psychic processes to grow in peace. It would be simple enough, if only simplicity were not the most difficult of all things. To begin with, the task consists solely in observing objectively how a fragment of fantasy develops. Nothing could be simpler, and yet right here the difficulties begin. Apparently one has no fantasy fragments – or yes, there's one, but it is too stupid! Dozens of good reasons are brought against it. One cannot concentrate on it – it is too boring – what would come of it anyway – it is 'nothing but' this or that, and so on. The conscious mind raises innumerable objections, in fact it often seems bent on blotting out the spontaneous fantasy activity in spite of real insight and in spite of the firm

determination to allow the psychic process to go forward without interference. Occasionally there is a veritable cramp of consciousness.

21   If one is successful in overcoming the initial difficulties, criticism is still
likely to start in afterwards in the attempt to interpret the fantasy, to
classify it, to aestheticize it, or to devalue it. The temptation to do this is
almost irresistible. After it has been faithfully observed, free rein can be
given to the impatience of the conscious mind; in fact it must be given, or
obstructive resistances will develop. But each time the fantasy material is
to be produced, the activity of consciousness must be switched off again.

22   In most cases the results of these efforts are not very encouraging at
first. Usually they consist of tenuous webs of fantasy that give no clear
indication of their origin or their goal. Also, the way of getting at the
fantasies varies with individuals. For many people, it is easiest to write
them down; others visualize them, and others again draw or paint them
with or without visualization. If there is a high degree of conscious cramp,
often only the hands are capable of fantasy; they model or draw figures
that are sometimes quite foreign to the conscious mind.

23   These exercises must be continued until the cramp in the conscious mind
is relaxed, in other words, until one can let things happen, which is the
next goal of the exercise. In this way a new attitude is created, an attitude
that accepts the irrational and the incomprehensible simply because it is
happening. This attitude would be poison for a person who is already
overwhelmed by the things that happen to him, but it is of the greatest
value for one who selects, from among the things that happen, only those
that are acceptable to his conscious judgment, and is gradually drawn out
of the stream of life into a stagnant backwater.

24   At this point, the way travelled by the two types mentioned earlier seems
to divide. Both have learned to accept what comes to them. (As Master Lü-
tse teaches: 'When occupations come to us, we must accept them; when
things come to us, we must understand them from the ground up.'[3]) One
man will now take chiefly what comes to him from outside, and the other
what comes from inside. Moreover, the law of life demands that what they
take from outside and inside will be the very things that were always
excluded before. This reversal of one's nature brings an enlargement, a
heightening and enrichment of the personality, if the previous values are
retained alongside the change – provided that these values are not mere
illusions. If they are not held fast, the individual will swing too far to the
other side, slipping from fitness into unfitness, from adaptedness into
unadaptedness, and even from rationality into insanity. The way is not
without danger. Everything good is costly, and the development of
personality is one of the most costly of all things. It is a matter of saying
yea to oneself, of taking oneself as the most serious of tasks, of being
conscious of everything one does, and keeping it constantly before one's
eyes in all its dubious aspects – truly a task that taxes us to the utmost.

25   A Chinese can always fall back on the authority of his whole civilization. If he starts on the long way, he is doing what is recognized as being the best thing he could possibly do. But the Westerner who wishes to set out on this way, if he is really serious about it, has all authority against him – intellectual, moral, and religious. That is why it is infinitely easier for him to imitate the Chinese way and leave the troublesome European behind him, or else to seek the way back to the medievalism of the Christian Church and barricade himself behind the wall separating true Christians from the poor heathen and other ethnographic curiosities encamped outside. Aesthetic or intellectual flirtations with life and fate come to an abrupt halt here: the step to higher consciousness leaves us without a rearguard and without shelter. The individual must devote himself to the way with all his energy, for it is only by means of his integrity that he can go further, and his integrity alone can guarantee that his way will not turn out to be an absurd misadventure.

26   Whether his fate comes to him from without or from within, the experiences and happenings on the way remain the same. Therefore I need say nothing about the manifold outer and inner events, the endless variety of which I could never exhaust in any case. Nor would this be relevant to the text under discussion. On the other hand, there is much to be said about the psychic states that accompany the process of development. These states are expressed symbolically in our text, and in the very same symbols that for many years have been familiar to me from my practice.

THE FUNDAMENTAL CONCEPTS

A. TAO

27   The great difficulty in interpreting this and similar texts[1] for the European is that the author always starts from the central point, from the point we would call the goal, the highest and ultimate insight he has attained. Thus our Chinese author begins with ideas that demand such a comprehensive understanding that a person of discriminating mind has the feeling he would be guilty of ridiculous pretension, or even of talking utter nonsense, if he should embark on an intellectual discourse on the subtle psychic experiences of the greatest minds of the East. Our text, for example, begins: 'That which exists through itself is called the Way.' The *Hui Ming Ching* begins with the words: 'The subtlest secret of the Tao is human nature and life.'

28   It is characteristic of the Western mind that it has no word for Tao. The Chinese character is made up of the sign for 'head' and the sign for 'going.' Wilhelm translates Tao by *Sinn* (Meaning). Others translate it as 'way,' 'providence,' or even as 'God,' as the Jesuits do. This illustrates our difficulty. 'Head' can be taken as consciousness,[2] and 'going' as travelling

a way, and the idea would then be: to go consciously, or the conscious
way. This is borne out by the fact that the 'light of heaven' which 'dwells
between the eyes' as the 'heart of heaven' is used synonymously with Tao.
Human nature and life are contained in the 'light of heaven' and, according
to the *Hui Ming Ching*, are the most important secrets of the Tao. 'Light'
is the symbolical equivalent of consciousness, and the nature of consciousness is expressed by analogies with light. The *Hui Ming Ching* is
introduced with the verses:

> If thou wouldst complete the diamond body with no outflowing,
> Diligently heat the roots of consciousness[3] and life.
> Kindle light in the blessed country ever close at hand,
> And there hidden, let thy true self always dwell.

29 These verses contain a sort of alchemical instruction as to the method
or way of producing the 'diamond body,' which is also mentioned in our
text. 'Heating' is necessary; that is, there must be an intensification of
consciousness in order that light may be kindled in the dwelling place of
the true self. Not only consciousness, but life itself must be intensified:
the union of these two produces conscious life. According to the *Hui Ming
Ching*, the ancient sages knew how to bridge the gap between consciousness and life because they cultivated both. In this way the *sheli*, the
immortal body, is 'melted out' and the 'great Tao is completed.'[4]

30 If we take the Tao to be the method or conscious way by which to unite
what is separated, we have probably come close to the psychological
meaning of the concept. At all events, the separation of consciousness and
life cannot very well be understood as anything else than what I described
earlier as an aberration or uprooting of consciousness. There can be no
doubt, either, that the realization of the opposite hidden in the unconscious
– the process of 'reversal' – signifies reunion with the unconscious laws
of our being, and the purpose of this reunion is the attainment of conscious
life or, expressed in Chinese terms, the realization of the Tao.

B. THE CIRCULAR MOVEMENT AND THE CENTRE

31 As I have pointed out, the union of opposites[5] on a higher level of
consciousness is not a rational thing, nor is it a matter of will; it is a process
of psychic development that expresses itself in symbols. Historically, this
process has always been represented in symbols, and today the development of personality is still depicted in symbolic form. I discovered this
fact in the following way. The spontaneous fantasy products I discussed
earlier become more profound and gradually concentrate into abstract
structures that apparently represent 'principles' in the sense of Gnostic
archai. When the fantasies take the form chiefly of thoughts, intuitive
formulations of dimly felt laws or principles emerge, which at first tend

to be dramatized or personified. (We shall come back to these again later.) If the fantasies are drawn, symbols appear that are chiefly of the *mandala*[6] type. *Mandala* means 'circle,' more especially a magic circle. Mandalas are found not only throughout the East but also among us. The early Middle Ages are especially rich in Christian mandalas; most of them show Christ in the centre, with the four evangelists, or their symbols, at the cardinal points. This conception must be a very ancient one, because Horus and his four sons were represented in the same way by the Egyptians.[7] It is known that Horus with his four sons has close connections with Christ and the four evangelists. An unmistakable and very interesting mandala can be found in Jakob Böhme's book *XL Questions concerning the Soule.*[8] It is clear that this mandala represents a psychocosmic system strongly coloured by Christian ideas. Böhme calls it the 'Philosophical Eye'[9] or the 'Mirror of Wisdom,' by which is obviously meant a *summa* of secret knowledge. Most mandalas take the form of a flower, cross, or wheel, and show a distinct tendency towards a quaternary structure reminiscent of the Pythagorean *tetraktys*, the basic number. Mandalas of this sort also occur as sand paintings in the religious ceremonies of the Pueblo and Navaho Indians.[10] But the most beautiful mandalas are, of course, those of the East, especially the ones found in Tibetan Buddhism, which also contain the symbols mentioned in our text. Mandala drawings are often produced by the mentally ill, among them persons who certainly did not have the least idea of any of the connections we have discussed.[11]

32   Among my patients I have come across cases of women who did not draw mandalas but danced them instead. In India there is a special name for this: *mandala nrithya*, the mandala dance. The dance figures express the same meanings as the drawings. My patients can say very little about the meaning of the symbols but are fascinated by them and find that they somehow express and have an effect on their subjective psychic state.

33   Our text promises to 'reveal the secret of the Golden Flower of the great *One.*' The golden flower is the light, and the light of heaven is the Tao. The golden flower is a mandala symbol I have often met with in the material brought me by my patients. It is drawn either seen from above as a regular geometric pattern, or in profile as a blossom growing from a plant. The plant is frequently a structure in brilliant fiery colours growing out of a bed of darkness, and carrying the blossom of light at the top, a symbol recalling the Christmas tree. Such drawings also suggest the origin of the golden flower, for according to the *Hui Ming Ching* the 'germinal vesicle' is the 'dragon castle at the bottom of the sea.'[12] Other synonyms are the 'yellow castle,' the 'heavenly heart,' the 'terrace of living,' the 'square inch field of the square foot house,' the 'purple hall of the city of jade,' the 'dark pass,' the 'space of former heaven.'[13] It is also called the 'boundary region of the snow mountains,' the 'primordial pass,' the 'kingdom of greatest joy,' the 'boundless country,' the 'altar upon which

consciousness and life are made.' 'If a dying man does not know this germinal vesicle,' says the *Hui Ming Ching*, 'he will not find the unity of consciousness and life in a thousand births, nor in ten thousand aeons.'[14]

34   The beginning, where everything is still one, and which therefore appears as the highest goal, lies at the bottom of the sea, in the darkness of the unconscious. In the germinal vesicle, consciousness and life (or human nature and life, *hsing-ming*) are still a 'unity, inseparably mixed like the sparks in the refining furnace.' 'Within the germinal vesicle is the fire of the ruler.' 'All the sages began their work at the germinal vesicle.'[15] Note the fire analogies. I know a series of European mandala drawings in which something like a plant seed surrounded by membranes is shown floating in the water. Then, from the depths below, fire penetrates the seed and makes it grow, causing a great golden flower to unfold from the germinal vesicle.

35   This symbolism refers to a quasi-alchemical process of refining and ennobling. Darkness gives birth to light; out of the 'lead of the water region' grows the noble gold; what is unconscious becomes conscious in the form of a living process of growth. (Indian Kundalini yoga offers a perfect analogy.[16]) In this way the union of consciousness and life takes place.

36   When my patients produce these mandala pictures, it is naturally not the result of suggestion; similar pictures were being made long before I knew their meaning or their connection with the practices of the East, which, at that time, were wholly unknown to me. The pictures arise quite spontaneously, and from two sources. One source is the unconscious, which spontaneously produces fantasies of this kind; the other is life, which, if lived with utter devotion, brings an intuition of the self, of one's own individual being. When the self finds expression in such drawings, the unconscious reacts by enforcing an attitude of devotion to life. For in complete agreement with the Eastern view, the mandala is not only a means of expression but also produces an effect. It reacts upon its maker. Age-old magical effects lie hidden in this symbol, for it is derived from the 'protective circle' or 'charmed circle,' whose magic has been preserved in countless folk customs.[17] It has the obvious purpose of drawing a *sulcus primigenius*, a magical furrow around the centre, the temple or *temenos* (sacred precinct), of the innermost personality, in order to prevent an 'outflowing' or to guard by apotropaic means against distracting influences from outside. Magical practices are nothing but projections of psychic events, which then exert a counter-influence on the psyche and put a kind of spell upon the personality. Through the ritual action, attention and interest are led back to the inner, sacred precinct, which is the source and goal of the psyche and contains the unity of life and consciousness. The unity once possessed has been lost, and must now be found again.

37   The unity of the two, life and consciousness, is the Tao, whose symbol

would be the central white light, also mentioned in the *Bardo Thödol*.[18] This light dwells in the 'square inch' or in the 'face,' that is, between the eyes. It is a visualization of the 'creative point,' of that which has intensity without extension, in conjunction with the 'field of the square inch,' the symbol for that which has extension. The two together make the Tao. Human nature (*hsing*) and consciousness (*hui*) are expressed in light symbolism, and therefore have the quality of intensity, while life (*ming*) would coincide with extensity. The one is *yang*-like, the other *yin*-like. The afore-mentioned mandala of a somnambulist girl, aged fifteen and a half, whom I had under observation some thirty years ago, shows in its centre a spring of 'Primary Force,' or life energy without extension, whose emanations clash with a contrary spatial principle – in complete analogy with the basic idea of our Chinese text.

38   The 'enclosure,' or *circumambulatio*, is expressed in our text by the idea of 'circulation.' The circulation is not merely movement in a circle, but means, on the one hand, the marking off of the sacred precinct and, on the other, fixation and concentration. The sun-wheel begins to turn; the sun is activated and begins its course – in other words, the Tao begins to work and takes the lead. Action is reversed into non-action; everything peripheral is subordinated to the command of the centre. Therefore it is said: 'Movement is only another name for mastery.' Psychologically, this circulation would be the 'movement in a circle around oneself,' so that all sides of the personality become involved. 'The poles of light and darkness are made to rotate,' that is, there is an alternation of day and night.

39   The circular movement thus has the moral significance of activating the light and dark forces of human nature, and together with them all psychological opposites of whatever kind they may be. It is nothing less than self-knowledge by means of self-brooding (Sanskrit *tapas*). A similar archetypal concept of a perfect being is that of the Platonic man, round on all sides and uniting within himself the two sexes.

40   One of the best modern parallels is the description which Edward Maitland, the biographer of Anna Kingsford,[19] gave of his central experience. He had discovered that when reflecting on an idea, related ideas became visible, so to speak, in a long series apparently reaching back to their source, which to him was the divine spirit. By concentrating on this series, he tried to penetrate to their origin. He writes:

> I was absolutely without knowledge or expectation when I yielded to the impulse to make the attempt. I simply experimented on a faculty . . . being seated at my writing-table the while in order to record the results as they came, and resolved to retain my hold on my outer and circumferential consciousness, no matter how far towards my inner and central consciousness I might go. For I knew not whether I should be able to regain the former if I once quitted my hold of it, or to recollect

the facts of the experience. At length I achieved my object, though only by a strong effort, the tension occasioned by the endeavour to keep both extremes of the consciousness in view at once being very great.

Once well started on my quest, I found myself traversing a succession of spheres or belts . . . the impression produced being that of mounting a vast ladder stretching from the circumference towards the centre of a system, which was at once my own system, the solar system, the universal system, the three systems being at once diverse and identical. . . . Presently, by a supreme, and what I felt must be a final effort . . . I suceeded in polarizing the whole of the convergent rays of my consciousness into the desired focus. And at the same instant, as if through the sudden ignition of the rays thus fused into a unity, I found myself confronted with a glory of unspeakable whiteness and brightness, and of a lustre so intense as well-nigh to beat me back. . . . But though feeling that I had to explore further, I resolved to make assurance doubly sure by piercing if I could the almost blinding lustre, and seeing what it enshrined. With a great effort I succeeded, and the glance revealed to me that which I had felt must be there. . . . It was the dual form of the Son . . . the unmanifest made manifest, the unformulate formulate, the unindividuate individuate, God as the Lord, proving through His duality that God is Substance as well as Force, Love as well as Will, Feminine as well as Masculine, Mother as well as Father.

41   He found that God is two in one, like man. Besides this he noticed something that our text also emphasizes, namely 'suspension of breathing.' He says ordinary breathing stopped and was replaced by an internal respiration, 'as if by breathing of a distinct personality within and other than the physical organism.' He took this being to be the 'entelechy' of Aristotle and the 'inner Christ' of the apostle Paul, the 'spiritual and substantial individuality engendered within the physical and phenomenal personality, and representing, therefore, the rebirth of man on a plane transcending the material.'

42   This genuine[20] experience contains all the essential symbols of our text. The phenomenon itself, the vision of light, is an experience common to many mystics, and one that is undoubtedly of the greatest significance, because at all times and places it proves to be something unconditioned and absolute, a combination of supreme power and profound meaning. Hildegard of Bingen, an outstanding personality quite apart from her mysticism, writes in much the same way about her central vision:

Since my childhood I have always seen a light in my soul, but not with the outer eyes, nor through the thoughts of my heart; neither do the five outer senses take part in this vision. . . . The light I perceive is not of a local kind, but is much brighter than the cloud which supports the sun. I cannot distinguish height, breadth, or length in it. . . . What

I see or learn in such a vision stays long in my memory. I see, hear, and know in the same moment. . . . I cannot recognize any sort of form in this light, although I sometimes see in it another light that is known to me as the living light. . . . While I am enjoying the spectacle of this light, all sadness and sorrow vanish from my memory.[21]

43   I myself know a few individuals who have had personal experience of this phenomenon. So far as I have been able to understand it, it seems to have to do with an acute state of consciousness, as intense as it is abstract, a 'detached' consciousness which, as Hildegard implies, brings into awareness areas of psychic happenings ordinarily covered in darkness. The fact that the general bodily sensations disappear during the experience suggests that their specific energy has been withdrawn and has apparently gone towards heightening the clarity of consciousness. As a rule, the phenomenon is spontaneous, coming and going on its own initiative. Its effect is astonishing in that it almost always brings about a solution of psychic complications and frees the inner personality from emotional and intellectual entanglements, thus creating a unity of being which is universally felt as 'liberation.'

44   Such a symbolic unity cannot be attained by the conscious will because consciousness is always partisan. Its opponent is the collective unconscious, which does not understand the language of the conscious mind. Therefore it is necessary to have the magic of the symbol which contains those primitive analogies that speak to the unconscious. The unconscious can be reached and expressed only by symbols, and for this reason the process of individuation can never do without the symbol. The symbol is the primitive exponent of the unconscious, but at the same time an idea that corresponds to the highest intuitions of the conscious mind.

45   The oldest mandala drawing known to me is a palaeolithic 'sun-wheel,' recently discovered in Rhodesia. It, too, is based on the quaternary principle. Things reaching so far back into human history naturally touch upon the deepest layers of the unconscious, and can have a powerful effect on it even when our conscious language proves itself to be quite impotent. Such things cannot be thought up but must grow again from the forgotten depths if they are to express the supreme insights of consciousness and the loftiest intuitions of the spirit, and in this way fuse the uniqueness of present-day consciousness with the age-old past of life.

NOTES

Pars. 17-26

1   [*The Secret of the Golden Flower* (1962 edn.), p. 42.]
2   [The Taoist idea of action through non-action. – C.F.B.]
3   [*The Secret of the Golden Flower* (1962 edn.), p. 51.]

The fundamental concepts, pars. 27-42

1 Cf. the *Hui Ming Ching* (Book of Consciousness and Life) in *The Secret of the Golden Flower* (1962 edn.), pp. 69ff.
2 The head is also the 'seat of heavenly light.'
3 In the *Hui Ming Ching*, 'human nature' (*hsing*) and 'consciousness' (*hui*) are used interchangeably.
4 *The Golden Flower* (1962 edn.), p. 70.
5 Cf. *Psychological Types* (CW6) ch. V.
6 [For a fuller discussion of the *mandala*, see 'A Study in the Process of Individuation' and 'Concerning Mandala Symbolism' in *The Archetypes and the Collective Unconscious* (CW9.I). – EDITORS.]
7 Cf. Wallis Budge, *The Gods of the Egyptians*.
8 [The mandala is reproduced in 'A Study in the Process of Individuation,' (CW 9.I) p. 297.]
9 Cf. the Chinese concept of the heavenly light between the eyes.
10 Matthews, 'The Mountain Chant: A Navajo Ceremony' (1887), and Stevenson, 'Ceremonial of Hasjelti Daijis' (1891).
11 The mandala of a somnambulist is reproduced in *Psychiatric Studies* (CW1) p. 40.
12 *The Golden Flower* (1962 edn.), p. 70.
13 [Ibid., p. 22.]
14 [Ibid., p. 70.]
15 [Ibid., p. 71.]
16 Cf. Avalon, *The Serpent Power*.
17 Cf. the excellent collection in Knuchel, *Die Umwandlung in Kult, Magie und Rechtsbrauch*.
18 Evans-Wentz, *The Tibetan Book of the Dead*.
19 *Anna Kingsford, Her Life, Letters, Diary, and Work*, pp. 129f. I am indebted for this reference to my colleague, Dr. Beatrice Hinkle, New York.
20 Such experiences are genuine, but their genuineness does not prove that all the conclusions or convictions forming their content are necessarily sound. Even in cases of lunacy one comes across perfectly valid psychic experiences. [Author's note added in the first (1931) English edition.]
21 [*Acta S. Hildegardis*, in Migne, *P.L.*, vol. 197, col. 18.]

5   The aims of psychotherapy[1]

From: The Practice of Psychotherapy (1931) (*CW* 16), pars. 66–113

66 It is generally agreed today that neuroses are functional psychic disturbances and are therefore to be cured preferably by psychological treatment. But when we come to the question of the structure of the neuroses and the principles of therapy, all agreement ends, and we have to acknowledge that we have as yet no fully satisfactory conception of the nature of the neuroses or of the principles of treatment. While it is true that two currents or schools of thought have gained a special hearing, they by no means exhaust the number of divergent opinions that actually exist. There are also numerous non-partisans who, amid the general conflict of opinion, have their own special views. If, therefore, we wanted to paint a comprehensive picture of this diversity, we should have to mix upon our palette all the hues and shadings of the rainbow. I would gladly paint such a picture if it lay within my power, for I have always felt the need for a conspectus of the many viewpoints. I have never succeeded in the long run in not giving divergent opinions their due. Such opinions could never arise, much less secure a following, if they did not correspond to some special disposition, some special character, some fundamental psychological fact that is more or less universal. Were we to exclude one such opinion as simply wrong and worthless, we should be rejecting this particular disposition or this particular fact as a misinterpretation – in other words, we should be doing violence to our own empirical material. The wide approval which greeted Freud's explanation of neurosis in terms of sexual causation and his view that the happenings in the psyche turn essentially upon infantile pleasure and its satisfaction should be instructive to the psychologist. It shows him that his manner of thinking and feeling coincides with a fairly widespread trend or spiritual current which, independently of Freud's theory, has made itself felt in other places, in other circumstances, in other minds, and in other forms. I should call it a manifestation of the collective psyche. Let me remind you here of the works of Havelock Ellis and August Forel and the contributors to *Anthropophyteia*;[2] then of the changed attitude to sex in Anglo-Saxon countries during the post-Victorian period, and the broad discussion of sexual matters in literature, which had already started with the French

realists. Freud is one of the exponents of a contemporary psychological fact which has a special history of its own; but for obvious reasons we cannot go into that here.

67   The acclaim which Adler, like Freud, has met with on both sides of the Atlantic points similarly to the undeniable fact that, for a great many people, the need for self-assertion arising from a sense of inferiority is a plausible basis of explanation. Nor can it be disputed that this view accounts for psychic actualities which are not given their due in the Freudian system. I need hardly mention in detail the collective psychological forces and social factors that favour the Adlerian view and make it their theoretical exponent. These matters are sufficiently obvious.

68   It would be an unpardonable error to overlook the element of truth in both the Freudian and the Adlerian viewpoints, but it would be no less unpardonable to take either of them as the sole truth. Both truths correspond to psychic realities. There are in fact some cases which by and large can best be described and explained by the one theory, and some by the other.

69   I can accuse neither of these two investigators of any fundamental error; on the contrary, I endeavour to apply both hypotheses as far as possible because I fully recognize their relative rightness. It would certainly never have occurred to me to depart from Freud's path had I not stumbled upon facts which forced me into modifications. And the same is true of my relation to the Adlerian viewpoint.

70   After what has been said it seems hardly necessary to add that I hold the truth of my own deviationist views to be equally relative, and feel myself so very much the mere exponent of another disposition that I could almost say with Coleridge: 'I believe in the one and only saving Church, of which at present I am the only member.'[3]

71   It is in applied psychology, if anywhere, that we must be modest today and bear with an apparent plurality of contradictory opinions; for we are still far from having anything like a thorough knowledge of the human psyche, that most challenging field of scientific inquiry. At present we have merely more or less plausible opinions that cannot be squared with one another.

72   If, therefore, I undertake to say something about my views I hope I shall not be misunderstood. I am not advertising a novel truth, still less am I announcing a final gospel. I can only speak of attempts to throw light on psychic facts that are obscure to me, or of efforts to overcome therapeutic difficulties.

73   And it is just with this last point that I should like to begin, for here lies the most pressing need for modifications. As is well known, one can get along for quite a time with an inadequate theory, but not with inadequate therapeutic methods. In my psychotherapeutic practice of nearly thirty years I have met with a fair number of failures which made a far deeper impression on me than my successes. Anybody can have successes in

psychotherapy, starting with the primitive medicine-man and faith-healer. The psychotherapist learns little or nothing from his successes, for they chiefly confirm him in his mistakes. But failures are priceless experiences because they not only open the way to a better truth but force us to modify our views and methods.

74   I certainly recognize how much my work has been furthered first by Freud and then by Adler, and in practice I try to acknowledge this debt by making use of their views, whenever possible, in the treatment of my patients. Nevertheless I must insist that I have experienced failures which, I felt, might have been avoided had I considered the facts that subsequently forced me to modify their views.

75   To describe all the situations I came up against is almost impossible, so I must content myself with singling out a few typical cases. It was with older patients that I had the greatest difficulties, that is, with persons over forty. In handling younger people I generally get along with the familiar viewpoints of Freud and Adler, for these tend to bring the patients to a certain level of adaptation and normality. Both views are eminently applicable to the young, apparently without leaving any disturbing after-effects. In my experience this is not so often the case with older people. It seems to me that the basic facts of the psyche undergo a very marked alteration in the course of life, so much so that we could almost speak of a psychology of life's morning and a psychology of its afternoon. As a rule, the life of a young person is characterized by a general expansion and a striving towards concrete ends; and his neurosis seems mainly to rest on his hesitation or shrinking back from this necessity. But the life of an older person is characterized by a contraction of forces, by the affirmation of what has been achieved, and by the curtailment of further growth. His neurosis comes mainly from his clinging to a youthful attitude which is now out of season. Just as the young neurotic is afraid of life, so the older one shrinks back from death. What was a normal goal for the young man becomes a neurotic hindrance to the old – just as, through his hesitation to face the world, the young neurotic's originally normal dependence on his parents grows into an incest-relationship that is inimical to life. It is natural that neurosis, resistance, repression, transference, 'guiding fictions,' and so forth should have one meaning in the young person and quite another in the old, despite apparent similarities. The aims of therapy should undoubtedly be modified to meet this fact. Hence the age of the patient seems to me a most important *indicium*.

76   But there are various *indicia* also within the youthful phase of life. Thus, in my estimation, it is a technical blunder to apply the Freudian viewpoint to a patient with the Adlerian type of psychology, that is, an unsuccessful person with an infantile need to assert himself. Conversely, it would be a gross misunderstanding to force the Adlerian viewpoint on a successful man with a pronounced pleasure-principle psychology. When in a quandary the resistances of the patient may be valuable signposts. I am inclined

to take deep-seated resistances seriously at first, paradoxical as this may sound, for I am convinced that the doctor does not necessarily know better than the patient's own psychic constitution, of which the patient himself may be quite unconscious. This modesty on the part of the doctor is altogether becoming in view of the fact that there is not only no generally valid psychology today but rather an untold variety of temperaments and of more or less individual psyches that refuse to fit into any scheme.

77   You know that in this matter of temperament I postulate two different basic attitudes in accordance with the typical differences already suspected by many students of human nature – namely, the extraverted and the introverted attitudes. These attitudes, too, I take to be important *indicia*, and likewise the predominance of one particular psychic function over the others.[4]

78   The extraordinary diversity of individual life necessitates constant modifications of theory which are often applied quite unconsciously by the doctor himself, although in principle they may not accord at all with his theoretical creed.

79   While we are on this question of temperament I should not omit to mention that there are some people whose attitude is essentially spiritual and others whose attitude is essentially materialistic. It must not be imagined that such an attitude is acquired accidentally or springs from mere misunderstanding. Very often they are ingrained passions which no criticism and no persuasion can stamp out; there are even cases where an apparently outspoken materialism has its source in a denial of religious temperament. Cases of the reverse type are more easily credited today, although they are not more frequent than the others. This too is an *indicium* which in my opinion ought not to be overlooked.

80   When we use the word *indicium* it might appear to mean, as is usual in medical parlance, that this or that treatment is indicated. Perhaps this should be the case, but psychotherapy has at present reached no such degree of certainty – for which reason our *indicia* are unfortunately not much more than warnings against one-sidedness.

81   The human psyche is a thing of enormous ambiguity. In every single case we have to ask ourselves whether an attitude or a so-called *habitus* is authentic, or whether it may not be just a compensation for its opposite. I must confess that I have so often been deceived in this matter that in any concrete case I am at pains to avoid all theoretical presuppositions about the structure of the neurosis and about what the patient can and ought to do. As far as possible I let pure experience decide the therapeutic aims. This may perhaps seem strange, because it is commonly supposed that the therapist has an aim. But in psychotherapy it seems to me positively advisable for the doctor not to have too fixed an aim. He can hardly know better than the nature and will to live of the patient. The great decisions in human life usually have far more to do with the instincts and other mysterious unconscious factors than with conscious will and well-meaning

reasonableness. The shoe that fits one person pinches another; there is no universal recipe for living. Each of us carries his own life-form within him – an irrational form which no other can outbid.

82   All this naturally does not prevent us from doing our utmost to make the patient normal and reasonable. If the therapeutic results are satisfactory, we can probably let it go at that. If not, then for better or worse the therapist must be guided by the patient's own irrationalities. Here we must follow nature as a guide, and what the doctor then does is less a question of treatment than of developing the creative possibilities latent in the patient himself.

83   What I have to say begins where the treatment leaves off and this development sets in. Thus my contribution to psychotherapy confines itself to those cases where rational treatment does not yield satisfactory results. The clinical material at my disposal is of a peculiar composition: new cases are decidedly in the minority. Most of them already have some form of psychotherapeutic treatment behind them, with partial or negative results. About a third of my cases are not suffering from any clinically definable neurosis, but from the senselessness and aimlessness of their lives. I should not object if this were called the general neurosis of our age. Fully two thirds of my patients are in the second half of life.

84   This peculiar material sets up a special resistance to rational methods of treatment, probably because most of my patients are socially well-adapted individuals, often of outstanding ability, to whom normalization means nothing. As for so-called normal people, there I really am in a fix, for I have no ready-made philosophy of life to hand out to them. In the majority of my cases the resources of the conscious mind are exhausted (or, in ordinary English, they are 'stuck'). It is chiefly this fact that forces me to look for hidden possibilities. For I do not know what to say to the patient when he asks me, 'What do you advise? What shall I do?' I don't know either. I only know one thing: when my conscious mind no longer sees any possible road ahead and consequently gets stuck, my unconscious psyche will react to the unbearable standstill.

85   This 'getting stuck' is a psychic occurrence so often repeated during the course of human history that it has become the theme of many myths and fairytales. We are told of the Open sesame! to the locked door, or of some helpful animal who finds the hidden way. In other words, getting stuck is a typical event which, in the course of time, has evoked typical reactions and compensations. We may therefore expect with some probability that something similar will appear in the reactions of the unconscious, as, for example, in dreams.

86   In such cases, then, my attention is directed more particularly to dreams. This is not because I am tied to the notion that dreams must always be called to the rescue, or because I possess a mysterious dream-theory which tells me how everything must shape itself; but quite simply from perplexity. I do not know where else to go for help, and so I try to find it in dreams.

These at least present us with images pointing to something or other, and that is better than nothing. I have no theory about dreams, I do not know how dreams arise. And I am not at all sure that my way of handling dreams even deserves the name of a 'method.' I share all your prejudices against dream-interpretation as the quintessence of uncertainty and arbitrariness. On the other hand, I know that if we meditate on a dream sufficiently long and thoroughly, if we carry it around with us and turn it over and over, something almost always comes of it. This something is not of course a scientific result to be boasted about or rationalized; but it is an important practical hint which shows the patient what the unconscious is aiming at. Indeed, it ought not to matter to me whether the result of my musings on the dream is scientifically verifiable or tenable, otherwise I am pursuing an ulterior – and therefore autoerotic – aim. I must content myself wholly with the fact that the result means something to the patient and sets his life in motion again. I may allow myself only one criterion for the result of my labours: Does it work? As for my scientific hobby – my desire to know *why* it works – this I must reserve for my spare time.

87   Infinitely varied are the contents of the initial dreams, that is, the dreams that come at the outset of the treatment. In many cases they point directly to the past and recall things lost and forgotten. For very often the standstill and disorientation arise when life has become one-sided, and this may, in psychological terms, cause a sudden loss of libido. All our previous activities become uninteresting, even senseless, and our aims suddenly no longer worth striving for. What in one person is merely a passing mood may in another become a chronic condition. In these cases it often happens that other possibilities for developing the personality lie buried somewhere or other in the past, unknown to anybody, not even to the patient. But the dream may reveal the clue.

88   In other cases the dream points to present facts, for example marriage or social position, which the conscious mind has never accepted as sources of problems or conflicts.

89   Both possibilities come within the sphere of the rational, and I daresay I would have no difficulty in making such initial dreams seem plausible. The real difficulty begins when the dreams do not point to anything tangible, and this they do often enough, especially when they hold anticipations of the future. I do not mean that such dreams are necessarily prophetic, merely that they feel the way, they 'reconnoitre.' These dreams contain inklings of possibilities and for that reason can never be made plausible to an outsider. Sometimes they are not plausible even to me, and then I usually say to the patient, 'I don't believe it, but follow up the clue.' As I have said, the sole criterion is the stimulating effect, but it is by no means necessary for me to understand why such an effect takes place.

90   This is particularly true of dreams that contain something like an 'unconscious metaphysics,' by which I mean mythological analogies that are sometimes incredibly strange and baffling.

91   Now, you will certainly protest: How on earth can I know that the dreams contain anything like an unconscious metaphysics? And here I must confess that I do not really know. I know far too little about dreams for that. I see only the effect on the patient, of which I would like to give you a little example.

92   In a long initial dream of one of my 'normal' patients, the illness of his sister's child played an important part. She was a little girl of two.

93   Some time before, this sister had in fact lost a boy through illness, but otherwise none of her children was ill. The occurrence of the sick child in the dream at first proved baffling to the dreamer, probably because it failed to fit the facts. Since there was no direct and intimate connection between the dreamer and his sister, he could feel in this image little that was personal to him. Then he suddenly remembered that two years earlier he had taken up the study of occultism, in the course of which he also discovered psychology. So the child evidently represented his interest in the psyche – an idea I should never have arrived at of my own accord. Seen purely theoretically, this dream image can mean anything or nothing. For that matter, does a thing or a fact ever mean anything in itself? The only certainty is that it is always man who interprets, who assigns meaning. And that is the gist of the matter for psychology. It impressed the dreamer as a novel and interesting idea that the study of occultism might have something sickly about it. Somehow the thought struck home. And this is the decisive point: the interpretation works, however we may elect to account for its working. For the dreamer the thought was an implied criticism, and through it a certain change of attitude was brought about. By such slight changes, which one could never think up rationally, things are set in motion and the dead point is overcome, at least in principle.

94   From this example I could say figuratively that the dream meant that there was something sickly about the dreamer's occult studies, and in this sense – since the dream brought him to such an idea – I can also speak of 'unconscious metaphysics.'

95   But I go still further: Not only do I give the patient an opportunity to find associations to his dreams, I give myself the same opportunity. Further, I present him with my ideas and opinions. If, in so doing, I open the door to 'suggestion,' I see no occasion for regret; for it is well known that we are susceptible only to those suggestions with which we are already secretly in accord. No harm is done if now and then one goes astray in this riddle-reading: sooner or later the psyche will reject the mistake, much as the organism rejects a foreign body. I do not need to prove that my interpretation of the dream is right (a pretty hopeless undertaking anyway), but must simply try to discover, with the patient, what *acts* for him – I am almost tempted to say, what is actual.

96   For this reason it is particularly important for me to know as much as possible about primitive psychology, mythology, archaeology, and comparative religion, because these fields offer me invaluable analogies with

which I can enrich the associations of my patients. Together, we can then find meaning in apparent irrelevancies and thus vastly increase the effectiveness of the dream. For the layman who has done his utmost in the personal and rational sphere of life and yet has found no meaning and no satisfaction there, it is enormously important to be able to enter a sphere of irrational experience. In this way, too, the habitual and the common-place come to wear an altered countenance, and can even acquire a new glamour. For it all depends on how we look at things, and not on how they are in themselves. The least of things with a meaning is always worth more in life than the greatest of things without it.

97   I do not think I underestimate the risk of this undertaking. It is as if one began to build a bridge out into space. Indeed, the ironist might even allege – and has often done so – that in following this procedure both doctor and patient are indulging in mere fantasy-spinning.

98   This objection is no counter-argument, but is very much to the point. I even make an effort to second the patient in his fantasies. Truth to tell, I have no small opinion of fantasy. To me, it is the maternally creative side of the masculine mind. When all is said and done, we can never rise above fantasy. It is true that there are unprofitable, futile, morbid, and un-satisfying fantasies whose sterile nature is immediately recognized by every person endowed with common sense; but the faulty performance proves nothing against the normal performance. All the works of man have their origin in creative imagination. What right, then, have we to disparage fantasy? In the normal course of things, fantasy does not easily go astray; it is too deep for that, and too closely bound up with the tap-root of human and animal instinct. It has a surprising way of always coming out right in the end. The creative activity of imagination frees man from his bondage to the 'nothing but'[5] and raises him to the status of one who plays. As Schiller says, man is completely human only when he is at play.

99   My aim is to bring about a psychic state in which my patient begins to experiment with his own nature – a state of fluidity, change, and growth where nothing is eternally fixed and hopelessly petrified. I can here of course adumbrate only the principles of my technique. Those of you who happen to be acquainted with my works can easily imagine the necessary parallels. I would only like to emphasize that you should not think of my procedure as entirely without aim or limit. In handling a dream or fantasy I make it a rule never to go beyond the meaning which is effective for the patient; I merely try to make him as fully conscious of this meaning as possible, so that he shall also become aware of its supra-personal con-nections. For, when something happens to a man and he supposes it to be personal only to himself, whereas in reality it is a quite universal experience, then his attitude is obviously wrong, that is, too personal, and it tends to exclude him from human society. By the same token we need to have not only a personal, contemporary consciousness, but also a supra-personal consciousness with a sense of historical continuity. However

abstract this may sound, practical experience shows that many neuroses are caused primarily by the fact that people blind themselves to their own religious promptings because of a childish passion for rational enlightenment. It is high time the psychologist of today recognized that we are no longer dealing with dogmas and creeds but with the religious attitude *per se*, whose importance as a psychic function can hardly be overrated. And it is precisely for the religious function that the sense of historical continuity is indispensable.

100　　Coming back to the question of my technique, I ask myself how far I am indebted to Freud for its existence. At all events I learned it from Freud's method of free association, and I regard it as a direct extension of that.

101　　So long as I help the patient to discover the effective elements in his dreams, and so long as I try to get him to see the general meaning of his symbols, he is still, psychologically speaking, in a state of childhood. For the time being he is dependent on his dreams and is always asking himself whether the next dream will give him new light or not. Moreover, he is dependent on my having ideas about his dreams and on my ability to increase his insight through my knowledge. Thus he is still in an undesirably passive condition where everything is rather uncertain and questionable; neither he nor I know the journey's end. Often it is not much more than a groping about in Egyptian darkness. In this condition we must not expect any very startling results – the uncertainty is too great for that. Besides which there is always the risk that what we have woven by day the night will unravel. The danger is that nothing permanent is achieved, that nothing remains fixed. It not infrequently happens in these situations that the patient has a particularly vivid or curious dream, and says to me, 'Do you know, if only I were a painter I would make a picture of it.' Or the dreams are about photographs, paintings, drawings, or illuminated manuscripts, or even about the films.

102　　I have turned these hints to practical account, urging my patients at such times to paint in reality what they have seen in dream or fantasy. As a rule I am met with the objection, 'But I am not a painter!' To this I usually reply that neither are modern painters, and that consequently modern painting is free for all, and that anyhow it is not a question of beauty but only of the trouble one takes with the picture. How true this is I saw recently in the case of a talented professional portraitist; she had to begin my way of painting all over again with pitiably childish efforts, literally as if she had never held a brush in her hand. To paint what we see before us is a different art from painting what we see within.

103　　Many of my more advanced patients, then, begin to paint. I can well understand that everyone will be profoundly impressed with the utter futility of this sort of dilettantism. Do not forget, however, that we are speaking not of people who still have to prove their social usefulness, but of those who can no longer see any sense in being socially useful and who have come upon the deeper and more dangerous question of the meaning of their own individual lives. To be a particle in the mass has meaning and charm only for the man who has not yet reached that stage, but none for the man who is sick to death of being a particle. The importance of what life means to the individual may be denied by those who are socially below the general level of adaptation, and is invariably denied by the educator whose ambition it is to breed mass-men. But those who belong to neither category will sooner or later come up against this painful question.

104   Although my patients occasionally produce artistically beautiful things that might very well be shown in modern 'art' exhibitions, I nevertheless treat them as completely worthless when judged by the canons of real art. As a matter of fact, it is essential that they should be considered worthless, otherwise my patients might imagine themselves to be artists, and the whole point of the exercise would be missed. It is not a question of art at all – or rather, it should not be a question of art – but of something more and other than mere art, namely the living effect upon the patient himself. The meaning of individual life, whose importance from the social stand-point is negligible, stands here at its highest, and for its sake the patient struggles to give form, however crude and childish, to the inexpressible.

105   But why do I encourage patients, when they arrive at a certain stage in their development, to express themselves by means of brush, pencil, or pen at all?

106   Here again my prime purpose is to produce an effect. In the state of psychological childhood described above, the patient remains passive; but now he begins to play an active part. To start off with, he puts down on paper what he has passively seen, thereby turning it into a deliberate act. He not only talks about it, he is actually doing something about it. Psychologically speaking, it makes a vast difference whether a man has an interesting conversation with his doctor two or three times a week, the results of which are left hanging in mid air, or whether he has to struggle for hours with refractory brush and colours, only to produce in the end something which, taken at its face value, is perfectly senseless. If it were really senseless to him, the effort to paint it would be so repugnant that he could scarcely be brought to perform this exercise a second time. But because his fantasy does not strike him as entirely senseless, his busying himself with it only increases its effect upon him. Moreover, the concrete shaping of the image enforces a continuous study of it in all its parts, so that it can develop its effects to the full. This invests the bare fantasy with an element of reality, which lends it greater weight and greater driving power. And these rough-and-ready pictures do indeed produce effects which, I must admit, are rather difficult to describe. For instance, a patient needs only to have seen once or twice how much he is freed from a wretched state of mind by working at a symbolical picture, and he will always turn to this means of release whenever things go badly with him. In this way something of inestimable importance is won – the beginning

of independence, a step towards psychological maturity. The patient can make himself creatively independent through this method, if I may call it such. He is no longer dependent on his dreams or on his doctor's knowledge; instead, by painting himself he gives shape to himself. For what he paints are active fantasies – that which is active within him. And that which is active within is himself, but no longer in the guise of his previous error, when he mistook the personal ego for the self; it is himself in a new and hitherto alien sense, for his ego now appears as the object of that which works within him. In countless pictures he strives to catch this interior agent, only to discover in the end that it is eternally unknown and alien, the hidden foundation of psychic life.

107   It is impossible for me to describe the extent to which this discovery changes the patient's standpoint and values, and how it shifts the centre of gravity of his personality. It is as though the earth had suddenly discovered that the sun was the centre of the planetary orbits and of its own earthly orbit as well.

108   But have we not always known this to be so? I myself believe that we have always known it. But I may know something with my head which the other man in me is far from knowing, for indeed and in truth I live as though I did not know it. Most of my patients knew the deeper truth, but did not live it. And why did they not live it? Because of that bias which makes us all live from the ego, a bias which comes from overvaluation of the conscious mind.

109   It is of the greatest importance for the young person, who is still unadapted and has as yet achieved nothing, to shape his conscious ego as effectively as possible, that is, to educate his will. Unless he is a positive genius he cannot, indeed he should not, believe in anything active within him that is not identical with his will. He must feel himself a man of will, and may safely depreciate everything else in him and deem it subject to his will, for without this illusion he could not succeed in adapting himself socially.

110   It is otherwise with a person in the second half of life who no longer needs to educate his conscious will, but who, to understand the meaning of his individual life, needs to experience his own inner being. Social usefulness is no longer an aim for him, although he does not deny its desirability. Fully aware as he is of the social unimportance of his creative activity, he feels it more as a way of working at himself to his own benefit. Increasingly, too, this activity frees him from morbid dependence, and he thus acquires an inner stability and a new trust in himself. These last achievements now redound to the good of the patient's social existence; for an inwardly stable and self-confident person will prove more adequate to his social tasks than one who is on a bad footing with his unconscious.

111   I have purposely avoided loading my lecture with theory, hence much must remain obscure and unexplained. But, in order to make the pictures produced by my patients intelligible, certain theoretical points must at

least receive mention. A feature common to all these pictures is a primitive symbolism which is conspicuous both in the drawing and in the colouring. The colours are as a rule quite barbaric in their intensity. Often an unmistakable archaic quality is present. These peculiarities point to the nature of the underlying creative forces. They are irrational, symbolistic currents that run through the whole history of mankind, and are so archaic in character that it is not difficult to find their parallels in archaeology and comparative religion. We may therefore take it that our pictures spring chiefly from those regions of the psyche which I have termed the collective unconscious. By this I understand an unconscious psychic functioning common to all men, the source not only of our modern symbolical pictures but of all similar products in the past. Such pictures spring from, and satisfy, a natural need. It is as if a part of the psyche that reaches far back into the primitive past were expressing itself in these pictures and finding it possible to function in harmony with our alien conscious mind. This collaboration satisfies and thus mitigates the psyche's disturbing demands upon the latter. It must, however, be added that the mere execution of the pictures is not enough. Over and above that, an intellectual and emotional understanding is needed; they require to be not only rationally integrated with the conscious mind, but morally assimilated. They still have to be subjected to a work of synthetic interpretation. Although I have travelled this path with individual patients many times, I have never yet succeeded in making all the details of the process clear enough for publication.[6] So far this has been fragmentary only. The truth is, we are here moving in absolutely new territory, and a ripening of experience is the first requisite. For very important reasons I am anxious to avoid hasty conclusions. We are dealing with a process of psychic life outside consciousness, and our observation of it is indirect. As yet we do not know to what depths our vision will plumb. It would seem to be some kind of centring process, for a great many pictures which the patients themselves feel to be decisive point in this direction. During this centring process what we call the ego appears to take up a peripheral position. The change is apparently brought about by an emergence of the historical part of the psyche. Exactly what is the purpose of this process remains at first sight obscure. We can only remark its important effect on the conscious personality. From the fact that the change heightens the feeling for life and maintains the flow of life, we must conclude that it is animated by a peculiar purposefulness. We might perhaps call this a new illusion. But what is 'illusion'? By what criterion do we judge something to be an illusion? Does anything exist for the psyche that we are entitled to call illusion? What we are pleased to call illusion may be for the psyche an extremely important life-factor, something as indispensable as oxygen for the body – a psychic actuality of overwhelming significance. Presumably the psyche does not trouble itself about our categories of reality; for it, everything that *works* is real. The investigator of the psyche must not confuse it with his consciousness, else he veils from his sight the object of his investigation. On the contrary, to recognize it at all, he must learn to see how different it is from consciousness. Nothing is more probable than that what we call illusion is very real for the psyche – for which reason we cannot take psychic reality to be commensurable with conscious reality. To the psychologist there is nothing more fatuous than the attitude of the missionary who pronounces the gods of the 'poor heathen' to be mere illusion. Unfortunately we still go blundering along in the same dogmatic way, as though *our* so-called reality were not equally full of illusion. In psychic life, as everywhere in our experience, all things that work are reality, regardless of the names man chooses to bestow on them. To take these realities for what they are – not foisting other names on them – that is our business. To the psyche, spirit is no less spirit for being named sexuality.

112   I must repeat that these designations and the changes rung upon them never even remotely touch the essence of the process we have described. It cannot be compassed by the rational concepts of the conscious mind, any more than life itself; and it is for this reason that my patients consistently turn to the representation and interpretation of symbols as the more adequate and effective course.

113   With this I have said pretty well everything I can say about my therapeutic aims and intentions within the broad framework of a lecture. It can be no more than an incentive to thought, and I shall be quite content if such it has been.

NOTES

1 [Delivered as a lecture, 'Ziele der Psychotherapie,' on April 12, 1929, at the 4th General Medical Congress for Psychotherapy, Bad Nauheim, and published in the *Bericht* of the Congress, 1929; republished in *Seelenprobleme der Gegenwart* (Zurich, 1931), pp. 87–114. Previously trans. by C. F. Baynes and W. S. Dell in *Modern Man in Search of a Soul* (London and New York, 1933. – EDITORS.]

2 [Published at Leipzig, 1904–13. – EDITORS.]

3 [The attribution to Coleridge is incorrect, according to Coleridgean scholars who were consulted. – EDITORS.]

4 [Viz., thinking, feeling, sensation, and intuition. – EDITORS.]

5 [The term 'nothing but' (*nichts als*) denotes the common habit of explaining something unknown by reducing it to something apparently known and thereby devaluing it. For instance, when a certain illness is said to be 'nothing but psychic,' it is explained as imaginary and is thus devalued. The expression is borrowed from James, *The Varieties of Religious Experience*, p. 12. – EDITORS.]

6 This has since been remedied. Cf. 'A Study in the Process of Individuation.' [Also cf. *Psychology and Alchemy* (CW12) Part II. – EDITORS.]

6 A study in the process of individuation[1]

Excerpts from: *The Archetypes and the Collective Unconscious* (1933/50) (*CW* 9.1), pars. 525–626

> Tao's working of things is vague and obscure.
> Obscure! Oh vague!
> In it are images.
> Vague! Oh obscure!
> In it are things.
> Profound! Oh dark indeed!
> In it is seed.
> Its seed is very truth.
> In it is trustworthiness.
> From the earliest Beginning until today
> Its name is not lacking
> By which to fathom the Beginning of all things.
> How do I know it is the Beginning of all things?
> Through *it!*
>
> Lao-tzu, *Tao Teh Ching*, ch. 21.

INTRODUCTORY

525 During the 1920s, I made the acquaintance in America of a lady with an academic education – we will call her Miss X – who had studied psychology for nine years. She had read all the more recent literature in this field. In 1928, at the age of fifty-five, she came to Europe in order to continue her studies under my guidance. As the daughter of an exceptional father she had varied interests, was extremely cultured, and possessed a lively turn of mind. She was unmarried, but lived with the unconscious equivalent of a human partner, namely the animus (the personification of everything masculine in a woman), in that characteristic liaison so often met with in women with an academic education. As frequently happens, this development of hers was based on a positive father complex: she was 'fille à papa' and consequently did not have a good relation to her mother. Her animus was not of the kind to give her cranky ideas. She was protected from this by her natural intelligence and by a remarkable readiness to tolerate the opinions of other people. This good quality, by no means to

be expected in the presence of an animus, had, in conjunction with some difficult experiences that could not be avoided, enabled her to realize that she had reached a limit and 'got stuck,' and this made it urgently necessary for her to look round for ways that might lead her out of the impasse. That was one of the reasons for her trip to Europe. Associated with this there was another – not accidental – motive. On her mother's side she was of Scandinavian descent. Since her relation to her mother left very much to be desired, as she herself clearly realized, the feeling had gradually grown up in her that this side of her nature might have developed differently if only the relation to her mother had given it a chance. In deciding to go to Europe she was conscious that she was turning back to her own origins and was setting out to reactivate a portion of her childhood that was bound up with the mother. Before coming to Zurich she had gone back to Denmark, her mother's country. There the thing that affected her most was the landscape, and unexpectedly there came over her the desire to paint – above all, landscape motifs. Till then she had noticed no such aesthetic inclinations in herself, also she lacked the ability to paint or draw. She tried her hand at watercolours, and her modest landscapes filled her with a strange feeling of contentment. Painting them, she told me, seemed to fill her with new life. Arriving in Zurich, she continued her painting efforts, and on the day before she came to me for the first time she began another landscape – this time from memory. While she was working on it, a fantasy-image suddenly thrust itself between her and the picture: she saw herself with the lower half of her body in the earth, stuck fast in a block of rock. The region round about was a beach strewn with boulders. In the background was the sea. She felt caught and helpless. Then she suddenly saw me in the guise of a medieval sorcerer. She shouted for help, I came along and touched the rock with a magic wand. The stone instantly burst open, and she stepped out uninjured. She then painted this fantasy-image instead of the landscape and brought it to me the following day.

PICTURE 1

526 As usually happens with beginners and people with no skill of hand, the drawing of the picture cost her considerable difficulties. In such cases it is very easy for the unconscious to slip its subliminal images into the painting. Thus it came about that the big boulders would not appear on the paper in their real form but took on unexpected shapes. They looked, some of them, like hardboiled eggs cut in two, with the yolk in the middle. Others were like pointed pyramids. It was in one of these that Miss X was stuck. Her hair, blown out behind her, and the movement of the sea suggested a strong wind.

527   The picture shows first of all her imprisoned state, but not yet the act of liberation. So it was there that she was attached to the earth, in the land

Picture 1

of her mother. Psychologically this state means being caught in the unconscious. Her inadequate relation to her mother had left behind something dark and in need of development. Since she succumbed to the magic of her motherland and tried to express this by painting, it is obvious that she is still stuck with half her body in Mother Earth: that is, she is still partly identical with the mother and, what is more, through that part of the body which contains just that secret of the mother which she had never inquired into.

528   Since Miss X had discovered all by herself the method of active imagination I have long been accustomed to use, I was able to approach the problem at just the point indicated by the picture: she is caught in the unconscious and expects magical help from me, as from a sorcerer. And since her psychological knowledge had made her completely *au fait* with certain possible interpretations, there was no need of even an understanding wink to bring to light the apparent *sous-entendu* of the liberating magician's wand. The sexual symbolism, which for many naïve minds is of such capital importance, was no discovery for her. She was far enough advanced to know that explanations of this kind, however true they might be in other respects, had no significance in her case. She did not want to

know how liberation might be possible in a *general* way, but how and in what way it could come about for *her*. And about this I knew as little as she. I know that such solutions can only come about in an individual way that cannot be foreseen. One cannot think up ways and means artificially, let alone know them in advance, for such knowledge is merely collective, based on average experience, and can therefore be completely inadequate, indeed absolutely wrong, in individual cases. And when, on top of that, we consider the patient's age, we would do well to abandon from the start any attempt to apply ready-made solutions and warmed-up generalities of which the patient knows just as much as the doctor. Long experience has taught me not to know anything in advance and not to know better, but to let the unconscious take precedence. Our instincts have ridden so infinitely many times, unharmed, over the problems that arise at this stage of life that we may be sure the transformation processes which make the transition possible have long been prepared in the unconscious and are only waiting to be released.

529   I had already seen from her previous history how the unconscious made use of the patient's inability to draw in order to insinuate its own suggestions. I had not overlooked the fact that the boulders had surreptitiously transformed themselves into *eggs*. The egg is a germ of life with a lofty symbolical significance. It is not just a cosmogonic symbol – it is also a 'philosophical' one. As the former it is the Orphic egg, the world's beginning; as the latter, the philosophical egg of the medieval natural philosophers, the vessel from which, at the end of the *opus alchymicum*, the homunculus emerges, that is, the Anthropos, the spiritual, inner and complete man, who in Chinese alchemy is called the *chen-yen* (literally, 'perfect man').[2]

530   From this hint, therefore, I could already see what solution the unconscious had in mind, namely individuation, for this is the transformation process that loosens the attachment to the unconscious. It is a definitive solution, for which all other ways serve as auxiliaries and temporary makeshifts. This knowledge, which for the time being I kept to myself, bade me act with caution. I therefore advised Miss X not to let it go at a mere fantasy-image of the act of liberation, but to try to make a picture of it. How this would turn out I could not guess, and that was a good thing, because otherwise I might have put Miss X on the wrong track from sheer helpfulness. She found this task terribly difficult owing to her artistic inhibitions. So I counselled her to content herself with what was possible and to use her fantasy for the purpose of circumventing technical difficulties. The object of this advice was to introduce as much fantasy as possible into the picture, for in that way the unconscious has the best chance of revealing its contents. I also advised her not to be afraid of bright colours, for I knew from experience that vivid colours seem to attract the unconscious. Thereupon, a new picture arose.

PICTURE 2

Picture 2

531 Again there are boulders, the round and pointed forms; but the round ones are no longer eggs, they are complete circles, and the pointed ones are tipped with golden light. One of the round forms has been blasted out of its place by a golden flash of lightning. The magician and magic wand are no longer there. The personal relationship to me seems to have ceased: the picture shows an impersonal natural process.

532 While Miss X was painting this picture she made all sort of discoveries. Above all, she had no notion of what picture she was going to paint. She tried to reimagine the initial situation; the rocky shore and the sea are proof of this. But the eggs turned into abstract spheres or circles, and the magician's touch became a flash of lightning cutting through her unconscious state. With this transformation she had rediscovered the historical synonym of the philosophical egg, namely the *rotundum*, the round, original form of the Anthropos (or στοιχεῖον στρογγύλον, 'round element,' as Zosimos calls it). This is an idea that has been associated with the Anthropos since ancient times.[3] The soul, too, according to tradition, has a round form. As the Monk of Heisterbach says, it is not only 'like to the sphere of the moon, but is furnished on all sides with eyes' (*ex omni parte oculata*). We shall come back to this motif of polyophthalmia later on. His remark refers in all probability to certain parapsychological

phenomena, the 'globes of light' or globular luminosities which, with remarkable consistency, are regarded as 'souls' in the remotest parts of the world.[4]

533   The liberating flash of lightning is a symbol also used by Paracelsus[5] and the alchemists for the same thing. Moses' rock-splitting staff, which struck forth the living water and afterwards changed into a serpent, may have been an unconsious echo in the background.[6] Lightning signifies a sudden, unexpected, and overpowering change of psychic condition.[7]

[. . .]

538   [. . .] [I]n our picture the lightning, striking into the darkness and 'hardness,' has blasted a *rotundum* out of the dark *massa confusa* and kindled a light in it. There can be no doubt that the dark stone means the blackness, i.e., the unconscious, just as the sea and sky and the upper half of the woman's figure indicate the sphere of consciousness. [. . .] The lightning has released the spherical form from the rock and so caused a kind of liberation. But, just as the magician has been replaced by the lightning, so the patient has been replaced by the sphere. The unconscious has thus presented her with ideas which show that she had gone on thinking without the aid of consciousness and that this radically altered the initial situation. It was again her inability to draw that led to this result. Before finding this solution, she had made two attempts to portray the act of liberation with human figures, but with no success. She had overlooked the fact that the initial situation, her imprisonment in the rock, was already irrational and symbolic and therefore could not be solved in a rational way. It had to be done by an equally irrational process. That was why I advised her, should she fail in her attempt to draw human figures, to use some kind of hieroglyph. It then suddenly struck her that the sphere was a suitable symbol for the individual human being. That it was a chance idea (*Einfall*) is proved by the fact that it was not her conscious mind that thought up this typification, but the unconscious, for an *Einfall* 'falls in' quite of its own accord. It should be noted that she represents only herself as a sphere, not me. I am represented only by the lightning, purely functionally, so that for her I am simply the 'precipitating' cause. As a magician I appeared to her in the apt role of Hermes Kyllenios, of whom the Odyssey says: 'Meanwhile Cyllenian Hermes was gathering in the souls of the suitors, armed with the splendid golden wand that he can use at will to cast a spell on our eyes or wake us from the soundest sleep.'[45] Hermes is the ψυχῶν αἴτιος, 'originator of souls.' He is also the ἡγήτωρ ὀνείρων, 'guide of dreams.'[46] For the following pictures it is of special importance that Hermes has the number 4 attributed to him. Martianus Capella says: 'The number four is assigned to the Cyllenian, for he alone is held to be a fourfold god.'[47]

539   The form the picture had taken was not unreservedly welcome to the patient's conscious mind. Luckily, however, while painting it Miss X had discovered that two factors were involved. These, in her own words, were

reason and the *eyes*. Reason always wanted to make the picture as *it* thought it ought to be; but the eyes held fast to their vision and finally forced the picture to come out as it actually did and not in accordance with rationalistic expectations. Her reason, she said, had really intended a daylight scene, with the sunshine melting the sphere free, but the eyes favoured a nocturne with 'shattering, dangerous lightning.' This realization helped her to acknowledge the actual result of her artistic efforts and to admit that it was in fact an objective and impersonal process and not a personal relationship.

540   For anyone with a personalistic view of psychic events, such as a Freudian, it will not be easy to see in this anything more than an elaborate repression. But if there was any repression here we certainly cannot make the conscious mind responsible for it, because the conscious mind would undoubtedly have preferred a personal imbroglio as being far more interesting. The repression must have been manoeuvred by the unconscious from the start. One should consider what this means: instinct, the most original force of the unconscious, is suppressed or turned back on itself by an arrangement stemming from this same unconscious! It would be idle indeed to talk of 'repression' here, since we know that the unconscious goes straight for its goal and that this does not consist solely in pairing two animals but in allowing an individual to become whole. For this purpose wholeness – represented by the sphere – is emphasized as the essence of personality, while I am reduced to the fraction of a second, the duration of a lightning flash.

541   The patient's association to lightning was that it might stand for *intuition*, a conjecture that is not far off the mark, since intuitions often come 'like a flash.' Moreover, there are good grounds for thinking that Miss X was a *sensation* type. She herself thought she was one. The 'inferior' function would then be intuition. As such, it would have the significance of a releasing or 'redeeming' function. We know from experience that the inferior function always compensates, complements, and balances the 'superior' function.[48] My psychic peculiarity would make me a suitable projection carrier in this respect. The inferior function is the one of which least conscious use is made. This is the reason for its undifferentiated quality, but also for its freshness and vitality. It is not at the disposal of the conscious mind, and even after long use it never loses its autonomy and spontaneity, or only to a very limited degree. Its role is therefore mostly that of a *deus ex machina*. It depends not on the ego but on the *self*. Hence it hits consciousness unexpectedly, like lightning, and occasionally with devastating consequences. It thrusts the ego aside and makes room for a supraordinate factor, the totality of a person, which consists of conscious and unconscious and consequently extends far beyond the ego. This self was always present,[49] but sleeping, like Nietzsche's 'image in the stone.'[50] It is, in fact, the secret of the stone, of the *lapis philosophorum*, in so far as this is the *prima materia*. In the stone

sleeps the spirit *Mercurius*, the 'circle of the moon,' the 'round and square,'[51] the homunculus, Tom Thumb and Anthropos at once,[52] whom the alchemists also symbolized as their famed *lapis philosophorum*.[53]

542   All these ideas and inferences were naturally unknown to my patient, and they were known to me at the time only in so far as I was able to recognize the circle as a *mandala*,[54] the psychological expression of the totality of the self. Under these circumstances there could be no question of my having unintentionally infected her with alchemical ideas. The pictures are, in all essentials, genuine creations of the unconscious; their inessential aspects (landscape motifs) are derived from conscious contents.

543   Although the sphere with its glowing red centre and the golden flash of lightning play the chief part, it should not be overlooked that there are several other eggs or spheres as well. If the sphere signifies the self of the patient, we must apply this interpretation to the other spheres, too. They must therefore represent other people who, in all probability, were her intimates. In both the pictures two other spheres are clearly indicated. So I must mention that Miss X had two women friends who shared her intellectual interests and were joined to her in a lifelong friendship. All three of them, as if bound together by fate, are rooted in the same 'earth,' i.e., in the collective unconscious, which is one and the same for all. It is probably for this reason that the second picture has the decidedly *nocturnal* character intended by the unconscious and asserted against the wishes of the conscious mind. It should also be mentioned that the pointed pyramids of the first picture reappear in the second, where their points are actually gilded by the lightning and strongly emphasized. I would interpret them as unconscious contents 'pushing up' into the light of consciousness, as seems to be the case with many contents of the collective unconscious.[55] In contrast to the first picture, the second is painted in more vivid colours, red and gold. Gold expresses sunlight, value, divinity even. It is therefore a favourite synonym for the *lapis*, being the *aurum philosophicum* or *aurum potabile* or *aurum vitreum*.[56]

544   As already pointed out, I was not at that time in a position to reveal anything of these ideas to Miss X, for the simple reason that I myself knew nothing of them. I feel compelled to mention this circumstance yet again, because the third picture, which now follows, brings a motif that points unmistakably to alchemy and actually gave me the definitive incentive to make a thorough study of the works of the old adepts.

PICTURE 3

545   The third picture, done as spontaneously as the first two, is distinguished most of all by its light colours. Free-floating in space, among clouds, is a dark blue sphere with a wine-red border. Round the middle runs a wavy silver band, which keeps the sphere balanced by 'equal and opposite

Picture 3

forces,' as the patient explained. To the right, above the sphere, floats a snake with golden rings, its head pointing at the sphere – an obvious development of the golden lightning in Picture 2. But she drew the snake in afterwards, on account of certain 'reflections.' The whole is 'a planet in the making.' In the middle of the silver band is the number 12. The band was thought of as being in rapid vibratory motion; hence the wave motif. It is like a vibrating belt that keeps the sphere afloat. Miss X compared it to the ring of Saturn. But unlike this, which is composed of disintegrated satellites, her ring was the origin of future moons such as Jupiter possesses. The black lines in the silver band she called 'lines of force'; they were meant to indicate that it was in motion. As if asking a question, I made the remark: 'Then it is the vibrations of the band that keep the sphere floating?' 'Naturally,' she said, 'they are the wings of Mercury, the messenger of the gods. The silver is *quicksilver!*' She went on at once: 'Mercury, that is Hermes, is the Nous, the mind or reason, and that is the animus, who is here outside instead of inside. He is like a veil that hides the true personality.'[57] We shall leave this latter remark alone for the moment and turn first to the wider context, which, unlike that of the two previous pictures, is especially rich.

546   While Miss X was painting this picture, she felt that two earlier dreams

were mingling with her vision. They were the two 'big' dreams of her life. She knew of the attribute 'big' from my stories of the dream life of African primitives I had visited. It has become a kind of 'colloquial term' for characterizing archetypal dreams, which as we know have a peculiar numinosity. It was used in this sense by the dreamer. Several years previously, she had undergone a major operation. Under narcosis she had the following dream-vision: *She saw a grey globe of the world. A silver band rotated about the equator and, according to the frequency of its vibrations, formed alternate zones of condensation and evaporation. In the zones of condensation appeared the numbers 1 to 3, but they had the tendency to increase up to 12.* These numbers signified 'nodal points' or 'great personalities' who played a part in man's historical development. 'The number 12 meant the most important nodal point or great man (still to come), because it denotes the climax or turning point of the process of development.' (These are her own words.)

547   The other dream that intervened had occurred a year before the first one: *She saw a golden snake in the sky. It demanded the sacrifice, from among a great crowd of people, of a young man, who obeyed this demand with an expression of sorrow.* The dream was repeated a little later, but this time *the snake picked on the dreamer herself. The assembled people regarded her compassionately, but she took her fate 'proudly' on herself.*

548   She was, as she told me, born immediately after midnight, so soon afterwards, indeed, that there was some doubt as to whether she came into the world on the 28th or on the 29th. Her father used to tease her by saying that she was obviously born before her time, since she came into the world just at the beginning of a new day, but 'only just,' so that one could almost believe she was born 'at the twelfth hour.' The number 12, as she said, meant for her the culminating point of her life, which she had only now reached. That is, she felt the 'liberation' as the climax of her life. It is indeed an hour of birth – not of the dreamer but of the self. This distinction must be borne in mind.

549   The context to Picture 3 here established needs a little commentary. First, it must be emphasized that the patient felt the moment of painting this picture as the 'climax' of her life and also described it as such. Second, two 'big' dreams have amalgamated in the picture, which heightens its significance still more. The sphere blasted from the rock in Picture 2 has now, in the brighter atmosphere, floated up to heaven. The nocturnal darkness of the earth has vanished. The increase of light indicates conscious realization: the liberation has become a fact that is integrated into consciousness. The patient has understood that the floating sphere symbolizes the 'true personality.' At present, however, it is not quite clear how she understands the relation of the ego to the 'true personality.' The term chosen by her coincides in a remarkable way with the Chinese *chen-yen*, the 'true' or 'complete' man, who has the closest affinity with the *homo quadratus*[58] of alchemy.[59] As we pointed out in the analysis of

Picture 2, the *rotundum* of alchemy is identical with Mercurius, the 'round and square.'[60] In Picture 3 the connection is shown concretely through the mediating idea of the wings of Mercury.

[. . .]

553   In our picture Mercurius forms a world-encircling band, usually represented by a snake.[70] Mercurius is a serpent or dragon in alchemy ('serpens mercurialis'). Oddly enough, this serpent is some distance away from the sphere and is aiming down at it, as if to strike. The sphere, we are told, is kept afloat by equal and opposite forces, represented by the quicksilver or somehow connected with it. According to the old view, Mercurius is duplex, i.e., he is himself an antithesis.[71] Mercurius or Hermes is a magician and god of magicians. As Hermes Trismegistus he is the patriarch of alchemy. His magician's wand, the caduceus, is entwined by two snakes. The same attribute distinguishes Asklepios, the god of physicians.[72] The archetype of these ideas was projected on to me by the patient before ever the analysis had begun.

554   The primordial image underlying the sphere girdled with quicksilver is probably that of the world egg encoiled by a snake.[73] But in our case the snake symbol of Mercurius is replaced by a sort of pseudo-physicistic notion of a field of vibrating molecules of quicksilver. This looks like an intellectual disguising of the true situation, that the self, or its symbol, is entwined by the mercurial serpent. As the patient remarked more or less correctly, the 'true personality' is veiled by it. This, presumably, would then be something like an Eve in the coils of the paradisal serpent. In order to avoid giving this appearance, Mercurius has obligingly split into his two forms, according to the old-established pattern: the *mercurius crudus* or *vulgi* (crude or ordinary quicksilver), and the *Mercurius Philosophorum* (the *spiritus mercurialis* or the spirit Mercurius, Hermes-Nous), who hovers in the sky as the golden lightning-snake or Nous Serpent, at present inactive. In the vibrations of the quicksilver band we may discern a certain tremulous excitement, just as the suspension expresses tense expectation: 'Hover and haver suspended in pain!' For the alchemists quicksilver meant the concrete, material manifestation of the spirit Mercurius, as the above-mentioned mandala in the scholia to the *Tractatus aureus* shows: the central point is Mercurius, and the square is Mercurius divided into the four elements. He is the *anima mundi*, the innermost point and at the same time the encompasser of the world, like the atman in the Upanishads. And just as quicksilver is a materialization of Mercurius, so the gold is a materialization of the sun in the earth.[74]

555   A circumstance that never ceases to astonish one is this: that at all times and in all places alchemy brought its conception of the *lapis* or its *minera* (raw material) together with the idea of the *homo altus* or *maximus*, that is, with the Anthropos.[75] Equally, one must stand amazed at the fact that here too the conception of the dark round stone blasted out of the rock should represent such an abstract idea as the psychic totality of man. The

earth and in particular the heavy cold stone is the epitome of materiality, and so is the metallic quicksilver which, the patient thought, meant the animus (mind, *nous*). We would expect pneumatic symbols for the idea of the self and the animus, images of air, breath, wind. The ancient formula λίθος οὐ λίθος (the stone that is no stone) expresses this dilemma: we are dealing with a *complexio oppositorum,* with something like the nature of light, which under some conditions behaves like particles and under others like waves, and is obviously in its essence both at once. Something of this kind must be conjectured with regard to these paradoxical and hardly explicable statements of the unconscious. They are not inventions of any conscious mind, but are spontaneous manifestations of a psyche not controlled by consciousness and obviously possessing all the freedom it wants to express views that take no account of our conscious intentions. The duplicity of Mercurius, his simultaneously metallic and pneumatic nature, is a paraellel to the symbolization of an extremely spiritual idea like the Anthropos by a corporeal, indeed metallic, substance (gold). One can only conclude that the unconscious tends to regard spirit and matter not merely as equivalent but as actually identical, and this in flagrant contrast to the intellectual one-sidedness of consciousness, which would sometimes like to spiritualize matter and at other times to materialize spirit. That the *lapis,* or in our case the floating sphere, has a double meaning is clear from the circumstance that it is characterized by two symbolical colours: red means blood and affectivity, the physiological reaction that joins spirit to body, and blue means the spiritual process (mind or *nous*). This duality reminds one of the alchemical duality *corpus* and *spiritus,* joined together by a third, the *anima* as the *ligamentum corporis et spiritus.*[. . .]

PICTURE 4

556 Picture 4 [. . .] shows a significant change: the sphere has divided into an outer membrane and an inner nucleus. The outer membrane is flesh coloured, and the originally rather nebulous red nucleus in Picture 2 now has a differentiated internal structure of a decidedly ternary character. The 'lines of force' that originally belonged to the band of quicksilver now run through the whole nuclear body, indicating that the excitation is no longer external only but has seized the innermost core. 'An enormous inner activity now began,' the patient told me. The nucleus with its ternary structure is presumbaly the female organ, stylized to look like a plant, in the act of fecundation: the spermatozoon is penetrating the nuclear membrane. Its role is played by the mercurial serpent: the snake is black, dark, chthonic, a subterranean and ithyphallic Hermes; but it has the golden wings of Mercury and consequently possesses his pneumatic nature. The alchemists accordingly represented their *Mercurius duplex* as the winged and wingless dragon, calling the former feminine and the latter masculine.

Picture 4

557   The serpent in our picture represents not so much the spermatozoon but, more accurately, the phallus. Leone Ebreo,[76] in his *Dialoghi d'amore*, calls the planet Mercury the *membrum virile* of heaven, that is, of the macrocosm conceived as the *homo maximus*.[77] The spermatozoon seems, rather, to correspond to the golden substance which the snake is injecting into the invaginated ectoderm of the nucleus.[78] The two silver petals (?) probably represent the receptive vessel, the moon-bowl in which the sun's seed (gold) is destined to rest.[79] Underneath the flower is a small violet circle inside the ovary, indicating by its colour that it is a 'united double nature,' spirit and body (blue and red).[80] The snake has a pale yellow halo, which is meant to express its numinosity.

558   Since the snake evolved out of the flash of lightning or is a modulated form of it, I would like to instance a parallel where the lightning has the same illuminating, vivifying, fertilizing, transforming and healing function that in our case falls to the snake [see Figure 6.1]. Two phases are represented: first, a black sphere, signifying a state of profound depression; and second, the lightning that strikes into this sphere. Ordinary speech makes use of the same imagery: something 'strikes home' in a 'flash of revelation.' The only difference is that generally the image comes first, and only afterwards the realization which enables the patient to say: 'This has struck home.'

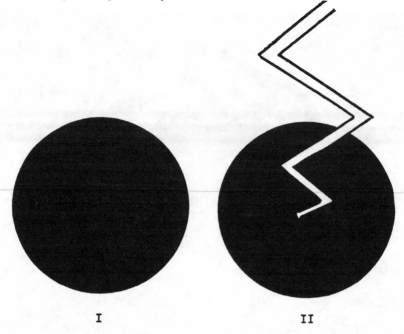

I   II

Figure 6.1 Sketch of a drawing by a young woman patient with psychogenic depression from the beginning of the treatment

I. State of black hopelessness / II. Beginning of the therapeutic effect

In an earlier picture the sphere lay on the bottom of the sea. As a series of pictures shows, it arose in the first place because a black snake had swallowed the sun. There then followed an eight-rayed, completely black mandala with a wreath of eight silver stars. In the centre was a black homunculus. Next the black sphere developed a red centre, from which red rays, or streams of blood, ran out into tentacle-like extremities. The whole thing looked rather like a crab or an octopus. As the later pictures showed, the patient herself was shut up in the sphere.

559   As to the context of Picture 4, Miss X emphasized that what disturbed her most was the band of quicksilver in Picture 3. She felt the silvery substance ought to be 'inside,' the black lines of force remaining outside to form a black snake. This would now encircle the sphere.[81] She felt the snake at first as a 'terrible danger,' as something threatening the 'integrity of the sphere.' At the point where the snake penetrates the nuclear membrane, fire breaks out (emotion). Her conscious mind interpreted this conflagration as a defensive reaction on the part of the sphere, and accordingly she tried to depict the attack as having been repulsed. But this attempt failed to satisfy the 'eyes,' though she showed me a pencil sketch of it. She was obviously in a dilemma: she could not accept the snake, because its sexual significance was only too clear to her without any assistance from me. I merely remarked to her: 'This is a well-known process[82] which you can safely accept,' and showed her from my collection a similar picture, done by a man, of a floating sphere being penetrated *from*

below by a black phallus-like object. Later she said: 'I suddenly understood the whole process in a more impersonal way.' It was the realization of a law of life to which sex is subordinated. 'The ego was not the centre, but, following a universal law, I circled round a sun.' Thereupon she was able to accept the snake 'as a necessary part of the process of growth' and finish the picture quickly and satisfactorily. Only one thing continued to give difficulty: she had to put the snake, she said, 'One hundred per cent at the top, in the middle, in order to satisfy the eyes.' Evidently the unconscious would only be satisfied with the most important position at the top and in the middle – in direct contrast to the picture I had previously shown her. This, as I said, was done by a man and showed the menacing black symbol entering the mandala from below. For a woman, the typical danger emanating from the unconscious comes *from above*, from the 'spiritual' sphere personified by the animus, whereas for a man it comes from the chthonic realm of the 'world and woman,' i.e., the anima projected on to the world.

[. . .]

561　　Let us remember that in Picture 3 *Mercurius vulgi*, ordinary quicksilver, encircles the sphere. This means that the mysterious sphere is enveloped or veiled by a 'vulgar' or crude understanding. The patient herself opined that 'the animus veils the true personality.' We shall hardly be wrong in assuming that a banal, everyday view of the world, allegedly biological, has here got hold of the sexual symbol and concretized it after the approved pattern. A pardonable error! Another, more correct view is so much more subtle that one naturally prefers to fall back on something well-known and ready to hand, thus gratifying one's own 'rational' expectations and earning the applause of one's contemporaries – only to discover that one has got hopelessly stuck and has arrived back at the point from which one set forth on the great adventure. It is clear what is meant by the ithyphallic serpent: from above comes all that is aerial, intellectual, spiritual, and from below all that is passionate, corporeal, and dark. The snake, contrary to expectation, turns out to be a pneumatic symbol,[87] a *Mercurius spiritualis* – a realization which the patient herself formulated by saying that the ego, despite its capricious manipulation of sexuality, is subject to a universal law. Sex in this case is therefore no problem at all, as it has been subjected to a higher transformation process and is contained in it; not repressed, only without an object.

562　　Miss X subsequently told me that she felt Picture 4 was the most difficult, as if it denoted the turning point of the whole process. In my view she may not have been wrong in this, because the clearly felt, ruthless setting aside of the so beloved and so important ego is no light matter. Not for nothing is this 'letting go' the *sine qua non* of all forms of higher spiritual development, whether we call it meditation, contemplation, yoga, or spiritual exercises. But, as this case shows, relinquishing the ego is not an act of the will and not a result arbitrarily produced; it is an event, an occurrence, whose inner, compelling logic can be disguised only by wilful self-deception.

563   In this case and at this moment the ability to 'let go' is of decisive importance. But since everything passes, the moment may come when the relinquished ego must be reinstated in its functions. Letting go gives the unconscious the opportunity it has been waiting for. But since it consists of opposites – day and night, bright and dark, positive and negative – and is good and evil and therefore ambivalent, the moment will infallibly come when the individual, like the exemplary Job, must hold fast so as not to be thrown catastrophically off balance – when the wave rebounds. The holding fast can be achieved only by a conscious will, i.e., by the ego. That is the great and irreplaceable significance of the ego, but one which, as we see here, is none the less relative. Relative, too, is the gain won by integrating the unconscious. We add to ourselves a bright and a dark, and more light means more night.[88] The urge of consciousness towards wider horizons, however, cannot be stopped; they must needs extend the scope of the personality, if they are not to shatter it.

PICTURE 5

564   Picture 5, Miss X said, followed naturally from Picture 4, with no difficulty. The sphere and the snake have drawn apart. The snake is sinking downwards and seems to have lost its threateningness. But the sphere has been fecundated with a vengeance: it has not only got bigger, but blossoms in the most vivid colours.[89] The nucleus has divided into four; something like a segmentation has occurred. This is not due to any conscious reflection, such as might come naturally to a biologically educated person; the division of the process or of the central symbol into four has always existed, beginning with the four sons of Horus, or the four seraphim of Ezekiel, or the birth of the four Aeons from the Metra (uterus) impregnated by the pneuma in Barbelo-Gnosis, or the cross formed by the lightning (snake) in Böhme's system,[90] and ending with the tetrameria of the *opus alchymicum* and its components (the four elements, qualities, stages, etc.).[91] In each case the quaternity forms a unity; here it is the green circle at the centre of the four. The four are undifferentiated, and each of them forms a vortex, apparently turning to the left. I think I am not mistaken in regarding it as probable that, in general, a leftward movement indicates movement towards the unconscious, while a rightward (clockwise) movement goes towards consciousness.[92] The one is 'sinister,' the other 'right,' 'rightful,' 'correct.' In Tibet, the leftward-moving swastika is a sign of the Bön religion, of black magic. Stupas and chörtens must therefore be circumambulated clockwise. The leftward-spinning eddies spin into the unconscious; the rightward-moving swastika in Tibet is therefore a Buddhist emblem.[93] [. . .]

Picture 5

565   For our patient the process appeared to mean, first and foremost, a differentiation of consciousness. From the treasures of her psychological knowledge she interpreted the four as the four orienting functions of consciousness: thinking, feeling, sensation, intuition. She noticed, however, that the four were all alike, whereas the four functions are all unlike. This raised no question for her, but it did for me. What are these four if they are *not* the four functional aspects of consciousness? I doubted whether this could be a sufficient interpretation of them. They seemed to be much more than that, and that is probably the reason why they are not different but identical. They do not form four functions, different by definition, but they might well represent the *a priori* possibility for the formation of the four functions. In this picture we have the quaternity, the archetypal 4, which is capable of numerous interpretations, as history shows and as I have demonstrated elsewhere. It illustrates the coming to consciousness of an unconscious content; hence it frequently occurs in cosmogonic myths. What is the precise significance of the fact that the four eddies are apparently turning to the left, when the division of the mandala into four denotes a process of becoming conscious, is a point about which I would rather not speculate. I lack the necessary material. Blue means air or pneuma, and the leftward movement an intensification of the unconscious

influence. Possibly this should be taken as a pneumatic compensation for the strongly emphasized red colour, which signifies affectivity.

566   The mandala itself is bright red, but the four eddies have in the main a cool, greenish-blue colour, which the patient associated with 'water.' This might hang together with the leftward movement, since water is a favourite symbol for the unconscious.[94] The green of the circle in the middle signifies life in the chthonic sense. It is the 'benedicta viriditas' of the alchemists.

567   The problematical thing about this picture is the fact that the black snake is outside the totality of the symbolic circle. In order to make the totality actual, it ought really to be inside. But if we remember the unfavourable significance of the snake, we shall understand why its assimilation into the symbol of psychic wholeness presents certain difficulties. If our conjecture about the leftward movement of the four eddies is correct, this would denote a trend towards the deep and dark side of the spirit,[95] by means of which the black snake could be assimilated. The snake, like the devil in Christian theology, represents the shadow, and one which goes far beyond anything personal and could therefore best be compared with a principle, such as the principle of evil.[96] It is the colossal shadow thrown by man, of which our age had to have such a devastating experience. It is no easy matter to fit this shadow into our cosmos. The view that we can simply turn our back on evil and in this way eschew it belongs to the long list of antiquated naïveties. This is sheer ostrich policy and does not affect the reality of evil in the slightest. Evil is the necessary opposite of good, without which there would be no good either. It is impossible even to think evil out of existence. Hence the fact that the black snake remains outside expresses the critical position of evil in our traditional view of the world.

568   The background of the picture is pale, the colour of parchment. I mention this fact in particular, as the pictures that follow show a characteristic change in this respect.

PICTURE 6

569   The background of Picture 6 is a cloudy grey. The mandala itself is done in the vividest colours, bright red, green, and blue. Only where the red outer membrane enters the blue-green nucleus does the red deepen to blood colour and the pale blue to a dark ultramarine. The wings of Mercury, missing in the previous picture, reappear here at the neck of the blood-red pistons (as previously on the neck of the black snake in Picture 4). But the most striking thing is the appearance of a swastika, undoubtedly wheeling to the right. (I should add that these pictures were painted in 1928 and had no direct connection with contemporary fantasies, which at that time were still unknown to the world at large.) Because of its green colour, the swastika suggests something plantlike, but at the same time it has the wavelike character of the four eddies in the previous picture.

Picture 6

570   In this mandala an attempt is made to unite the opposites red and blue, outside and inside. Simultaneously, the rightward movement aims at bringing about an ascent into the light of consciousness, presumably because the background has become noticeably darker. The black snake has disappeared, but has begun to impart its darkness to the entire background. To compensate this, there is in the mandala an upwards movement towards the light, apparently an attempt to rescue consciousness from the darkening of the environment. The picture was associated with a dream that occurred a few days before. Miss X dreamt that *she returned to the city after a holiday in the country. To her astonishment she found a tree growing in the middle of the room where she worked. She thought: 'Well, with its thick bark this tree can withstand the heat of an apartment.'* Associations to the tree led to its maternal significance. The tree would explain the plant motif in the mandala, and its sudden growth represents the higher level or freeing of consciousness induced by the movement to the right. For the same reason the 'philosophical' tree is a symbol of the alchemical *opus*, which we know is an individuation process.

   [. . .]

PICTURE 7

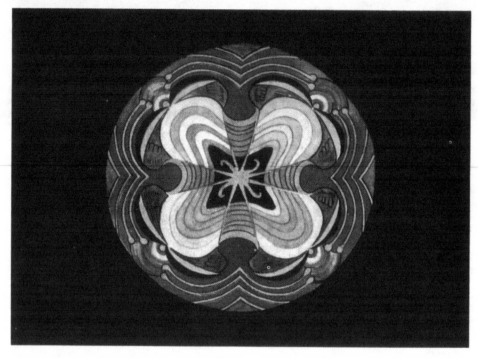

Picture 7

574 In Picture 7 it has indeed turned to night: the entire sheet which the mandala is painted on is black. All the light is concentrated in the sphere. The colours have lost their brightness but have gained in intensity. It is especially striking that the black has penetrated as far as the centre, so that something of what we feared has already occurred: the blackness of the snake and of the sombre surroundings has been assimilated by the nucleus and, at the same time, as the picture shows, is compensated by a golden light radiating out from the centre. The rays form an equal-armed cross, to replace the swastika of the previous picture, which is here represented only by four hooks suggesting a rightwards rotation. With the attainment of absolute blackness, and particularly its presence in the centre, the upward movement and rightward rotation seem to have come to an end. On the other hand, the wings of Mercury have undergone a noticeable differentiation, which presumably means that the sphere has sufficient power to keep itself afloat and not sink down into total darkness. The golden rays forming the cross bind the four together.[111] This produces an inner bond and consolidation as a defence against destructive influences[112] emanating from the black substance that has penetrated to the centre. For us the cross symbol always has the connotation of *suffering*, so we are probably not wrong in assuming that the mood of this picture is

one of more or less painful *suspension* – remember the wings – over the dark abyss of inner loneliness.

[. . .]

576   The numerous wavy lines or layers in the mandala could be interpreted as representing the formation of *layers of skin*, giving protection against outside influences. They serve the same purpose as the inner consolidation. These cortices probably have something to do with the dream of the tree in the workroom, which had a 'thick bark.' The formation of skins is also found in other mandalas, and it denotes a hardening or sealing off against the outside, the production of a regular rind or 'hide.' It is possible that this phenomenon would account for the cortices or *putamina* ('shards') mentioned in the cabala.[114] 'For such is the name for that which abides outside holiness,' such as the seven fallen kings and the four Achurayim.[115] From them come the 'klippoth' or cortices. As in alchemy, these are the scoriae or slag, to which adheres the quality of plurality and of death. In our mandala the cortices are boundary lines marking off the inner unity and protecting it against the outer blackness with its disintegrating influences, personified by the snake.[116] The same motif is expressed by the petals of the lotus and by the skins of the onion: the outer layers are withered and desiccated, but they protect the softer, inner layers. The lotus seat of the Horus-child, of the Indian divinities, and of the Buddha must be understood in this sense. Hölderlin makes use of the same image:

> Fateless, like the sleeping
> Infant, breathe the heavenly ones,
> Chastely guarded
> In modest bud; their spirits
> Blossom eternally . . . [117]

[. . .]

580   [In] our mandala [. . .] the original four eddies have coalesced into the wavy squares in the middle of the picture. Their place is taken by golden points at the outer rim (developed from the previous picture), emitting rainbow colours. These are the colours of the *peacock's eye*, which play a great role as the *cauda pavonis* in alchemy.[124] The appearance of these colours in the opus represents an intermediate stage preceding the definitive end result. Böhme speaks of a 'love-desire or a Beauty of Colours; and here all Colours arise.'[125] In our mandala, too, the rainbow colours spring from the red layer that means affectivity.

[. . .]

583   [. . .] The golden lines that end in pistons recapitulate the spermatozoon motif and therefore have a spermatic significance, suggesting that the quaternity will be reproduced in a new and more distinct form. In so far as the quaternity has to do with conscious realization, we can infer from these symptoms an intensification of the latter, as is also suggested by the golden light radiating from the centre. Probably a kind of inner illumination is meant.

584   Two days before painting this picture, Miss X dreamt that *she was in her father's room in their country house.* 'But my mother had moved my bed away from the wall into the middle of the room and had slept in it. I was furious, and moved the bed back to its former place. In the dream the bed-cover was red – exactly the red reproduced in the picture.'

585   The mother significance of the tree in her previous dream has here been taken up by the unconscious: this time the mother has slept in the middle of the room. This seems to be for Miss X an annoying intrusion into her sphere, symbolized by the room of her father, who has an animus significance for her. Her sphere is therefore a spiritual one, and she has usurped it just as she usurped her father's room. She has thus identified with the 'spirit.' Into this sphere her mother has intruded and installed herself in the centre, at first under the symbol of the tree. She therefore stands for physis opposed to spirit, i.e., for the natural feminine being which the dreamer also is, but which she would not accept because it appeared to her as a black snake. Although she remedied the intrusion at once, the dark chthonic principle, the black substance, has nevertheless penetrated to the centre of her mandala, as Picture 7 shows. But just because of this the golden light can appear. [. . .] The collision between the paternal and the maternal principle (spirit and nature) works like a shock.

586   After this picture, she felt the renewed penetration of the red colour, which she associated with feeling, as something disturbing, and she now discovered that her 'rapport' with me, her analyst (= father), was unnatural and unsatisfactory. She was giving herself airs, she said, and was posing as an intelligent, understanding pupil (usurpation of spirituality!). But she had to admit that she felt very silly and was very silly, regardless of what I thought about it. This admission brought her a feeling of great relief and helped her to see at last that sex was 'not, on the one hand, merely a mechanism for producing children and not, on the other, only an expression of supreme passion, but was also banally physiological and autoerotic.' This belated realization led her straight into a fantasy state where she became conscious of a series of obscene images. At the end she saw the image of a large bird, which she called the 'earth bird,' and which alighted on the earth. Birds, as aerial beings, are well-known spirit symbols. It represented the transformation of the 'spiritual' image of herself into a more earthy version that is more characteristic of women. This 'tailpiece' confirms our suspicion that the intensive upward and rightward movement has come to a halt: the bird is coming down to earth. [. . .] Through this differentiation consciousness is not only widened but also brought face to face with the reality of things, so that the inner experience is tied, so to speak, to a definite spot.

587   On the days following, the patient was overcome by feelings of self-pity. It became clear to her now how much she regretted never having had any children. She felt like a neglected animal or a lost child. This mood grew

into a regular *Weltschmerz*, and she felt like the 'all-compassionate Tathagata' (Buddha). Only when she had completely given way to these feelings could she bring herself to paint another picture. Real liberation comes not from glossing over or repressing painful states of feeling, but only from experiencing them to the full.

PICTURE 8

Picture 8

588 The thing that strikes us at once in Picture 8 is that almost the whole interior is filled with the black substance. The blue-green of the water has condensed to a dark blue quaternity, and the golden light in the centre turns in the reverse direction, anti-clockwise: the bird is coming down to earth. That is, the mandala is moving towards the dark, chthonic depths. It is still floating – the wings of Mercury show this – but it has come much closer to the blackness. The inner, undifferentiated quaternity is balanced by an outer, differentiated one, which Miss X equated with the four functions of consciousness. To these she assigned the following colours: yellow = intuition, light blue = thinking, flesh pink = feeling, brown = sensation.[134] Each of these quarters is divided into three, thus producing the number 12 again. The separation and characterization of the two quaternities is worth noting. The outer quaternity of wings appears as a differentiated

realization[135] of the undifferentiated inner one, which really represents the archetype. In the cabala this relationship corresponds to the quaternity of Merkabah[136] on the one hand and of the Achurayim on the other, and in Böhme they are the four Spirits of God[137] and the four elements.

589   The plantlike form of the cross in the middle of the mandala, also noted by the patient, refers back to the tree ('tree of the cross') and the mother.[138] She thus makes it clear that this previously taboo element has been accepted and now holds the central place. She was fully conscious of this – which of course was a great advance on her previous attitude.

590   In contrast to the previous picture there are no inner cortices. This is a logical development, because the thing they were meant to exclude is now in the centre, and defence has become superfluous. Instead, the cortices spread out into the darkness as golden rings, expanding concentrically like waves. This would mean a far-reaching influence on the environment emanating from the sealed-off self.

591   Four days before she painted this mandala she had the following dream: '*I drew a young man to the window and, with a brush dipped in white oil, removed a black fleck from the cornea of his eye. A little golden lamp then became visible in the centre of the pupil. The young man felt greatly relieved, and I told him he should come again for treatment. I woke up saying the words: "If therefore thine eye be single, thy whole body shall be full of light."*' (Matthew 6: 22.)

592   This dream describes the change: the patient is no longer identical with her animus. The animus has, so to speak, become *her* patient, since he has eye trouble. As a matter of fact the animus usually sees things 'cock-eyed' and often very unclearly. Here a black fleck on the cornea obscures the golden light shining from inside the eye. He has 'seen things too blackly.'
[. . .]

593   Our mandala is indeed an 'eye,' the structure of which symbolizes the centre of order in the unconscious. The eye is a hollow sphere, black inside, and filled with a semi-liquid substance, the vitreous humour. Looking at it from outside, one sees a round, coloured surface, the iris, with a dark centre, from which a golden light shines. Böhme calls it a 'fiery eye,' in accordance with the old idea that seeing emanates from the eye. The eye may well stand for consciousness (which is in fact an organ of perception), looking into its own background. It sees its own light there, and when this is clear and pure the whole body is filled with light. Under certain conditions consciousness has a purifying effect. This is probably what is meant by Matthew 6: 22ff., an idea expressed even more clearly in Luke 11: 33ff.

594   The eye is also a well-known symbol for God. Hence Böhme calls his 'Philosophique Globe' the 'Eye of Eternity,' the 'Essence of all Essences,' the 'Eye of God.'[140]

595   By accepting the darkness, the patient has not, to be sure, changed it into light, but she has kindled a light that illuminates the darkness within.

By day no light is needed, and if you don't know it is night you won't light one, nor will any light be lit for you unless you have suffered the horror of darkness. This is not an edifying text but a mere statement of the psychological facts. The transition from Picture 7 to Picture 8 gives one a working idea of what I mean by 'accepting the dark principle.' It has sometimes been objected that nobody can form a clear conception of what this means, which is regrettable, because it is an ethical problem of the first order. Here, then, is a practical example of this 'acceptance,' and I must leave it to the philosophers to puzzle out the ethical aspects of the process.[141]

PICTURE 9

Picture 9

596 In Picture 9 we see for the first time the blue 'soul-flower,' on a red background, also described as such by Miss X[. . . .][142] In the centre is the golden light in the form of a lamp, as she herself stated. The cortices are very pronounced, but they consist of light (at least in the upper half of the mandala) and radiate outwards.[143] The light is composed of the rainbow hues of the rising sun; it is a real *cauda pavonis*. There are six sets of sunbeams. This recalls the Buddha's Discourse on the Robe, from the Collection of the Pali Canon:

His heart overflowing with lovingkindness . . . with compassion . . . with joyfulness . . . with equanimity, he abides, raying forth loving-kindness, compassion, joyfulness, equanimity, towards one quarter of space, then towards the second, then towards the third, then towards the fourth, and above and below, thus, all around. Everywhere, into all places the wide world over, his heart overflowing with compassion streams forth, wide, deep, illimitable, free from enmity, free from all ill-will. . . .[144]

597   But a parallel with the Buddhist East cannot be carried through here, because the mandala is divided into an upper and a lower half.[145] Above, the rings shine many-hued as a rainbow; below, they consist of brown earth. Above, there hover three white birds (*pneumata* signifiying the Trinity); below, a goat is rising up, accompanied by two ravens (Wotan's birds)[146] and twining snakes. This is not the sort of picture a Buddhist holy man would make, but that of a Western person with a Christian back-ground, whose light throws a dark shadow. What is more, the three birds float in a jet black sky, and the goat, rising out of dark clay, is shown against a field of bright orange. This, oddly enough, is the colour of the Buddhist monk's robe, which was certainly not a conscious intention of the patient. The underlying thought is clear: no white without black, and no holiness without the devil. Opposites are brothers, and the Oriental seeks to liberate himself from them by his *nirdvandva* ('free from the two') and his *neti neti* ('not this, not that'), or else he puts up with them in some mysterious fashion, as in Taoism. The connection with the East is deliberately stressed by the patient, through her painting into the mandala four hexagrams from the *I Ching*.[147]

598   The sign in the left top half is 'Yü, ENTHUSIASM' (No. 16). It means 'Thunder comes resounding out of the earth,' i.e., a movement coming from the unconscious, and expressed by music and dancing. Confucius comments as follows:

Firm as a rock, what need of a whole day?
The judgment can be known.
The superior man knows what is hidden and what is evident.
He knows weakness, he knows strength as well.
Hence the myriads look up to him.
Enthusiasm can be the source of beauty, but it can also delude.

599   The second hexagram at the top is 'Sun, DECREASE' (No. 41). The upper trigram means Mountain, the lower trigram means Lake. The mountain towers above the lake and 'restrains' it. That is the 'image' whose interpretation points to self-restraint and reserve, i.e., a seeming decrease of oneself. This is significant in the light of 'ENTHUSIASM.' In the top line of the hexagram, 'But [one] no longer has a separate home,' the homelessness of the Buddhist monk is meant. On the psychological

level this does not, of course, refer to so drastic a demonstration of renunciation and independence, but to the patient's irreversible insight into the conditioned quality of all relationships, into the relativity of all values, and the transience of all things.

600   The sign in the bottom half to the right is 'Sheng, PUSHING UPWARD' (No. 46). 'Within the earth, wood grows: The image of Pushing Upward.' It also says: 'One pushes upward into an empty city,' and 'The king offers him Mount Ch'i.' So this hexagram means growth and development of the personality, like a plant pushing out of the earth – a theme already anticipated by the plant motif in an earlier mandala. This is an allusion to the important lesson which Miss X has learnt from her experience: that there is no development unless the shadow is accepted.

601   The hexagram to the left is 'Ting, THE CAULDRON' (No. 50). This is a bronze sacrificial vessel equipped with handles and legs, which held the cooked viands used for festive occasions. The lower trigram means Wind and Wood, the upper one Fire. The 'Cauldron' is thus made up of 'fire over wood,' just as the alchemical vessel consists of fire or water.[148] There is 'delicious food' in it (the 'fat of the pheasant'), but it is not eaten because 'the handle of the *ting* is altered' and its 'legs are broken,' making it unusable. But, as a result of 'constant self-abnegation,' the personality becomes differentiated ('the *ting* has golden carrying rings' and even 'rings of jade') and purified, until it acquires the 'hardness and soft lustre' of precious jade.[149]

602   Though the four hexagrams were put into the mandala on purpose, they are authentic results of preoccupation with the *I Ching*. The phases and aspects of my patient's inner process of development can therefore express themselves easily in the language of the *I Ching*, because it too is based on the psychology of the individuation process that forms one of the main interests of Taoism and of Zen Buddhism.[150] Miss X's interest in Eastern philosphy was due to the deep impression which a better knowledge of her life and of herself had made upon her – an impression of the tremendous contradictions in human nature. The insoluble conflict she was faced with makes her preoccupation with Eastern therapeutic systems, which seem to get along without conflict, doubly interesting. It may be partly due to this acquaintance with the East that the opposites, irreconcilable in Christianity, were not blurred or glossed over, but were seen in all their sharpness, and in spite (or perhaps just because) of this, were brought together into the unity of the mandala. Böhme was never able to achieve this union; on the contrary, in his mandala the bright and dark semi-circles are turned back to back. [. . .]

603   Böhme's starting-point was philosophical alchemy, and to my knowledge he was the first to try to organize the Christian cosmos, as a total reality, into a mandala.[152] The attempt failed, inasmuch as he was unable to unite the two halves in a circle. Miss X's mandala, on the other hand, comprises and contains the opposites, as a result, we may suppose, of the

support afforded by the Chinese doctrine of Yang and Yin, the two metaphysical principles whose co-operation makes the world go round. The hexagrams, with their firm (yang) and yielding (yin) lines, illustrate certain phases of this process. It is therefore right that they should occupy a mediating position between above and below. Lao-tzu says: 'High stands on low.' This indisputable truth is secretly suggested in the mandala: the three white birds hover in a black field, but the grey-black goat has a bright orange-coloured background. Thus the Oriental truth insinuates itself and makes possible – at least by symbolic anticipation – a union of opposites within the irrational life process formulated by the *I Ching*. That we are really concerned here with opposite phases of one and the same process is shown by the picture that now follows.

PICTURE 10

Picture 10

604   In Picture 10, begun in Zurich but only completed when Miss X again visited her motherland, we find the same division as before into above and below. The 'soul-flower'[153] in the centre is the same, but it is surrounded on all sides by a dark blue night sky, in which we see the four phases of the moon, the new moon coinciding with the world of darkness below. The three birds have become two. Their plumage has darkened, but on the other

hand the goat has turned into two semi-human creatures with horns and light faces, and only two of the four snakes remain. A notable innovation is the appearance of two *crabs* in the lower, chthonic hemisphere that also represents the body. The crab has essentially the same meaning as the astrological sign Cancer.[154] Unfortunately Miss X gave no context here. In such cases it is usually worth investigating what use has been made in the past of the object in question. In earlier, pre-scientific ages hardly any distinction was drawn between long-tailed crabs (*Macrura*, crayfish) and short-tailed crabs (*Brachyura*). As a zodiacal sign Cancer signifies *resurrection*, because the crab sheds its shell.[155] The ancients had in mind chiefly *Pagurus bernhardus*, the hermit crab. It hides in its shell and cannot be attacked. Therefore it signifies *caution* and *foresight, knowledge of coming events*.[156] It 'depends on the moon, and waxes with it.'[157] It is worth noting that the crab appears just in the mandala in which we see the phases of the moon for the first time. Astrologically, Cancer is the house of the moon. Because of its backwards and sideways movement, it plays the role of an unlucky animal in superstition and colloquial speech ('crabbed,' 'catch a crab,' etc.). Since ancient times cancer (καρκίνος) has been the name for a malignant tumour of the glands. Cancer is the zodiacal sign in which the sun begins to retreat, when the days grow shorter. Pseudo-Kallisthenes relates that crabs dragged Alexander's ships down into the sea.[158] 'Karkinos' was the name of the crab that bit Heracles in the foot in his fight with the Lernaean monster. In gratitude, Hera set her accomplice among the stars.[159]

605   In astrology, Cancer is a feminine and watery sign,[160] and the summer solstice takes place in it. In the *melothesiae*[161] it is correlated with the *breast*. It rules over the *Western sea*. In Propertius it makes a sinister appearance: 'Octipedis Cancri terga sinistra time' (Fear thou the ill-omened back of the eight-footed crab).[162] De Gubernatis says: 'The crab . . . causes now the death of the solar hero and now that of the monster.'[163] The *Panchatantra* (V, 2) relates how a crab, which the mother gave to her son as apotropaic magic, saved his life by killing a black snake.[164] As De Gubernatis thinks, the crab stands now for the sun and now for the moon,[165] according to whether it goes forwards or backwards.

606   Miss X was born in the first degrees of Cancer (actually about 3°). She knew her horoscope and was well aware of the significance of the moment of birth; that is, she realized that the degree of the rising sun (the ascendant) conditions the individuality of the horoscope. Since she obviously guessed the horoscope's affinity with the mandala, she introduced her individual sign into the painting that was meant to express her psychic self.[166]

607   The essential conclusion to be drawn from Picture 10 is that the dualities which run through it are always inwardly balanced, so that they lose their sharpness and incompatibility. As Multatuli says: 'Nothing is quite true, and even that is not quite true.' But this loss of strength is counterbalanced

by the unity of the centre, where the lamp shines, sending out coloured rays to the eight points of the compass.[167]

608   Although the attainment of inner balance through symmetrical pairs of opposites was probably the main intention of this mandala, we should not overlook the fact that the *duplication motif* also occurs when unconscious contents are about to become conscious and differentiated. They then split, as often happens in dreams, into two identical or slightly different halves corresponding to the conscious and still unconscious aspects of the nascent content. I have the impression, from this picture, that it really does represent a kind of solstice or climax, where decision and division take place. The dualities are, at bottom, Yes and No, the irreconcilable opposites, but they *have* to be held together if the balance of life is to be maintained. This can only be done by holding unswervingly to the centre, where action and suffering balance each other. It is a path 'sharp as the edge of a razor.' A climax like this, where universal opposites clash, is at the same time a moment when a wide perspective often opens out into the past and future. This is the psychological moment when, as the *consensus gentium* has established since ancient times, synchronistic phenomena occur – that is, when the far appears near: sixteen years later, Miss X became fatally ill with cancer of the breast.[168]

Picture 11

PICTURE 11

609 Here I will only mention that the coloured rays emanating from the centre have become so rarified that, in the next few pictures, they disappear altogether. Sun and moon are now outside, no longer included in the microcosm of the mandala. The sun is not golden, but has a dull, ochrous hue and in addition is clearly turning to the left: it is moving towards its own obscuration, as had to happen after the cancer picture (solstice). The moon is in the first quarter. The roundish masses near the sun are probably meant to be cumulous clouds, but with their grey-red hues they look suspiciously like bulbous swellings. The interior of the mandala now contains a quincunx of stars, the central star being silver and gold. The division of the mandala into an aerial and an earthy hemisphere has transferred itself to the outside world and can no longer be seen in the interior. The silvery rim of the aerial hemisphere in the preceding picture now runs round the entire mandala and recalls the band of quicksilver that, as *Mercurius vulgaris*, 'veils the true personality.' At all events, it is probable that the influence and importance of the outside world are becoming so strong in this picture as to bring about an impairment and devaluation of the mandala. It does not break down or burst (as can easily happen under similar circumstances), but is removed from the telluric influence through the symbolical constellation of stars and heavenly bodies.

PICTURES 12–19

610 In Picture 12 the sun is in fact sinking below the horizon and the moon is coming out of the first quarter. The radiation of the mandala has ceased altogether, but the equivalents of sun and moon, and also of the earth, have been assimilated into it. A remarkable feature is its sudden inner animation by two human figures and various animals. The constellation character of the centre has vanished and given way to a kind of flower motif. What this animation means cannot be established, unfortunately, as we have no commentary.

611   In Picture 13 the source of radiation is no longer in the mandala but outside, in the shape of the full moon, from which rings of rainbow-coloured light radiate in concentric circles. The mandala is laced together by four black and golden snakes, the heads of three of them pointing to the centre, while the fourth rears upwards. In between the snakes and the centre there are indications of the spermatozoon motif. This may mean an intensive penetration on the part of the outside world, but it could also mean magical protection. The breaking down of the quaternity into 3 plus 1 is in accord with the archetype.[169]

612   In Picture 14 the mandala is suspended over the lit-up ravine of Fifth Avenue, New York, whither Miss X in the meantime returned. On the blue

Picture 12

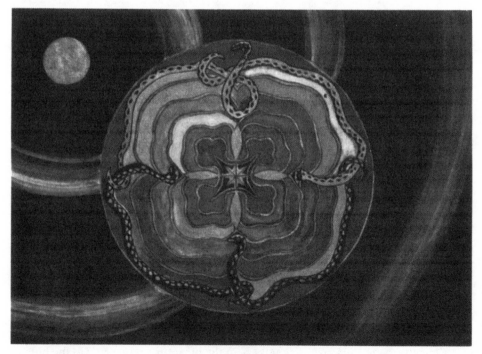

Picture 13

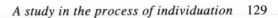

Picture 14

Picture 15

flower in the centre the *coniunctio* of the 'royal' pair is represented by the sacrificial fire burning between them. The King and Queen are assisted by two kneeling figures of a man and a woman. It is a typical marriage quaternio, and for an understanding of its psychology I must refer the reader to my account in the 'Psychology of Transference.'[170] This inner bond should be thought of as a compensatory 'consolidation' against disintegrating influences from without.

613   In Picture 15 the mandala floats between Manhattan and the sea. It is daylight again, and the sun is just rising. Out of the blue centre blue snakes penetrate into the red flesh of the mandala: the enantiodromia is setting in, after the introversion of feeling caused by the shock of New York had passed its climax. The blue colour of the snakes indicates that they have acquired a pneumatic nature.

Picture 16

614   From Picture 16 onwards, the drawing and painting technique shows a decided improvement. The mandalas gain in aesthetic value. In Picture 17 a kind of *eye motif* appears, which I have also observed in the mandalas of other persons. It seems to me to link up with the motif of *polyophthalmia* and to point to the peculiar nature of the unconscious, which can be regarded as a 'multiple consciousness.' I have discussed this question in detail elsewhere.[171][. . .]

Picture 17

Picture 18

Picture 19

615   The enantiodromia only reached its climax the following year, in Picture 19.[172] In that picture the red substance is arranged round the golden, four-rayed star in the centre, and the blue substance is pushing everywhere to the periphery. Here the rainbow-coloured radiation of the mandala begins again for the first time, and from then on was maintained for over ten years (in mandalas not reproduced here).

616   I will not comment on the subsequent pictures, nor reproduce them all – as I say, they extend over more than ten years – because I feel I do not understand them properly. In addition, they came into my hands only recently, after the death of the patient, and unfortunately without text or commentary. Under these circumstances the work of interpretation becomes very uncertain, and is better left unattempted. Also, this case was meant only as an example of how such pictures come to be produced, what they mean, and what reflections and observations their interpretation requires. It is not intended to demonstrate how an entire lifetime expresses itself in symbolic form. The individuation process has many stages and is subject to many vicissitudes, as the fictive course of the *opus alchymicum* amply shows.

CONCLUSION

617   Our series of pictures illustrates the initial stages of the way of individuation. It would be desirable to know what happens afterwards. But,
just as neither the philosophical gold nor the philosophers' stone was ever
made in reality, so nobody has ever been able to tell the story of the whole
way, at least not to mortal ears, for it is not the story-teller but death who
speaks the final 'consummatum est.' Certainly there are many things worth
knowing in the later stages of the process, but, from the point of view of
teaching as well as of therapy, it is important not to skip too quickly over
the initial stages. As these pictures are intuitive anticipations of future
developments, it is worth while lingering over them for a long time, in
order, with their help, to integrate so many contents of the unconscious
into consciousness that the latter really does reach the stage it sees ahead.
These psychic evolutions do not as a rule keep pace with the tempo of
intellectual developments. Indeed, their very first goal is to bring a
consciousness that has hurried too far ahead into contact again with the
unconscious background with which it should be connected. This was the
problem in our case too. Miss X had to turn back to her 'motherland' in
order to find her earth again – *vestigia retro*! It is a task that today faces
not only individuals but whole civilizations. What else is the meaning of
the frightful regressions of our time? The tempo of the development of
consciousness through science and technology was too rapid and left the
unconscious, which could no longer keep up with it, far behind, thereby
forcing it into a defensive position which expresses itself in a universal
will to destruction. The political and social isms of our day preach every
conceivable ideal, but, under this mask, they pursue the goal of lowering
the level of our culture by restricting or altogether inhibiting the possibilities of individual development. They do this partly by creating a
chaos controlled by terrorism, a primitive state of affairs that affords only
the barest necessities of life and surpasses in horror the worst times of the
so-called 'Dark' Ages. It remains to be seen whether this experience of
degradation and slavery will once more raise a cry for greater spiritual
freedom.

618   This problem cannot be solved collectively, because the masses are not
changed unless the individual changes. At the same time, even the best-
looking solution cannot be forced upon him, since it is a good solution
only when it is combined with a natural process of development. It is
therefore a hopeless undertaking to stake everything on collective recipes
and procedures. The bettering of a general ill begins with the individual,
and then only when he makes himself and not others responsible. This is
naturally only possible in freedom, but not under a rule of force, whether
this be exercised by a self-elected tyrant or by one thrown up by the mob.

619   The initial pictures in our series illustrate the characteristic psychic
processes which set in the moment one gives a mind to that part of the

personality which has remained behind, forgotten. Scarcely has the connection been established when symbols of the self appear, trying to convey a picture of the total personality. As a result of this development, the unsuspecting modern gets into paths trodden from time immemorial – the *via sancta*, whose milestones and signposts are the religions.[173] He will think and feel things that seem strange to him, not to say unpleasant. Apuleius relates that in the Isis mysteries he 'approached the very gates of death and set one foot on Proserpina's threshold, yet was permitted to return, rapt through all the elements. At midnight I saw the sun shining as if it were noon; I entered the presence of the gods of the underworld and the gods of the upper world, stood near and worshipped them.'[174] Such experiences are also expressed in our mandalas: that is why we find in religious literature the best parallels to the symbols and moods of the situations they formulate. These situations are intense inner experiences which can lead to lasting psychic growth and a ripening and deepening of the personality, if the individual affected by them has the moral capacity for πίστις, loyal trust and confidence. They are the age-old psychic experiences that underlie 'faith' and ought to be its unshakable foundation – and not of faith alone, but also of knowledge.

620   Our case shows with singular clarity the spontaneity of the psychic process and the transformation of a personal situation into the problem of individuation, that is, of becoming whole, which is the answer to the great question of our day: How can consciousness, our most recent acquisition, which has bounded ahead, be linked up again with the oldest, the unconscious, which has lagged behind? The oldest of all is the instinctual foundation. Anyone who overlooks the instincts will be ambuscaded by them, and anyone who does not humble himself will be humbled, losing at the same time his freedom, his most precious possession.

621   Always when science tries to describe a 'simple' life-process, the matter becomes complicated and difficult. So it is no wonder that the details of a transformation process rendered visible through active imagination make no small demands on our understanding. In this respect they may be compared with all other biological processes. These, too, require specialized knowledge to become comprehensible. Our example also shows, however, that this process can begin and run its course without any special knowledge having to stand sponsor to it. But if one wants to understand anything of it and assimilate it into consciousness, then a certain amount of knowledge is needed. If the process is not understood at all, it has to build up an unusual intensity so as not to sink back again into the unconscious without result. But if its affects rise to an unusual pitch, they will enforce some kind of understanding. It depends on the correctness of this understanding whether the consequences turn out more pathologically or less. Psychic experiences, according to whether they are rightly or wrongly understood, have very different effects on a person's development. It is one of the duties of the psychotherapist to acquire such

knowledge of these things as will enable him to help his patient to an adequate understanding. Experiences of this kind are not without their dangers, for they are also, among other things, the matrix of the psychoses. Stiffnecked and violent interpretations should under all circumstances be avoided, likewise a patient should never be forced into a development that does not come naturally and spontaneously. But once it has set in, he should not be talked out of it again, unless the possibility of a psychosis has been definitely established. Thorough psychiatric experience is needed to decide this question, and it must constantly be borne in mind that the constellation of archetypal images and fantasies is not in itself patho-logical. The pathological element only reveals itself in the way the individual reacts to them and how he interprets them. The characteristic feature of a pathological reaction is, above all, *identification with the archetype*. This produces a sort of inflation and possession by the emergent contents, so that they pour out in a torrent which no therapy can stop. Identification can, in favourable cases, sometimes pass off as a more or less harmless inflation. But in all cases identification with the unconscious brings a weakening of consciousness, and herein lies the danger. You do not 'make' an identification, you do not 'identify yourself,' but you experience your identity with the archetype in an unconscious way and so are possessed by it. Hence in more difficult cases it is far more necessary to strengthen and consolidate the ego than to understand and assimilate the products of the unconscious. The decision must be left to the diagnostic and therapeutic tact of the analyst.

622   This paper is a groping attempt to make the inner processes of the mandala more intelligible. They are, as it were, self-delineations of dimly sensed changes going on in the background, which are perceived by the 'reversed eye' and rendered visible with pencil and brush, just as they are, un-comprehended and unknown. The pictures represent a kind of ideogram of unconscious contents. I have naturally used this method on myself too and can affirm that one can paint very complicated pictures without having the least idea of their real meaning. While painting them, the picture seems to develop out of itself and often in opposition to one's conscious intentions. It is interesting to observe how the execution of the picture frequently thwarts one's expectations in the most surprising way. The same thing can be observed, sometimes even more clearly, when writing down the products of active imagination.[175]

623   The present work may also serve to fill a gap I myself have felt in my exposition of therapeutic methods. I have written very little on active imagination, but have talked about it a great deal. I have used this method since 1916, and I sketched it out for the first time in 'The Relations between the Ego and the Unconscious'. I first mentioned the mandala in 1929, in *The Secret of the Golden Flower*.[176] For at least thirteen years I kept quiet about the results of these methods in order to avoid any

suggestion. I wanted to assure myself that these things – mandalas especially – really are produced spontaneously and were not suggested to the patient by my own fantasy. I was then able to convince myself, through my own studies, that mandalas were drawn, painted, carved in stone, and built, at all times and in all parts of the world, long before my patients discovered them. I have also seen to my satisfaction that mandalas are dreamt and drawn by patients who were being treated by psychotherapists whom I had not trained. In view of the importance and significance of the mandala symbol, special precautions seemed to be necessary, seeing that this motif is one of the best examples of the universal operation of an archetype. In a seminar on children's dreams, which I held in 1939–40,[177] I mentioned the dream of a ten-year-old girl who had absolutely no possibility of ever hearing about the quaternity of God. The dream was written down by the child herself and was sent to me by an acquaintance: '*Once in a dream I saw an animal that had lots of horns. It spiked up other little animals with them. It wriggled like a snake and that was how it lived. Then a blue fog came out of all the four corners, and it stopped eating. Then God came, but there were really four Gods in the four corners. Then the animal died, and all the animals it had eaten came out alive again.*'

624   This dream describes an unconscious individuation process: all the animals are eaten by the one animal. Then comes the enantiodromia: the dragon changes into pneuma, which stands for a divine quaternity. Thereupon follows the apocatastasis, a resurrection of the dead. This exceedingly 'unchildish' fantasy can hardly be termed anything but archetypal. Miss X, in Picture 12, also put a whole collection of animals into her mandala – two snakes, two tortoises, two fishes, two lions, two pigs, a goat and a ram.[178] Integration gathers many into one. To the child who had this dream, and to Miss X likewise, it was certainly not known that Origen had already said (speaking of the sacrificial animals): 'Seek these sacrifices within thyself, and thou wilt find them within thine own soul. Understand that thou has within thyself flocks of cattle . . . flocks of sheep and flocks of goats. . . . Understand that the birds of the sky are also within thee. Marvel not if we say that these are within thee, but understand that thou thyself art even another little world, and hast within thee the sun and the moon, and also the stars.'[179]

625   The same idea occurs again in another passage, but this time it takes the form of a psychological statement: 'For look upon the countenance of a man who is at one moment angry, at the next sad, a short while afterward joyful, then troubled again, and then contented. . . . See how he who thinks himself one is not one, but seems to have as many personalities as he has moods, as also the Scripture says: A fool is changed as the moon. . . .[180] God, therefore, is unchangeable, and is called one for the reason that he changes not. Thus also the true imitator of God, who is made after God's image, is called one and the selfsame (*unus et ipse*) when he comes to perfection, for he also, when he is fixed on the summit of virtue, is not

changed, but remains always one. For every man, while he is in wickedness (*malitia*), is divided among many things and torn in many directions; and while he is in many kinds of evil he cannot be called one.'[181]

626   Here the many animals are affective states to which man is prone. The individuation process, clearly alluded to in this passage, subordinates the many to the One. But the One is God, and that which corresponds to him in us is the *imago Dei*, the God-image. But the God-image [. . .] expresses itself in the mandala.

NOTES

1 [Translated from 'Zur Empirie des Individuationsprozesses,' *Gestaltungen des Unbewussten* (Zurich, 1950), where it carries the author's note that it is a 'thoroughly revised and enlarged version of the lecture of the same title first published in the *Eranos-Jahrbuch 1933*,' i.e., in 1934. The original version was translated by Stanley Dell and published in *The Integration of the Personality* (New York, 1939; London, 1940). The motto by Lao-tzu is from a translation by Carol Baumann in her article 'Time and Tao,' *Spring*, 1951, p. 30.–EDITORS.]

2 Cf. *Psychology and Alchemy*, pars. 138f., 306, in CW12; and Wei Po-yang, 'An Ancient Chinese Treatise on Alchemy.'

3 *Psychology and Alchemy*, par. 109, n. 38 in CW12.

4 Caesarius of Heisterbach, *The Dialogue on Miracles*, trans. by Scott and Bland, Dist. IV. c. xxxiv (p. 231) and Dist. I, c. xxxii (p. 42): 'His soul was like a glassy spherical vessel, that had eyes before and behind.' A collection of similar reports in Bozzano, *Popoli primitivi e Manifestazioni supernormali*.

5 Cf. my 'Paracelsus as a Spiritual Phenomenon,' par. 190 in CW13. It is Hermes Kyllenios, who calls up the souls. The caduceus corresponds to the phallus. Cf. Hippolytus, *Elenchos*, V, 7, 30.

6 The same association in *Elenchos*, V, 16, 8: serpent = δύναμις of Moses.

7 Ruland (*Lexicon*, 1612) speaks of 'the gliding of the mind or spirit into another world.' In the *Chymical Wedding* of Rosencreutz the lightning causes the royal pair to come alive. The Messiah appears as lightning in the Syrian Apocalypse of Baruch (Charles, *Apocrypha*, II, p. 510). Hippolytus (*Elenchos*, VIII, 10, 3) says that, in the view of the Docetists, the Monogenes drew together 'like the greatest lightning-flash into the smallest body' (because the Aeons could not stand the effulgence of the Pleroma), or like 'light under the eyelids.' In this form he came into the world through Mary (VIII, 10, 5). Lactantius (*Works*, trans. by Fletcher, I, p. 470) says: '. . . the light of the descending God may be manifest in all the world as lightning.' This refers to Luke 17: 24: '. . . as the lightning that lighteneth . . . so shall the Son of man be in his day.' Similarly Zach. 9: 14: 'And the Lord God . . . his dart shall go forth as lightning' (DV). [. . .]

45 Rieu trans., p. 351.

46 Hippolytus, *Elenchos*, V, 7, 30; Kerényi, 'Hermes der Seelenführer,' p. 29.

47 Ibid., p. 30.

48 The pairs of functions are thinking/feeling, sensation/intuition. See *Psychological Types*, definitions in CW6.

49 Cf. *Psychology and Alchemy*, par. 329, in CW12 for the *a priori* presence of the mandala symbol.

50 Details in ibid., par. 406.

51 Preisendanz, *Papyri Graecae Magicae*, II, p. 139.

52 'The Spirit Mercurius,' pars. 267ff. in CW13.
53 *Psychology and Alchemy*, Part III, ch. 5 (CW12).
54 Cf. Wilhelm and Jung, *The Secret of the Golden Flower*.
55 Though we talk a great deal and with some justice about the resistance which the unconscious puts up against becoming conscious, it must also be emphasized that it has a kind of gradient towards consciousness, and this acts as an urge to become conscious.
56 The last-named refers to Rev. 21: 21.
57 Miss X was referring to my remarks in 'The Relations between the Ego and the Unconscious,' (in CW7) which she knew in its earlier version in *Collected Papers on Analytical Psychology* (2nd. edn., 1920).
58 The expressions 'square,' 'four-square,' are used in English in this sense.
59 The 'squared figure' in the centre of the alchemical mandala, symbolizing the *lapis*, and whose midpoint is Mercurius, is called the 'mediator making peace between the enemies or elements.' [Cf. *Aion* (CW9.II), pars. 377f. – EDITORS.]
60 So called in an invocation to Hermes. Cf. Preisendanz, II, p. 139. Further particulars in *Psychology and Alchemy*, par. 172; fig. 214 is a repetition of the *quadrangulum secretum sapientum* from the *Tractatus aureus* (1610), p. 43. Cf. also my 'The Spirit Mercurius,' par. 272 in CW13.
[. . .]
70 Cf. the 'account . . . of a many-coloured and many-shaped sphere' from the Cod. Vat. 190 (cited by Cumont in *Textes et monuments figurés relatifs aux mystères de Mithra*), which says: 'The all-wise God fashioned an immensely great dragon of gigantic length, breadth and thickness, having its dark-coloured head . . . towards sunrise, and its tail . . . towards sunset.' Of the dragon the text says: 'Then the all-wise Demiurge, by his highest command, set in motion the great dragon with the spangled crown, I mean the twelve signs of the zodiac which it carried on its back.' Eisler (*Weltenmantel und Himmelszelt*, p. 389) connects this zodiacal serpent with Leviathan. For the dragon as symbol of the year, see the Mythographus Vaticanus III, in *Classicorum Auctorum e Vaticanis Codicibus Editorum*, VI (1831), p. 162. There is a similar association in Horapollo, *Hieroglyphica*, trans. by Boas, p. 57.
71 'The Spirit Mercurius,' ch. 6 (CW13).
72 Meier, *Antike Inkubation und moderne Psychotherapie*.
73 Vishnu is described as *dāmodara*, 'bound about the body with a rope.' I am not sure whether this symbol should be considered here; I mention it only for the sake of completeness.
74 Michael Maier, *De circulo physico quadrato* (1616), ch. I.
75 Christ in medieval alchemy. Cf. *Psychology and Alchemy*, Part III, ch. 5 (CW12).
76 The writings of the physician and philosopher Leone Ebreo (*c.* 1460–1520) enjoyed a widespread popularity in the sixteenth century and exercised a far-reaching influence on his contemporaries and their successors. His work is a continuation of the Neoplatonist thought developed by the physician and alchemist Marsilio Ficino (1433–99) in his commentary on Plato's *Symposium*. Ebreo's real name was Don Judah Abrabanel, of Lisbon. (Sometimes the texts have Abrabanel, sometimes Abarbanel.)
77 Cf. the English version, *The Philosophy of Love* by Leone Ebreo, trans. by Friedeberg-Seeley and Barnes, pp. 92 and 94. The source of this view can be found in the cabalistic interpretation of Yesod (Knorr von Rosenroth, *Kabbala Denudata*, 1677–84).
78 This pseudo-biological terminology fits in with the patient's scientific education.
79 Another alchemical idea: the *synodos Lunae cum Sole*, or hierogamy of sun and moon. Cf. 'The Psychology of the Transference,' par. 421, n. 17 (CW16).
80 More on this in 'On the Nature of the Psyche,' par. 498 in CW8.

81 Here one must think of the world-encircling Ocean and the world-snake hidden in it: Leviathan, the 'dragon in the sea,' which, in accordance with the Egyptian tradition of Typhon (Set) and the sea he rules over, is the devil. 'The devil . . . surrounds the seas and the ocean on all sides' (St. Jerome, *Epistolae*, Part I, p. 12). Further particulars in Rahner, 'Antenna Crucis II: Das Meer der Welt,' pp. 89ff.

82 We find the same motif in the two mandalas published by Esther Harding in *Psychic Energy: Its Source and Its Transformation* [Pls. XVI, XVII].
[. . .]

87 In accordance with the classical view that the snake is πνευματικώτατον ζῷον, 'the most spiritual animal.' For this reason it was a symbol for the Nous and the Redeemer.

88 Cf. what St. John of the Cross says about the 'dark night of the soul.' His interpretation is as helpful as it is psychological.

89 Hence the alchemical mandala was likened to a *rosarium* (rose-garden).

90 In Buddhism the 'four great kings' (*lokapata*), the world-guardians, form the quaternity. Cf. the *Samyutta-Nikaya*, in *Dialogues of the Buddha*, Part II, p. 242.

91 'God separated and divided this primordial water by a kind of mystical distillation into four parts and regions' (Sendivogius, *Epist.* XIII, in Manget, *Bibliotheca chemica*, 1702, II, p. 496). In Christianos (Berthelot, *Alch. grecs*, VI, ix, 1 and x 1) the egg, and matter itself, consist of four components. (Cited from Xenocrates, ibid., VI, xv, 8.)

92 In Taoist philosophy, movement to the right means a 'falling' life-process, as the spirit is then under the influence of the feminine *p'o*-soul, which embodies the *yin* principle and is by nature passionate. Its designation as the anima (cf. my 'Commentary on *The Secret of the Golden Flower*,' pars. 57ff. in CW13) is psychologically correct, although this touches only one aspect of it. The *p'o*-soul entangles *hun*, the spirit, in the world-process and in reproduction. A leftward or backward movement, on the other hand, means the 'rising' movement of life. A 'deliverance from outward things' occurs and the spirit obtains control over the anima. This idea agrees with my findings, but it does not take account of the fact that a person can easily have the spirit outside and the anima inside.

93 This was told to me by the Rimpoche of Bhutia Busty, Sikkim.

94 Water also symbolizes the 'materiality' of the spirit when it has become a 'fixed' doctrine. One is reminded, too, of the blue-green colour in Böhme, signifying 'Liberty.'

95 For the double nature of the spirit (*Mercurius duplex* of the alchemists) see 'The Phenomenology of the Spirit in Fairytales,' in CW 9.I.

96 Cf. the fiery serpent of Lucifer in Böhme.

97 Cf. 'A Psychological Approach to the Dogma of the Trinity,' pars. 243ff. in CW11
[. . .]

111 This interpretation was confirmed for me by my Tibetan mentor, Lingdam Gomchen, abbot of Bhutia Busty: the swastika, he said, is that which 'cannot be broken, divided, or spoilt.' Accordingly, it would amount to an inner consolidation of the mandala.

112 Cf. the similar motif in the mandala of the *Amitāyur-dhyāna Sūtra*, in 'The Psychology of Eastern Meditation,' pars. 917, 930.
[. . .]

114 [Cf. 'Answer to Job,' *Psychology and Religion*, par. 595, n. 8 in CW11 – EDITORS.]

115 The seven kings refer to previous aeons, 'perished' worlds, and the four Achurayim are the so-called 'back of God': 'All belong to Malkhuth; which is so called because it is last in the system of Aziluth . . . they exist in the depths of the Shekinah' (*Kabbala Denudata*, I, p. 72). They form a masculine-feminine quaternio 'of the Father and Mother of the highest, and of the Senex Israel and

Tebhunah' (I, p. 675). The Senex is Ain-Soph or Kether (I, p. 635), Tebhunah is Binah, intelligence (I, p. 726). The shards also mean unclean spirits.

116 *Kabbala Denudata*, I, pp. 675f. The shards also stand for evil. (*Zohar*, I, 137aff., II, 34b.). According to a Christian interpretation from the 17th century, Adam Belial is the body of the Messiah, the 'entire body or the host of shards.' (Cf. II Cor. 6:15.) In consequence of the Fall, the host of shards irrupted into Adam's body, its outer layers being more infected than the inner ones. The 'Anima Christi' fought and finally destroyed the shards, which signify matter. In connection with Adam Belial the text refers to Proverbs 6:12: 'A naughty person, a wicked man, walketh with a froward mouth' (AV). (*Kabbala Denudata*, II, Appendix, cap. IX, sec. 2, p. 56).

117 'Hyperion's Song of Fate,' in *Gedichte*, p. 315. (Trans. as in Jung, *Symbols of Transformation*, p. 399)
    [. . .]

124 The *cauda pavonis* is identified by Khunrath with Iris, the 'nuncia Dei.' Dorn ('De transmutatione metallorum,' *Theatr. Chem.*, I, p. 599) explains it as follows: 'This is the bird which flies by night without wings, which the early dew of heaven, continually acting by upward and downward ascent and descent, turns into the head of a crow (*caput corvi*), then into the tail of a peacock, and afterwards it acquires the bright wings of a swan, and lastly an extreme redness, an index of its fiery nature.' In Basilides (Hippolytus, *Elenchos*, X, 14, 1) the peacock's egg is synonymous with the *sperma mundi*, the κόκκος σινάπεως. It contains the 'fullness of colours,' 365 of them. The golden colour should be produced from the peacock's eggs, we are told in the Cyranides (Delatte, *Textes latins et vieux français relatifs aux Cyanides*, p. 171). The light of Mohammed has the form of a peacock, and the angels were made out of the peacock's sweat (Aptowitzer, 'Arabisch-Jüdische Schöpfungstheorien,' pp. 209, 233).

125 Sig. rer., XIV, 10ff., pp. 112f. [Jakob Böhme (1575–1624) was a German philosopher and protestant mystic. His books describe evil as a necessary opposite to good. See the original version by Jung in *CW* 9.1 for further symbolic amplification that links the images and ideas in this study to the works of Böhme. – J.C.]
    [. . .]

134 The colour correlated with sensation in the mandalas of other persons is usually green.

135 Cf. the Achurayim quaternity.

136 Chochmah (= face of the man), Binah (= eagle), Gedulah (= lion), Gebhurah (= bull), the four symbolical angels in Ezekiel's vision.

137 He gives them the names of planets and describes them as the 'four Bailiffs, who hold government in the Mother, the Birth-giver.' They are Jupiter, Saturn, Mars, and Sun. 'In these four Forms the Spirit's Birth consists, viz. the true Spirit both in the inward and outward Being' (*Sig. rer.*, IX, 9ff., p. 61).

138 The connection between tree and mother, especially in Christian tradition, is discussed at length in *Symbols of Transformation*, Part II in CW 5.
    [. . .]

140 *Forty Questions*, pp. 24ff (Böhme).

141 I do not feel qualified to go into the ethics of what 'venerable Mother Nature' has to do in order to unfold her precious flower. Some people can, and those whose temperament makes them feel an ethical compulsion must do this in order to satisfy a need that is also felt by others. Erich Neumann has discussed these problems in a very interesting way in his *Tiefenpsychologie und Neue Ethik*. It will be objected that my respect for Nature is a very unethical attitude, and I shall be accused of shirking 'decisions.' People who think like this evidently know all about good and evil, and why and for what one has to decide. Unfortunately I do

not know all this so precisely, but I hope for my patients and for myself that everything, light and darkness, decision and agonizing doubt, may turn to 'good' – and by 'good' I mean a development such as is here described, an unfolding, which does no damage to either of them but conserves the possibilities of life.

142 *The Secret of the Golden Flower* (1962 edition) had not been published then. Picture 9 was reproduced in it. (Also see in CW13).

143 Cf. *Kabbala Denudata*, Appendix, ch. IV, sec. 2, p. 26: 'The beings created by the infinite Deity through the First Adam were all spiritual beings, viz. they were simple, shining acts, being one in themselves, partaking of a being that may be thought of as the midpoint of a sphere, and partaking of a life that may be imagined as a sphere emitting rays.'

144 'Parable of the Cloth,' in *The First Fifty Discourses from the Collection of the Middle-Length Discourses (Majjhima Nikaya) of Gotama the Buddha*, I, pp. 39f., modified. This reference to the Buddha is not accidental, since the figure of the Tathagata in the lotus seat occurs many times in the patient's mandalas.

145 Tibetan mandalas are not so divided, but very often they are embedded between heaven and hell, i.e., between the benevolent and the wrathful deities.

146 This is the lower triad that corresponds to the Trinity, just as the devil is occasionally depicted with three heads. Cf. 'Phenomenology of the Spirit in Fairytales', pars. 425 and 436ff. in CW 9.I.

147 Trans. by Wilhelm and Baynes (1967), pp. 67ff.

148 *Psychology and Alchemy*, par. 338 (CW12).

149 The same idea as the transformation into the *lapis*. Cf. ibid., par. 378.

150 Good examples are *The Secret of the Golden Flower* and Suzuki, *Introduction to Zen Buddhism*.
    [. . .]

152 I am purposely disregarding the numerous arrangements in a circle such as the *rex gloriae* with the four evangelists, Paradise with its four rivers, the heavenly hierarchies of Dionysius the Areopagite, etc. These all ignore the reality of evil, because they regard it as a mere *privatio boni* and thereby dismiss it with a euphemism. [For Böhme's Mandala see CW 9.I, fig. 1, p. 297]

153 Cf. Rahner, 'Die seelenheilende Blume.'

154 Cf. Bouché-Leclercq, *L'Astrologie grecque*, p. 136: Cancer = 'crabe ou écrevisse.' The constellation was usually represented as a tailless crab.

155 'The crab is wont to change with the changing seasons; casting off its old shell, it puts on a new and fresh one.' This, says Picinelli, is an 'emblema' of the resurrection of the dead, and cites Ephesians 4: 23: '. . . be renewed in the spirit of your minds' (RSV). (*Mondo simbolico*, Lib. VI, No. 45.)

156 Foreseeing the flooding of the Nile, the crabs (like the tortoises and crocodiles) bring their eggs in safety to a higher place. 'They foresee the future in their mind long before it comes.' Caussin, *Polyhistor symbolicus* (1618), p. 442.

157 Masenius, *Speculum imaginum veritatis occultae* (1714), cap. LXVII, 30, p. 768.

158 De Gubernatis, *Zoological Mythology*, II, p. 355.

159 Roscher, *Lexikon*, II, col. 959, s.v. 'Karkinos.' The same motif occurs in a dream described in *Two Essays on Analytical Psychology*, pars. 80ff. (CW7).

160 In Egypt, the heliacal rising of Cancer indicates the beginning of the annual flooding of the Nile and hence the beginning of the year. Bouché-Leclercq, p. 137.

161 [Cf. 'Psychology and Religion,' p. 67, n. 5. – EDITORS.] CW11.

162 *Propertius*, trans. by Butler, p. 275.

163 De Gubernatis, II, p. 356.

164 *The Panchatantra Reconstructed*, ed. by Edgerton, II, pp. 403f. Cf. also Hoffmann-Krayer et al., *Handwörterbuch des Deutschen Aberglaubens*, V, col. 448, s.v. 'Krebs.'

165 De Gubernatis, II, p. 356.

166 Her horoscope shows four earth signs but no air sign. The danger coming from the animus is reflected in ☽ ☐ ☿.

167 Cf. the Buddhist conception of the 'eight points of the compass' in the *Amitāyur-dhyāna Sūtra*; cf. 'The Psychology of Eastern Meditation,' pp. 560ff. in CW11.

168 I do not hesitate to take the synchronistic phenomena that underlie astrology seriously. Just as there is an eminently psychological reason for the existence of alchemy, so too in the case of astrology. Nowadays it is no longer interesting to know how far these two fields are aberrations; we should rather investigate the psychological foundations on which they rest. [Cf. Jung, 'Synchronicity: An Acausal Connecting Principle,' *passim* in CW8 – EDITORS.]

169 An instance of the axiom of Maria. Other well-known examples are Horus and his 4 (or 3 + 1) sons, the 4 symbolical figures in Ezekiel, the 4 evangelists and – last but not least – the 3 synoptic gospels and the 1 gospel of St. John.

170 [Ch. 2, pp. 211ff. in CW16 – EDITORS.]

171 'On the Nature of the Psyche,' sec. 6 in CW8.

172 Pictures 18–19 were painted by the patient after the termination of analytical work. The dates of the entire series of pictures were as follows: 1–6, Oct. 1928; 7–9, Nov. 1928; 10, Jan.; 11, Feb.; 12, June; 13, Aug.; 14, Sept.; 15, Oct.; 16, 17, Nov., all 1929; 18, Feb. 1930; 19, Aug. 1930.

173 Isaiah 45: 8, 'And a highway shall be there, and it shall be called the Holy Way' (RSV).

174 *The Golden Ass*, by Apuleius, trans. by Graves, p. 286.

175 Case material in Meier, 'Spontanmanifestationen des kollektiven Unbewussten,' 284ff.; Bänziger, 'Persönliches und Archetypisches im Individuations prozess,' p. 272; Gerhard Adler, *Studies in Analytical Psychology*, pp. 90ff.

176 Active imagination is also mentioned in 'The Aims of Psychotherapy,' pars. 101ff. Cf. also 'The Transcendent Function' (see above).

177 [*Psychologische Interpretation von Kinderträumen*, winter semester, 1939–40, Federal Polytechnic Institute, Zurich (mimeographed stenographic record). The same dream is discussed by Dr Jacobi in *Complex/Archetype/Symbol*, pp. 139ff – EDITORS.]

178 One thinks here of a Noah's Ark that crosses over the waters of death and leads to a rebirth of all life.

179 *In Leviticum Homiliae*, V, 2 (Migne, *P.G.*, vol. 12, col. 449).

180 Ecclesiasticus 27: 11.

181 *In libros Regnorum homilae*, I, 4 (Migne, *P.G.*, vol. 12, cols. 998–99).

7   The Tavistock lectures

Excerpts from: *The Symbolic Life* (1935) (*CW* 18), par. 4 and pars. 390–415

[. . .]

4 Now as to our procedure, I should like to give you first a short idea of my programme. We have two main topics to deal with, namely, on the one side the concepts concerning the *structure of the unconscious mind* and its *contents*; on the other, the *methods* used in the *investigation* of contents originating in the unconscious psychic processes. The second topic falls into three parts, first, the word-association method; second, the method of dream-analysis; and third, the method of active imagination.

[. . .]

Dr J.A.Hadfield:

390 Would Professor Jung give us a short account of the technique of active imagination?

Professor Jung:

391 That was the subject I really wanted to tell you about today in consequence of the analysis of the Toledo dream, so I am very glad to take it up. You will realize that I shall not be able to present any empirical material, but I may succeed in giving you an idea of the method. I believe that the best way is to tell you of a case where it was very difficult to teach the patient the method.

392 I was treating a young artist, and he had the greatest trouble in understanding what I meant by active imagination. He tried all sorts of things but he could not get at it. The difficulty with him was that he could not think. Musicians, painters, artists of all kinds, often can't think at all, because they never intentionally use their brain. This man's brain too was always working for itself; it had its artistic imaginations and he couldn't use it psychologically, so he couldn't understand. I gave him every chance to try, and he tried all sorts of stunts. I cannot tell you all the things he did, but I will tell you how he finally succeeded in using his imagination psychologically.

393 I live outside the town, and he had to take the train to get to my place. It starts from a small station, and on the wall of that station was a poster. Each time he waited for his train he looked at that poster. The poster was

an advertisement for Mürren in the Bernese Alps, a colourful picture of the waterfalls, of a green meadow and a hill in the centre, and on that hill were several cows. So he sat there staring at that poster and thinking that he could not find out what I meant by active imagination. And then one day he thought: 'Perhaps I could start by having a fantasy about that poster. I might for instance imagine that I am myself in the poster, that the scenery is real and that I could walk up the hill among the cows and then look down on the other side, and then I might see what there is behind that hill.'

394   So he went to the station for that purpose and imagined that he was in the poster. He saw the meadow and the road and walked up the hill among the cows, and then he came up to the top and looked down, and there was the meadow again, sloping down, and below was a hedge with a stile. So he walked down and over the stile, and there was a little footpath that ran round a ravine, and a rock, and when he came round that rock, there was a small chapel, with its door standing a little ajar. He thought he would like to enter, and so he pushed the door open and went in, and there upon an altar decorated with pretty flowers stood a wooden figure of the Mother of God. He looked up at her face, and in that exact moment something with pointed ears disappeared behind the altar. He thought, 'Well, that's all nonsense,' and instantly the whole fantasy was gone.

395   He went away and said, 'Now again I haven't understood what active imagination is.' And then, suddenly, the thought struck him: 'Well, perhaps that really *was* there; perhaps that thing behind the Mother of God, with the pointed ears, that disappeared like a flash, really happened.' Therefore he said to himself: 'I will just try it all over as a test.' So he imagined that he was back in the station looking at the poster, and again he fantasied that he was walking up the hill. And when he came to the top of the hill, he wondered what he would see on the other side. And there was the hedge and the stile and the hill sloping down. He said, 'Well, so far so good. Things haven't moved since, apparently.' And he went round the rock, and there was the chapel. He said: 'There is the chapel, that at least is no illusion. It is all quite in order.' The door stood ajar and he was quite pleased. He hesitated a moment and said: 'Now, when I push that door open and I see the Madonna on the altar, then that thing with the pointed ears should jump down behind the Madonna, and if it doesn't then the whole thing is bunk!' And so he pushed the door open and looked – and there it all was and the thing jumped down, as before, and then he was convinced. From then on he had the key and knew he could rely on his imagination, and so he learned to use it.

396   There is no time to tell you about the development of his images, nor how other patients arrive at the method. For of course everybody gets at it in his own way. I can only mention that it might also be a dream or an impression of a hypnagogic nature from which active imagination can start. I really prefer the term 'imagination' to 'fantasy,' because there is a difference between the two which the old doctors had in mind when they

said that 'opus nostrum,' our work, ought to be done 'per veram imaginationem et non phantastica' – by true imagination and not by a fantastical one.[13] In other words, if you take the correct meaning of this definition, fantasy is mere nonsense, a phantasm, a fleeting impression; but imagination is active, purposeful creation. And this is exactly the distinction I make too.

397 A fantasy is more or less your own invention, and remains on the surface of personal things and conscious expectations. But active imagination, as the term denotes, means that the images have a life of their own and that the symbolic events develop according to their own logic – that is, of course, if your conscious reason does not interfere. You begin by concentrating upon a starting point. I will give you an example from my own experience. When I was a little boy, I had a spinster aunt who lived in a nice old-fashioned house. It was full of beautiful old coloured engravings. Among them was a picture of my grandfather on my mother's side. He was a sort of bishop, and he was represented as coming out of his house and standing on a little terrace. There were handrails and stairs coming down from the terrace, and a footpath leading to the cathedral. He was in full regalia, standing there at the top of the terrace. Every Sunday morning I was allowed to pay a call on my aunt, and then I knelt on a chair and looked at that picture until grandfather came down the steps. And each time my aunt would say, 'But, my dear, he doesn't walk, he is still standing there.' But I knew I had seen him walking down.

398 You see how it happened that the picture began to move. And in the same way, when you concentrate on a mental picture, it begins to stir, the image becomes enriched by details, it moves and develops. Each time, naturally, you mistrust it and have the idea that you have just made it up, that it is merely your own invention. But you have to overcome that doubt, because it is not true. We can really produce precious little by our conscious mind. All the time we are dependent upon the things that literally fall into our consciousness; therefore in German we call them *Einfälle*. For instance, if my unconscious should prefer not to give me ideas, I could not proceed with my lecture, because I could not invent the next step. You all know the experience when you want to mention a name or a word which you know quite well, and it simply does not present itself; but some time later it drops into your memory. We depend entirely upon the benevolent co-operation of our unconscious. If it does not co-operate, we are completely lost. Therefore I am convinced that we cannot do much in the way of conscious invention; we over-estimate the power of intention and the will. And so when we concentrate on an inner picture and when we are careful not to interrupt the natural flow of events, our unconscious will produce a series of images which make a complete story.

399 I have tried that method with many patients and for many years, and I possess a large collection of such 'opera.' It is most interesting to watch the process. Of course I don't use active imagination as a panacea; there

have to be definite indications that the method is suitable for the individual, and there are a number of patients with whom it would be wrong to force it upon them. But often in the later stage of analysis, the objectivation of images replaces the dreams. The images anticipate the dreams, and so the dream-material begins to peter out. The unconscious becomes deflated in so far as the conscious mind relates to it. Then you get all the material in a creative form and this has great advantages over dream-material. It quickens the process of maturation, for analysis is a process of quickened maturation. This definition is not my own invention; the old professor Stanley Hall invented the term.

400   Since by active imagination all the material is produced in a conscious state of mind, the material is far more rounded out than the dreams with their precarious language. And it contains much more than dreams do; for instance, the feeling-values are in it, and one can judge it by feeling. Quite often, the patients themselves feel that certain material contains a tendency to visibility. They say, for instance: 'That dream was so impressive, if I only could paint I would try to express its atmosphere.' Or they feel that a certain idea should be expressed not rationally but in symbols. Or they are gripped by an emotion which, if given form, would be explainable, and so on. And so they begin to draw, to paint, or to shape their images plastically, and women sometimes do weaving. I have even had one or two women who danced their unconscious figures. Of course, they can also be expressed in writing.

401   I have many complete series of such pictures. They yield an enormous amount of archetypal material. Just now I am about to work out the historical parallels of some of them. I compare them with the pictorial material produced in similar attempts in past centuries, particularly in the early Middle Ages. Certain elements of the symbolism go back to Egypt. In the East we find many interesting parallels to our unconscious material, even down to the last details. This comparative work gives us a most valuable insight into the structure of the unconscious. You have to hand the necessary parallels to the patients too, not of course in such an elaborate way as you would present it in a scientific study, but as much as each individual needs in order to understand his archetypal images. For he can see their real meaning only when they are not just a queer subjective experience with no external connections, but a typical, ever-recurring expression of the objective facts and processes of the human psyche. By objectifying his impersonal images, and understanding their inherent ideas, the patient is able to work out all the values of his archetypal material. Then he can really see it, and the unconscious becomes understandable to him. Whatever he has put into it works back on him and produces a change of attitude which I tried to define by mentioning the non-ego centre.

402   I will give you an interesting example. I had a case, a university man, a very one-sided intellectual. His unconscious had become troubled and

activated; so it projected itself into other men who appeared to be his enemies, and he felt terribly lonely, because everybody seemed to be against him. Then he began to drink in order to forget his troubles, but he got exceedingly irritable and in these moods he began to quarrel with other men, and several times he had very disagreeable encounters, and once he was thrown out of a restaurant and got beaten up. And there were more incidents of that sort. Then things became really too thick for his endurance, and he came to me to ask my advice about what he should do. In that interview, I got a very definite impression of him: I saw that he was chock-full of archaic material, and I said to myself: 'Now I am going to make an interesting experiment to get that material absolutely pure, without any influence from myself, and therefore I won't touch it.' So I sent him to a woman doctor who was then just a beginner and who did not know much about archetypal material. Thus I was absolutely sure that she would not tamper with it. The patient was in such low spirits that he did not object to my proposition. So he worked with her and did everything she said.[14]

403   She told him to watch his dreams, and he wrote them all down carefully, from the first to the last. I now have a series of about thirteen hundred dreams of his. They contain the most marvellous series of archetypal images. And quite naturally, without being told to do so, he began to draw a number of pictures which he saw in his dreams, because he felt them to be very important. And in this work on his dreams and on these pictures he did exactly the kind of work which other patients do by active imagination. He even invented active imagination for himself in order to work out certain most intricate problems which his dreams presented him with, as for instance how to balance the contents of a circle, and more things like this. He worked out the problem of the *perpetuum mobile*, not in a crazy way but in a symbolic way. He worked on all the problems which medieval philosophy was so keen on and of which our rational mind says, 'That is all nonsense.' Such a statement only shows that we do not understand. They did understand; we are the fools, not they.

404   In the course of this analysis, which took him through about the first four hundred dreams, he was not under my surveillance. After the first interview I did not see him at all for eight months. He was five months with that doctor, and then for three months he was doing the work all by himself, continuing the observation of his unconscious with minute accuracy. He was very gifted in this respect. In the end, for about two months he had a number of interviews with me. But I did not have to explain much of the symbolism to him.

405   The effect of this work with his unconscious was that he became a perfectly normal and reasonable person. He did not drink any more, he became completely adapted and in every respect completely normal. The reason for this is quite obvious: that man – he was not married – had lived in a very one-sided intellectual way, and naturally had certain desires and

needs also. But he had no chance with women at all, because he had no differentiation of feeling whatsoever. So he made a fool of himself with women at once, and of course they had no patience with him. And he made himself very disagreeable to men, so he was frightfully lonely. But now he had found something that fascinated him; he had a new centre of interest. He soon discovered that his dreams pointed to something very meaningful, and so his whole intuitive and scientific interest was aroused. Instead of feeling like a lost sheep, he thought: 'Ah, when I am through with my work in the evening, I go to my study, and then I shall see what happens. I will work over my dreams, and then I shall discover extraordinary things.' And so it was. Of course rational judgment would say that he just fell violently into his fantasies. But that was not the case at all. He did a real bit of hard work on his unconscious, and he worked out his images scientifically. When he came to me after his three months alone, he was already almost normal. Only he still felt uncertain; he was troubled because he could not understand some of the material he had dug up from the unconscious. He asked my advice about it, and I most carefully gave him certain hints as to its meaning, but only so far as this could help him to keep on with the work and carry it through.

406   At the end of the year I am going to publish a selection from his first four hundred dreams, where I show the development of one motif only, the central motif of these archetypal images.[15] There will be an English translation later, and then you will have the opportunity to see how the method works in a case absolutely untouched by myself, or by any other outside suggestion. It is a most amazing series of images and really shows what active imagination can do. You understand, in this case it was only partially a method for objectifying the images in plastic form, because many of the symbols appeared directly in the dreams; but all the same it shows the kind of atmosphere which active imagination can produce. I have patients who, evening after evening, work at these images, painting and shaping their observations and experiences. The work has a fascination for them; it is the fascination which the archetypes always exert upon consciousness. But by objectifying them, the danger of their inundating consciousness is averted and their positive effect is made accessible. It is almost impossible to define this effect in rational terms; it is a sort of 'magical' effect, that is, a suggestive influence which goes out from the images to the individual, and in this way his unconscious is extended and is changed.

407   I am told that Dr Bennet has brought some pictures by a patient. Will he be so kind as to show them?

This picture [Figure 7.1] is meant to represent a bowl or vase. Of course it is very clumsily expressed and is a mere attempt, a suggestion of a vase or bowl. The motif of the vessel is itself an archetypal image which has a certain purpose, and I can prove from this picture what the purpose is. A

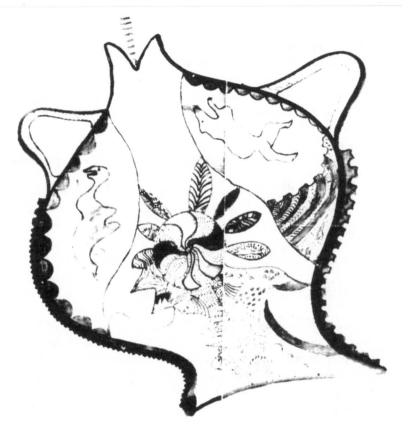

Figure 7.1 Painting by a patient

vessel is an instrument for containing things. It contains for instance liquids, and prevents them from getting dispersed. Our German word for vessel is *Gefäss*, which is the noun of *fassen*, that is, to set, to contain, to take hold of. The word *Fassung* means the setting, and also, metaphorically, composure, to remain collected. So the vessel in this picture indicates the movement of containing in order to gather in and to hold together. You have to hold something together which otherwise would fall asunder. From the way this picture is composed, and from certain features in it, it is obvious that the psychology of this man contains a number of disparate elements. It is a picture characteristic of a schizophrenic condition. I do not know the case at all, but Dr Bennet confirms that my conclusion is correct. You see the disparate elements all over the picture; there are a number of things which are not motivated and which don't belong together. Moreover, you see peculiar lines dividing the field. These lines are characteristic of a schizophrenic mentality; I call them the breaking lines. When a schizophrenic paints a picture of himself, he naturally expresses the schizophrenic split in his own mental structure, and so you find these breaking lines which often go right through a particular figure, like the breaking lines in a mirror. In this picture, the figures themselves show no breaking lines; they only go all over the field.

408   This man, then, tries to gather in all the disparate elements into the vessel. The vessel is meant to be the receptacle for his whole being, for all the incompatible units. If he tried to gather them into his ego, it would be an impossible task, because the ego can be identified only with one part at a time. So he indicates by the symbol of the vessel that he is trying to find a container for everything, and therefore he gives a hint at a non-ego centre by that sort of ball or globe in the middle.

409   The picture is an attempt at self-cure. It brings all the disparate elements into the light, and it also tries to put them together into that vessel. This idea of a receptacle is an archetypal idea. You find it everywhere, and it is one of the central motifs of unconscious pictures. It is the idea of the magic circle which is drawn round something that has to be prevented from escaping or protected against hostile influences. The magic circle as an apotropaic charm is an archaic idea which you still find in folklore. For instance, if a man digs for a treasure, he draws the magic circle round the field in order to keep the devil out. When the ground-plan of a city was set out, there used to be a ritual walk or ride round the circumference in order to protect the place within. In some Swiss villages, it is still the custom for the priest and the town council to ride round the fields when the blessing is administered for the protection of the harvest. In the centre of the magic circle or sacred precinct is the temple. One of the most wonderful examples of this idea is the temple of Borobudur in Java. The walk round, the *circumambulatio*, is done in a spiral; the pilgrims pass the figures of all the different lives of the Buddha, until on the top there is the invisible Buddha, the Buddha yet to come. The ground-plan of Borobudur is a circle within a square. This structure is called in Sanskrit a mandala. The word means a circle, particularly a magic circle. In the East, you find the mandala not only as the ground-plan of temples, but as pictures in the temples, or drawn for the day of certain religious festivals. In the very centre of the mandala there is the god, or the symbol of divine energy, the diamond thunderbolt. Round this innermost circle is a cloister with four gates. Then comes a garden, and round this there is another circle which is the outer circumference.

410   The symbol of the mandala has exactly this meaning of a holy place, a *temenos*, to protect the centre. And it is a symbol which is one of the most important motifs in the objectivation of unconscious images.[16] It is a means of protecting the centre of the personality from being drawn out and from being influenced from outside.

411   This picture by Dr Bennet's patient is an attempt to draw such a mandala. It has a centre, and it contains all his psychic elements, and the

vase would be the magic circle, the *temenos*, round which he has to do the *circumambulatio*. Attention is thus directed towards the centre, and at the same time all the disparate elements come under observation and an attempt is made to unify them. The *circumambulatio* had always to be done clockwise. If one turned round in the other direction it was very unfavourable. The idea of the *circumambulatio* in this picture is the patient's first attempt to find a centre and a container for his whole psyche. But he does not succeed. The design shows no balance, and the vase is toppling over. It even topples over towards the left, towards the side of the unconscious. So the unconscious is still too powerful. If he wants his apotropaic magic to work, he must do it in a different way. We shall see what he does in the next picture.

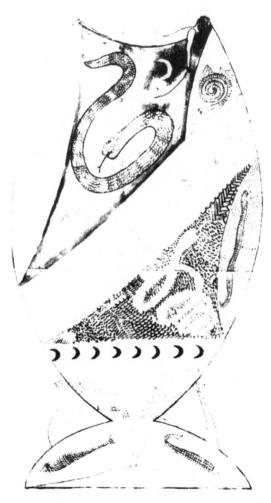

Figure 7.2 Painting by a patient

412   In this picture [Figure 7.2] he makes an attempt at symmetry. Now these disparate, monstrous things which he could not grasp before are collected and assimilated into more favourable, less pathological forms. He can now gather the living units of his unconscious, in the form of snakes, into the sacred vase. And the vase stands firm, it does not topple over any more, and its shape has improved. He does not succeed yet with his intention; but at least he can give his animals some form. They are all animals of the underworld, fishes that live in the deep sea, and snakes of the darkness. They symbolize the lower centres of his psychology, the sympathetic system. A most remarkable thing is that he also gathers in the stars. That means that the cosmos, his world, is collected into the picture. It is an allusion to the unconscious astrology which is in our bones, though we are unaware of it. At the top of the whole picture is the personification of the unconscious, a naked anima-figure who turns her back. That is a typical position; in the beginning of the objectivation of these images the anima-figure often turns her back. At the foot of the vase are eight figures of the crescent moon; the moon is also a symbol of the unconscious. A man's unconscious is the lunar world, for it is the night world, and this is characterized by the moon, and Luna is a feminine designation, because the unconscious is feminine. There are still various breaking lines which disturb the harmony. But I should assume that if no particular trouble interferes, the patient will most likely continue along this constructive line. I should say that there is hope that he might come round altogether, because the appearance of the anima is rather a positive sign. She also is a sort of vase, for in the beginning she incorporates the whole of the unconscious, instead of its being scattered in all the various units. Also, the patient tries to separate the motifs to the right and to the left, and this indicates an attempt at conscious orientation. The ball or globe in the first picture has disappeared, but this is not a negative sign. The whole vessel is the centre, and he has corrected the toppling over of the vase, it stands quite firmly on its base. All this shows that he is really making an attempt to put himself right.

413   The pictures should be given back to the patient because they are very important. You can get copies; patients like to do copies for the doctor. But he should leave the originals with the patients, because they want to look at them; and when they look at them they feel that their unconscious is expressed. The objective form works back on them and they become enchanted. The suggestive influence of the picture reacts on the psychological system of the patient and induces the same effect which he puts into the picture. That is the reason for idols, for the magic use of sacred images, of icons. They cast their magic into our system and put us right, provided we put ourselves into them. If you put yourself into the icon, the icon will speak to you. Take a Lamaic mandala which has a Buddha in the centre, or a Shiva, and, to the extent that you can put yourself into it, it answers and comes into you. It has a magic effect.

414 Because these pictures of the unconscious express the actual psychological condition of the individual, you can use them for the purpose of
diagnosis. You can tell right away from such a picture where the patient
stands, whether he has a schizophrenic disposition or is merely neurotic.
You can even tell what his prognosis is. It only needs some experience to
make these paintings exceedingly helpful. Of course, one should be
careful. One should not be dogmatic and say to every patient, 'Now you
paint.' There are people who think: 'Dr Jung's treatment consists in telling
his patients to paint,' just as formerly they thought: 'He divides them into
introverts and extraverts and says "you should live in such and such a way,
because you belong to this type or that."' That is certainly not treatment.
Each patient is a new problem for the doctor, and he will only be cured of
his neurosis if you help him to find his individual way to the solution of
his conflicts.

The Chairman:

415 Ladies and Gentlemen, you have been expressing by your applause
something of what you feel about Professor Jung. This is the last time in
this group of talks that we will have the honour and pleasure and privilege
of hearing Professor Jung. We have only inadequate ways of expressing
our thanks to him for these lectures which have been so stimulating, so
challenging, which have left us with so many things to think about in the
future, things which to all of us, especially those who are practising
psychotherapy, are enormously suggestive. I think that is what you meant
to do for us, Sir, and that is what you have done. We in this Institute are
extremely proud to have had you here talking to us, and all of us, I think,
are harbouring the idea that before long you will be back in England to
talk to us again and make us think more about these great problems.

NOTES

13 [Cf. *Psychology and Alchemy* (*C.W.*, vol. 12), par. 360.]
14 [This case provided the material for Part II of *Psychology and Alchemy*.]
15 'Traumsymbole des Individuationsprozesses,' in the *Eranos-Jahrbuch 1935*.
[Now Part II of *Psychology and Alchemy*.]
16 [Cf. 'Commentary on *The Secret of the Golden Flower*' (C.W., vol. 13) and
'Concerning Mandala Symbolism' (C.W. vol. 9, 1).]

8   The psychological aspects of the Kore

Excerpt from: *The Archetypes and the Collective Unconscious* (1940) (*CW* 9.1), pars. 319–34

[...]

319   It does not seem to me superfluous to give a number of examples from my case histories which bring out the occurrence of archetypal images in dreams or fantasies. Time and again with my public I come across the difficulty that they imagine illustration by 'a few examples' to be the simplest thing in the world. In actual fact it is almost impossible, with a few words and one or two images torn out of their context, to demonstrate anything. This only works when dealing with an expert. What Perseus has to do with the Gorgon's head would never occur to anyone who did not know the myth. So it is with the individual images: they need a context, and the context is not only a myth but an individual anamnesis. Such contexts, however, are of enormous extent. Anything like a complete series of images would require for its proper presentation a book of about two hundred pages. My own investigation of the Miller fantasies gives some idea of this.[9] It is therefore with the greatest hesitation that I make the attempt to illustrate from case-histories. The material I shall use comes partly from normal, partly from slightly neurotic, persons. It is part dream, part vision, or dream mixed with vision. These 'visions' are far from being hallucinations or ecstatic states; they are spontaneous, visual images of fantasy or so-called *active imagination*. The latter is a method (devised by myself) of introspection for observing the stream of interior images. One concentrates one's attention on some impressive but unintelligible dream-image, or on a spontaneous visual impression, and observes the changes taking place in it. Meanwhile, of course, all criticism must be suspended and the happenings observed and noted with absolute objectivity. Obviously, too, the objection that the whole thing is 'arbitrary' or 'thought up' must be set aside, since it springs from the anxiety of an ego-consciousness which brooks no master besides itself in its own house. In other words, it is the inhibition exerted by the conscious mind on the unconscious.

320   Under these conditions, long and often very dramatic series of fantasies ensue. The advantage of this method is that it brings a mass of unconscious

material to light. Drawing, painting, and modelling can be used to the same end. Once a visual series has become dramatic, it can easily pass over into the auditive or linguistic sphere and give rise to dialogues and the like. With slightly pathological individuals, and particularly in the not infrequent cases of latent schizophrenia, the method may, in certain circumstances, prove to be rather dangerous and therefore requires medical control. It is based on a deliberate weakening of the conscious mind and its inhibiting effect, which either limits or suppresses the unconscious. The aim of the method is naturally therapeutic in the first place, while in the second it also furnishes rich empirical material. Some of our examples are taken from this. They differ from dreams only by reason of their better form, which comes from the fact that the contents were perceived not by a dreaming but by a waking consciousness. The examples are from women in middle life.

CASE X (SPONTANEOUS VISUAL IMPRESSIONS, IN CHRONOLOGICAL ORDER)

321   i. '*I saw a white bird with outstretched wings. It alighted on the figure of a woman, clad in blue, who sat there like an* antique statue. *The bird perched on her hand, and in it she held a* grain of wheat. *The bird took it in its beak and flew into the sky again.*'

322   For this X painted a picture: a blue-clad, archaically simple 'Mother'-figure on a white marble base. Her maternity is emphasized by the large breasts.

323   ii. *A bull lifts a child up from the ground and carries it to the antique statue of a woman. A naked young girl with a wreath of flowers in her hair appears, riding on a white bull. She takes the child and throws it into the air like a ball and catches it again. The white bull carries them both to a temple. The girl lays the child on the ground, and so on (initiation follows).*

324   In this picture the *maiden* appears, rather in the form of Europa. (Here a certain school knowledge is being made use of.) Her nakedness and the wreath of flowers point to Dionysian abandonment. The game of ball with the child is the motif of some secret rite which always has to do with 'child-sacrifice.' (Cf. the accusations of ritual murder levelled by the pagans against the Christians and by the Christians against the Jews and Gnostics; also the Phoenician child-sacrifices, rumours about the Black Mass, etc., and 'the ball-game in church.')[10]

325   iii. '*I saw a golden pig on a pedestal. Beast-like beings* danced *round it in a circle. We made haste to dig* a hole in the ground. *I reached in and found* water. *Then a man appeared in a golden carriage. He jumped into the hole and began swaying back and forth, as if dancing. . . . I swayed in rhythm with him. Then he suddenly leaped out of the hole, raped me, and got me with child.*'

326   X is identical with the young girl, who often appears as a *youth,* too. This youth is an animus-figure, the embodiment of the masculine element in a woman. Youth and young girl together form a syzygy or *coniunctio* which symbolizes the essence of wholeness (as also does the Platonic hermaphrodite, who later became the symbol of perfected wholeness in alchemical philosophy). X evidently dances with the rest, hence '*we* made haste.' The parallel with the motifs stressed by Kerényi seems to me remarkable.

327   iv. '*I saw a beautiful youth with golden cymbals, dancing and leaping in joy and abandonment. . . . Finally he fell to the ground and buried his face in the flowers. Then he sank into the lap of a* very old mother. *After a time he got up and jumped into the water, where he sported like a* dolphin. . . . *I saw that his hair was golden. Now we were leaping together, hand in hand. So we came to a* gorge. . . .' *In leaping the gorge the youth falls into the chasm. X is left alone and comes to a river where a white* sea-horse *is waiting for her with a golden boat.*

328   In this scene X is the youth; therefore he disappears later, leaving her the sole heroine of the story. She is the child of the 'very old mother,' and is also the dolphin, the youth lost in the gorge, and the bride evidently expected by Poseidon. The peculiar overlapping and displacement of motifs in all this individual material is about the same as in the mythological variants. X found the youth in the lap of the mother so impressive that she painted a picture of it. The figure is the same as in item i; only, instead of the grain of wheat in her hand, there is the body of the youth lying completely exhausted in the lap of the gigantic mother.

329   v. *There now follows a sacrifice of sheep, during which a game of ball is likewise played with the sacrificial animal. The participants* smear themselves with the sacrificial blood, *and afterwards bathe in the pulsing gore. X is thereupon transformed into a* plant.

330   vi. *After that X comes to a* den of snakes, *and the snakes wind all round her.*

331   vii. *In a den of snakes beneath the sea there is a* divine woman, *asleep.* (She is shown in the picture as much larger than the others.) *She is wearing a blood-red garment that covers only the lower half of her body. She has a dark skin, full red lips, and seems to be of great physical strength. She kisses X, who is obviously in the role of the young girl, and hands her as a present to the many men who are standing by, etc.*

332   This chthonic goddess is the typical Earth Mother as she appears in so many modern fantasies.

333   viii. *As X emerged from the depths and saw the light again, she experienced a kind of illumination: white flames played about her head as she walked through waving* fields of grain.

334   With this picture the Mother-episode ended.
       [. . .]

NOTES

9 Cf. *Symbols of Transformation* (CW5). H. G. Baynes' book, *The Mythology of the Soul*, runs to 939 pages and endeavours to do justice to the material provided by only two cases.

10 [Cf. 'On the Psychology of the Trickster-Figure' in *CW* 9.1, pars. 456–88. – EDITORS.]

9　On the nature of the psyche

Excerpt from: *The Structure and Dynamics of the Psyche* (1947) (*CW* 8), pars. 397–404

[. . .]

397　We have stated that the lower reaches of the psyche begin where the function emancipates itself from the compulsive force of instinct and becomes amenable to the will, and we have defined the will as disposable energy. But that, as said, presupposes a disposing subject, capable of judgment, and endowed with consciousness. In this way we arrived at the position of proving, as it were, the very thing that we started by rejecting, namely the identification of psyche with consciousness. This dilemma resolves itself once we realize how very relative consciousness is, since its contents are conscious and unconscious at the same time, i.e., conscious under one aspect and unconscious under another. As is the way of paradoxes, this statement is not immediately comprehensible.[111] We must, however, accustom ourselves to the thought that conscious and unconscious have no clear demarcations, the one beginning where the other leaves off. It is rather the case that the psyche is a conscious-unconscious whole. As to the no man's land which I have called the 'personal unconscious,' it is fairly easy to prove that its contents correspond exactly to our definition of the psychic. But – as we define 'psychic' – is there a psychic unconscious that is not a 'fringe of consciousness' and not personal?

398　I have already mentioned that Freud established the existence of archaic vestiges and primitive modes of functioning in the unconscious. Subsequent investigations have confirmed this result and brought together a wealth of observational material. In view of the structure of the body, it would be astonishing if the psyche were the only biological phenomenon not to show clear traces of its evolutionary history, and it is altogether probable that these marks are closely connected with the instinctual base. Instinct and the archaic mode meet in the biological conception of the 'pattern of behaviour.' There are, in fact, no amorphous instincts, as every instinct bears in itself the pattern of its situation. Always it fulfils an image, and the image has fixed qualities. The instinct of the leaf-cutting ant fulfils the image of ant, tree, leaf, cutting, transport, and the little ant-garden of fungi.[112] If any one of these conditions is lacking, the instinct does not function, because it cannot exist without its total pattern, without its image. Such an image is an *a priori* type. It is inborn in the ant prior to any activity, for there can be no activity at all unless an instinct of corresponding pattern initiates and makes it possible. This schema holds true of all instincts and is found in identical form in all individuals of the same species. The same is also true of man: he has in him these *a priori* instinct-types which provide the occasion and the pattern for his activities, in so far as he functions instinctively. As a biological being he has no choice but to act in a specifically human way and fulfil his pattern of behaviour. This sets narrow limits to his possible range of volition, the more narrow the more primitive he is, and the more his consciousness is dependent upon the instinctual sphere. Although from one point of view it is quite correct to speak of the pattern of behaviour as a still-existing archaic vestige, as Nietzsche did in respect of the function of dreams, such an attitude does scant justice to the biological and psychological meaning of these types. They are not just relics or vestiges of earlier modes of functioning; they are the ever-present and biologically necessary regulators of the instinctual sphere, whose range of action covers the whole realm of the psyche and only loses its absoluteness when limited by the relative freedom of the will. We may say that the image represents the *meaning* of the instinct.

399   Although the existence of an instinctual pattern in human biology is probable, it seems very difficult to prove the existence of distinct types empirically. For the organ with which we might apprehend them – consciousness – is not only itself a transformation of the original instinctual image, but also its transformer. It is therefore not surprising that the human mind finds it impossible to specify precise types for man similar to those we know in the animal kingdom. I must confess that I can see no direct way to solve this problem. And yet I have succeeded, or so I believe, in finding at least an indirect way of approach to the instinctual image.

400   In what follows, I would like to give a brief description of how this discovery took place. I had often observed patients whose dreams pointed to a rich store of fantasy-material. Equally, from the patients themselves, I got the impression that they were stuffed full of fantasies, without their being able to tell me just where the inner pressure lay. I therefore took up a dream-image or an association of the patient's, and, with this as a point of departure, set him the task of elaborating or developing his theme by giving free rein to his fantasy. This, according to individual taste and talent, could be done in any number of ways, dramatic, dialectic, visual, acoustic, or in the form of dancing, painting, drawing, or modelling. The result of this technique was a vast number of complicated designs whose diversity puzzled me for years, until I was able to recognize that in this method I was witnessing the spontaneous manifestation of an unconscious process which was merely assisted by the technical ability of the patient, and to which I later gave the name 'individuation process.' But, long

before this recognition dawned upon me, I had made the discovery that this method often diminished, to a considerable degree, the frequency and intensity of the dreams, thus reducing the inexplicable pressure exerted by the unconscious. In many cases, this brought a large measure of therapeutic success, which encouraged both myself and the patient to press forward despite the baffling nature of the results.[113] I felt bound to insist that they were baffling, if only to stop myself from framing, on the basis of certain theoretical assumptions, interpretations which I felt were not only inadequate but liable to prejudice the ingenuous productions of the patient. The more I suspected these configurations of harbouring a certain purposefulness, the less inclined I was to risk any theories about them. This reticence was not made easy for me, since in many cases I was dealing with patients who needed an intellectual *point d'appui* if they were not to get totally lost in the darkness. I had to try to give provisional interpretations at least, so far as I was able, interspersing them with innumerable 'perhaps' and 'ifs' and 'buts' and never stepping beyond the bounds of the picture lying before me. I always took good care to let the interpretation of each image tail off into a question whose answer was left to the free fantasy-activity of the patient.

401   The chaotic assortment of images that at first confronted me reduced itself in the course of the work to certain well-defined themes and formal elements, which repeated themselves in identical or analagous form with the most varied individuals. I mention, as the most salient characteristics, chaotic multiplicity and order; duality; the opposition of light and dark, upper and lower, right and left; the union of opposites in a third; the quaternity (square, cross); rotation (circle, sphere); and finally the centring process and a radial arrangement that usually followed some quaternary system. Triadic formations, apart from the *complexio oppositorum* in a third, were relatively rare and formed notable exceptions which could be explained by special conditions.[114] The centring process is, in my experience, the never-to-be-surpassed climax of the whole development,[115] and is characterized as such by the fact that it brings with it the greatest possible therapeutic effect. The typical features listed above go to the limits of abstraction, yet at the same time they are the simplest expressions of the formative principles here at work. In actual reality, the patterns are infinitely more variegated and far more concrete than this would suggest. Their variety defies description. I can only say that there is probably no motif in any known mythology that does not at some time appear in these configurations. If there was any conscious knowledge of mythological motifs worth mentioning in my patients, it is left far behind by the ingenuities of creative fantasy. In general, my patients had only a minimal knowledge of mythology.

402   These facts show in an unmistakable manner how fantasies guided by unconscious regulators coincide with the records of man's mental activity as known to us from tradition and ethnological research. All the abstract

features I have mentioned are in a certain sense conscious: everyone can count up to four and knows what a circle is and a square; but, as formative principles, they are unconscious, and by the same token their psychological meaning is not conscious either. My most fundamental views and ideas derive from these experiences. First I made the observations, and only then did I hammer out my views. And so it is with the hand that guides the crayon or brush, the foot that executes the dance-step, with the eye and the ear, with the word and the thought: a dark impulse is the ultimate arbiter of the pattern, an unconscious *a priori* precipitates itself into plastic form, and one has no inkling that another person's consciousness is being guided by these same principles at the very point where one feels utterly exposed to the boundless subjective vagaries of chance. Over the whole procedure there seems to reign a dim foreknowledge not only of the pattern but of its meaning.[116] Image and meaning are identical; and as the first takes shape, so the latter becomes clear. Actually, the pattern needs no interpretation: it portays its own meaning. There are cases where I can let interpretation go as a therapeutic requirement. Scientific knowledge, of course, is another matter. Here we have to elicit from the sum total of our experience certain concepts of the greatest possible general validity, which are not given *a priori*. This particular work entails a translation of the timeless, ever-present operative archetype into the scientific language of the present.

403　　These experiences and reflections lead me to believe that there are certain collective unconscious conditions which act as regulators and stimulators of creative fantasy-activity and call forth corresponding formations by availing themselves of the existing conscious material. They behave exactly like the motive forces of dreams, for which reason active imagination, as I have called this method, to some extent takes the place of dreams. The existence of these unconscious regulators – I sometimes refer to them as 'dominants'[117] because of their mode of funtioning – seemed to me so important that I based upon it my hypothesis of an impersonal collective unconscious. The most remarkable thing about this method, I felt, was that it did not involve a *reductio in primam figuram*, but rather a synthesis – supported by an attitude voluntarily adopted, though for the rest wholly natural – of passive conscious material and unconscious influences, hence a kind of spontaneous amplification of the archetypes. The images are not to be thought of as a reduction of conscious contents to their simplest denominator, as this would be the direct road to the primordial images which I said previously was unimaginable; they make their appearance only in the course of amplification.

404　　On this natural amplification process I also based my method of eliciting the meaning of dreams, for dreams behave in exactly the same way as active imagination; only the support of conscious contents is lacking. To the extent that the archetypes intervene in the shaping of conscious contents by regulating, modifying, and motivating them, they act like the instincts. It is therefore very natural to suppose that these factors are connected with the instincts and to inquire whether the typical situational patterns which these collective form-principles apparently represent are not in the end identical with the instinctual patterns, namely, with the patterns of behaviour. I must admit that up to the present I have not laid hold of any argument that would finally refute this possibility.

NOTES

111 Freud also arrived at similar paradoxical conclusions. Thus, in his article 'The Unconscious' (p. 177): he says: 'An instinct can never become an object of consciousness – only the idea that represents the instinct can. *Even in the unconscious, moreover, an instinct cannot be represented otherwise than by an idea.*' (My italics.) As in my above account we were left asking, 'Who is the subject of the unconscious will?' so we must ask here, 'Exactly *who* has the idea of the instinct in the unconscious state?' For 'unconscious' ideation is a *contradictio in adjecto.*

112 For details see C. Lloyd Morgan, *Habit and Instinct.*

113 Cf. 'The Aims of Psychotherapy,' pars. 101ff.; and 'The Technique of Differentiation Between the Ego and the Figures of the Unconscious' in *Two Essays on Analytical Psychology*, pars. 343ff. [Also 'The Transcendent Function,' pars. 166ff.] see above.

114 The same applies to the pentadic figures.

115 So far as the development can be ascertained from the objective material.

116 Cf. *Psychology and Alchemy*, par. 329 in CW12.

117 Cf. *Two Essays on Analytical Psychology*, par. 151 in CW7.

10 Three letters to Mr O. (1947)

From: *Letters vol. 1*, pp. 458–61

To Mr O.

[ORIGINAL IN ENGLISH]

Dear Mr O.,

30 April 1947

Having studied your dream-material and having had a personal impression of your actual state of mind I have come to the conclusion that there is something wrong in the whole handling of your case, in spite of the fact that everything seems to be correct. The fact is that you have an uncannily extensive material one can hardly hope to cope with, at least I couldn't muster the amount of energy that would be required to deal with your dreams properly. In order to keep up with them one would need at least 3 hours a week. As you know, the principle of my technique does not consist only in analysis and interpretation of such materials as are produced by the unconscious, but also in their synthesis by active imagination. Of the latter I have seen nothing yet. But this is precisely the 'technique' which seems to be indicated in your situation. You are not only informed enough but also intelligent enough to go on for a long stretch on the assumption that I'm buried and that there is no analyst for you under the changing moon except the one that is in your own heart. As you will understand, this does not mean at all that you analyse and interpret your dreams according to the rules of the thumb, but that you do what we call in the German language the 'Auseinandersetzung mit dem Unbewussten,'[1] which is a dialectical procedure you carry through with yourself with the aid of active imagination. This is the best means I know to reduce an inordinate production of the unconscious. It doesn't seem right that a man like yourself is still dependent upon analysts. It is also not good for you, because it produces again and again a most unwholesome dissociation of your opposites, namely pride and humility. It will be good for your humility if you can accept the gifts of the unconscious guide that dwells in yourself, and it is good for your pride to humiliate itself to such an extent that you can accept what you receive. I don't intend to behave as if I were a corpse already. I'm therefore quite willing to help in your attempt in this direction, but I refuse in your own interest to plague myself with your material which is only helpful when you acquire its understanding by your own effort. Pride is a wonderful thing when you know how to fulfil its expectations. Did you never ask yourself who my analyst is? Yet, when it comes to the last issue, we must be able to stand alone *vis à vis* the unconscious for better or worse.

Yours sincerely, C. G. JUNG

To Mr O.

[ORIGINAL IN ENGLISH]

My dear Mr O.,   2 May 1947

I'm somewhat astonished that you haven't learned yet to apply what I call 'active imagination,' as this is the indispensable second part of any analysis that is really meant to go to the roots. I wish you would carefully study what I have written about it in *Die Beziehungen zwischen dem Ich und dem Unbewussten.*[1] It is true, not much has been published about this subject. Most is contained in my Seminars. It is too difficult a subject to deal with before a merely intellectual public.

The dream[2] you write about is suggestive in that respect: it is a *massa informis*[3] which is meant to be shaped. It shouldn't go down the sink as it is always expected to do, it must remain on the surface, because it is the *prima materia*[4] of whatever you are going to do about it. The point is that you start with any image, for instance just with that yellow mass in your dream. Contemplate it and carefully observe how the picture begins to unfold or to change. Don't try to make it into something, just do nothing but observe what its spontaneous changes are. Any mental picture you contemplate in this way will sooner or later change through a spontaneous association that causes a slight alteration of the picture. You must carefully avoid impatient jumping from one subject to another. Hold fast to the one image you have chosen and wait until it changes by itself. Note all these changes and eventually step into the picture yourself, and if it is a speaking figure at all then say what you have to say to that figure and listen to what he or she has to say.

Thus you can not only analyse your unconscious but you also give your unconscious a chance to analyse yourself, and therewith you gradually create the unity of conscious and unconscious without which there is no individuation at all. If you apply this method, then I can come in as an occasional adviser, but if you don't apply it, then my existence is of no use for you.

Yours sincerely, C. G. JUNG

To Mr O.

[ORIGINAL IN ENGLISH]

My dear O.,   7 May 1947

Your material is, as I feared, much too rich! It needs a tremendous amount of mental work to reduce it.

Your first vision where your Beatrice appears contains a point where I can show you how you can come in. Beatrice, as an anima figure, is most certainly a personification; that means, a personal being created in this shape by the unconscious. You can safely assume that this is the shape your anima has chosen in order to demonstrate to you how she looks. Such a huge Beatrice is surely an unexpected sight. Instead of reacting to this rather amazing sight, you are satisfied with continuing your vision. But the natural thing would be that you make use of the opportunity and start some dialogue with your anima. Anybody who feels natural about such things would follow his surprise and put a question or two to her: why she appears as Beatrice? why is she so big? why are you so small? why she nurses your wife and not yourself? Etc. You also might ask her – since she is the 'messenger of the grail' – what that funny thing is with that orange? what the magic ring means? what is the matter with all those animals? Treat her as a person, if you like as a patient or a goddess, but above all treat her as something that does exist. Moreover, in this vision you get right under the influence of your anima, and that's the reason why she begins to feed your wife, because your wife becomes underfed when you fall for your anima. Therefore you must talk to this person in order to see what she is about and to learn what her thoughts and character are. If you yourself step into your fantasy, then that overabundance of material will soon come to more reasonable proportions. But since you are giving free rein to your intuitions you are just swamped by it. Keep your head and your own personality over against the overwhelming multitude of images and aspects. You can do that, as I tell you, by stepping into the picture with your ordinary human reactions and emotions. It is a very good method to treat the anima as if she were a patient whose secret you ought to get at.

Yours sincerely, C.G. JUNG

NOTES

Letter 1 (30 April 1947)

1 This term is usually translated in *CW* as 'coming to terms with the unconscious.'

Letter 2 (2 May 1947)

1 'The Relations between the Ego and the Unconscious,' *CW* 7.
2 A mass of yellow substance grew under the hand of the dreamer. He tried to wash it down the kitchen sink but the drain was blocked and the mass didn't go down.
3 Alchemical term for the original chaos containing the divine seeds of life.
4 The term *prima materia* is often used synonymously with that of the *massa informis* (or *massa confusa*). Cf. *Psychology and Alchemy*, Index (CW12).

11 Mysterium Coniunctionis

Excerpts from: *CW 14*, (1955) pars. 705–11
and pars. 749–56

[. . .]

705 The production of the *caelum** is a symbolic rite performed in the laboratory. Its purpose was to create, in the form of a substance, that 'truth,' the celestial balsam or life principle, which is identical with the God-image. Psychologically, it was a representation of the individuation process by means of chemical substances and procedures, or what we today call active imagination. This is a method which is used spontaneously by nature herself or can be taught to the patient by the analyst. As a rule it occurs when the analysis has constellated the opposites so powerfully that a union or synthesis of the personality becomes an imperative necessity. Such a situation is bound to arise when the analysis of the psychic contents, of the patient's attitude and particularly of his dreams, has brought the compensatory or complementary images from the unconscious so insistently before his mind that the conflict between the conscious and the unconscious personality becomes open and critical. When this confrontation is confined to partial aspects of the unconscious the conflict is limited and the solution simple: the patient, with insight and some resignation or a feeling of resentment, places himself on the side of reason and convention. Though the unconscious motifs are repressed again, as before, the unconscious is satisfied to a certain extent, because the patient must now make a conscious effort to live according to its principles and, in addition, is constantly reminded of the existence of the repressed by annoying resentments. But if his recognition of the shadow is as complete as he can make it, then conflict and disorientation ensue, an equally strong Yes and No which he can no longer keep apart by a rational decision. He cannot transform his clinical neurosis into the less conspicuous neurosis of cynicism; in other words, he can no longer hide the conflict behind a mask. It requires a real solution and necessitates a third thing in which the opposites can unite. Here the logic of the intellect usually fails, for in a logical antithesis there is no third. The 'solvent' can only be of an irrational nature. In nature the resolution of opposites is always an energic process: she acts *symbolically* in the truest sense of the word,[126] doing something that expresses both sides, just as the waterfall visibly mediates between

above and below. The waterfall itself is then the incommensurable third. In an open and unresolved conflict dreams and fantasies occur which, like the waterfall, illustrate the tension and nature of the opposites, and thus prepare the synthesis.

706   This process can, as I have said, take place spontaneously or be artificially induced. In the latter case you choose a dream, or some other fantasy-image, and concentrate on it by simply catching hold of it and looking at it. You can also use a bad mood as a starting-point, and then try to find out what sort of fantasy-image it will produce, or what image expresses this mood. You then fix this image in the mind by concentrating your attention. Usually it will alter, as the mere fact of contemplating it animates it. The alterations must be carefully noted down all the time, for they reflect the psychic processes in the unconscious background, which appear in the form of images consisting of conscious memory material. In this way conscious and unconscious are united, just as a waterfall connects above and below. A chain of fantasy ideas develops and gradually takes on a dramatic character: the passive process becomes an action. At first it consists of projected figures, and these images are observed like scenes in the theatre. In other words, you dream with open eyes. As a rule there is a marked tendency simply to enjoy this interior entertainment and to leave it at that. Then, of course, there is no real progress but only endless variations on the same theme, which is not the point of the exercise at all. What is enacted on the stage still remains a background process; it does not move the observer in any way, and the less it moves him the smaller will be the cathartic effect of this private theatre. The piece that is being played does not want merely to be watched impartially, it wants to compel his participation. If the observer understands that his own drama is being performed on this inner stage, he cannot remain indifferent to the plot and its dénouement. He will notice, as the actors appear one by one and the plot thickens, that they all have some purposeful relationship to his conscious situation, that he is being addressed by the unconscious, and that *it* causes these fantasy-images to appear before him. He therefore feels compelled, or is encouraged by his analyst, to take part in the play and, instead of just sitting in a theatre, really have it out with his alter ego. For nothing in us ever remains quite uncontradicted, and consciousness can take up no position which will not call up, somewhere in the dark corners of the psyche, a negation or a compensatory effect, approval or resentment. This process of coming to terms with the Other in us is well worth while, because in this way we get to know aspects of our nature which we would not allow anybody else to show us and which we ourselves would never have admitted.[127] It is very important to fix this whole procedure in writing at the time of its occurrence, for you then have ocular evidence that will effectively counteract the ever-ready tendency to self-deception. A running commentary is absolutely necessary in dealing with the shadow, because otherwise its actuality cannot be fixed. Only in this painful way

is it possible to gain a positive insight into the complex nature of one's own personality.

707

SELF-KNOWLEDGE

Expressed in the language of Hermetic philosophy, the ego-personality's coming to terms with its own background, the shadow, corresponds to the union of spirit and soul in the *unio mentalis*, which is the first stage of the coniunctio. What I call coming to terms with the unconscious the alchemists called 'meditation.' Ruland says of this: 'Meditation: The name of an Internal Talk of one person with another who is invisible, as in the invocation of the Deity, or communion with one's self, or with one's good angel.'[128] This somewhat optimistic definition must immediately be qualified by a reference to the adept's relations with his *spiritus familiaris*, who we can only hope was a good one. In this respect Mercurius is a rather unreliable companion, as the testimony of the alchemists agrees. In order to understand the second stage, the union of the *unio mentalis* with the body, psychologically, we must bear in mind what the psychic state resulting from a fairly complete recognition of the shadow looks like. The shadow, as we know, usually presents a fundamental contrast to the conscious personality. This contrast is the prerequisite for the difference of potential from which psychic energy arises. Without it, the necessary tension would be lacking. Where considerable psychic energy is at work, we must expect a corresponding tension and inner opposition. The opposites are necessarily of a characterological nature: the existence of a positive virtue implies victory over its opposite, the corresponding vice. Without its counterpart virtue would be pale, ineffective, and unreal. The extreme opposition of the shadow to consciousness is mitigated by complementary and compensatory processes in the unconscious. Their impact on consciousness finally produces the uniting symbols.

708   Confrontation with the shadow produces at first a dead balance, a standstill that hampers moral decisions and makes convictions ineffective or even impossible. Everything becomes doubtful, which is why the alchemists called this stage *nigredo, tenebrositas*, chaos, melancholia. It is right that the magnum opus should begin at this point, for it is indeed a well-nigh unanswerable question how one is to confront reality in this torn and divided state. Here I must remind the reader who is acquainted neither with alchemy nor with the psychology of the unconscious that nowadays one very seldom gets into such a situation. Nobody now has any sympathy with the perplexities of an investigator who busies himself with magical substances, and there are relatively few people who have experienced the effects of an analysis of the unconscious on themselves, and almost nobody hits on the idea of using the objective hints given by dreams as a theme for meditation. If the ancient art of meditation is practised at all today, it

is practised only in religious or philosophical circles, where a theme is subjectively chosen by the meditant or prescribed by an instructor, as in the Ignatian *Exercitia* or in certain theosophical exercises that developed under Indian influence. These methods are of value only for increasing concentration and consolidating consciousness, but have no significance as regards effecting a synthesis of the personality. On the contrary, their purpose is to shield consciousness from the unconscious and to suppress it. They are therefore of therapeutic value only in cases where the conscious is liable to be overwhelmed by the unconscious and there is the danger of a psychotic interval.

709   In general, meditation and contemplation have a bad reputation in the West. They are regarded as a particularly reprehensible form of idleness or as pathological narcissism. No one has time for self-knowledge or believes that it could serve any sensible purpose. Also, one knows in advance that it is not worth the trouble to know oneself, for any fool can know what he is. We believe exclusively in doing and do not ask about the doer, who is judged only by achievements that have collective value. The general public seems to have taken cognizance of the existence of the unconscious psyche more than the so-called experts, but still nobody has drawn any conclusions from the fact that Western man confronts himself as a stranger and that self-knowledge is one of the most difficult and exacting of the arts.

710   When meditation is concerned with the objective products of the unconscious that reach consciousness spontaneously, it unites the conscious with contents that proceed not from a conscious causal chain but from an essentially unconscious process. We cannot know what the unconscious psyche is, otherwise it would be conscious. We can only conjecture its existence, though there are good enough grounds for this. Part of the unconscious contents is projected, but the projection as such is not recognized. Meditation or critical introspection and objective investigation of the object are needed in order to establish the existence of projections. If the individual is to take stock of himself it is essential that his projections should be recognized, because they falsify the nature of the object and besides this contain items which belong to his own personality and should be integrated with it. This is one of the most important phases in the wearisome process of self-knowledge. And since projections involve one in an inadmissible way in externalities, Dorn rightly recommends an almost ascetic attitude to the world, so that the soul may be freed from its involvement in the world of the body. Here only the 'spirit' can help it, that is, the drive for knowledge of the self, on a plane beyond all the illusion and bemusement caused by projection.

711   The *unio mentalis*, then, in psychological as well as in alchemical language, means knowledge of oneself. In contradistinction to the modern prejudice that self-knowledge is nothing but a knowledge of the ego, the alchemists regarded the self as a substance incommensurable with the ego,

hidden in the body, and identical with the image of God.[129] This view fully accords with the Indian idea of *purusha-atman*.[130] The psychic preparation of the magisterium as described by Dorn is therefore an attempt, uninfluenced by the East, to bring about a union of opposites in accordance with the great Eastern philosophies, and to establish for this purpose a principle freed from the opposites and similar to the *atman* or *tao*. Dorn called this the *substantia coelestis*, which today we would describe as a transcendental principle. This 'unum' is *nirdvandva* (free from the opposites), like the *atman* (self).

[. . .]

749   What the alchemist sought, then, to help him out of his dilemma was a chemical operation which we today would describe as a symbol. The procedure he followed was obviously an allegory of his postulated *substantia coelestis* and its chemical equivalent. To that extent the operation was not symbolical for him but purposive and rational. For us, who know that no amount of incineration, sublimation, and centrifuging of the vinous residue can ever produce an 'air-coloured' quintessence, the entire procedure is fantastic if taken literally. We can hardly suppose that Dorn, either, meant a real wine but, after the manner of the alchemists, *vinum ardens*, *acetum*, *spiritualis sanguis*, etc., in other words *Mercurius non vulgi*, who embodied the *anima mundi*. Just as the air encompasses the earth, so in the old view the soul is wrapped round the world. As I have shown, we can most easily equate the concept of Mercurius with that of the unconscious. If we add this term to the recipe, it would run: Take the unconscious in one of its handiest forms, say a spontaneous fantasy, a dream, an irrational mood, an affect, or something of the kind, and operate with it. Give it your special attention, concentrate on it, and observe its alterations objectively. Spare no effort to devote yourself to this task, follow the subsequent transformations of the spontaneous fantasy attentively and carefully. Above all, don't let anything from outside, that does not belong, get into it, for the fantasy-image has 'everything it needs.'[222] In this way one is certain of not interfering by conscious caprice and of giving the unconscious a free hand. In short, the alchemical operation seems to us the equivalent of the psychological process of active imagination.

750   Ordinarily, the only thing people know about psychotherapy is that it consists in a certain technique which the analyst applies to his patient. Specialists know how far they can get with it. One can use it to cure the neuroses, and even the milder psychoses, so that nothing more remains of the illness except the general human problem of how much of yourself you want to forget, how much psychic discomfort you have to take on your shoulders, how much you may forbid or allow yourself, how much or how little you may expect of others, how far you should give up the meaning of your life or what sort of meaning you should give it. The analyst has a right to shut his door when a neurosis no longer produces any clinical

symptoms and has debouched into the sphere of general human problems. The less he knows about these the greater his chances are of coming across comparatively reasonable patients who can be weaned from the transference that regularly sets in. But if the patient has even the remotest suspicion that the analyst thinks rather more about these problems than he says, then he will not give up the transference all that quickly but will cling to it in defiance of all reason – which is not so unreasonable after all, indeed quite understandable. Even adult persons often have no idea how to cope with the problem of living, and on top of that are so unconscious in this regard that they succumb in the most uncritical way to the slightest possibility of finding some kind of answer or certainty. Were this not so, the numerous sects and -isms would long since have died out. But, thanks to unconscious, infantile attachments, boundless uncertainty and lack of self-reliance, they all flourish like weeds.

751   The analyst who is himself struggling for all those things which he seeks to inculcate into his patients will not get round the problem of the transference so easily. The more he knows how difficult it is for him to solve the problems of his own life, the less he can overlook the fear and uncertainty or the frivolity and dangerously uncritical attitude of his patients. Even Freud regarded the transference as a neurosis at second hand and treated it as such. He could not simply shut the door, but honestly tried to analyze the transference away. This is not so simple as it sounds when technically formulated. Practice often turns out to be rather different from theory. You want, of course, to put a whole man on his feet and not just a part of him. You soon discover that there is nothing for him to stand on and nothing for him to hold on to. Return to the parents has become impossible, so he hangs on to the analyst. He can go neither backwards nor forwards, for he sees nothing before him that could give him a hold. All so-called reasonable possibilities have been tried out and have proved useless. Not a few patients then remember the faith in which they were brought up, and some find their way back to it, but not all. They know, perhaps, what their faith ought to mean to them, but they have found to their cost how little can be achieved with will and good intentions if the unconscious does not lend a hand. In order to secure its co-operation the religions have long turned to myths for help, or rather, the myths always flung out bridges between the helpless consciousness and the effective *idées forces* of the unconscious. But you cannot, artificially and with an effort of will, believe the statements of myth if you have not previously been gripped by them. If you are honest, you will doubt the truth of the myth because our present-day consciousness has no means of understanding it. Historical and scientific criteria do not lend themselves to a recognition of mythological truth; it can be grasped only by the intuitions of faith or by psychology, and in the latter case although there may be insight it remains ineffective unless it is backed by experience.

752   Thus the modern man cannot even bring about the *unio mentalis* which

would enable him to accomplish the second degree of conjunction. The analyst's guidance in helping him to understand the statements of his unconscious in dreams, etc. may provide the necessary insight, but when it comes to the question of real experience the analyst can no longer help him: he himself must put his hand to the work. He is then in the position of an alchemist's apprentice who is inducted into the teachings by the Master and learns all the tricks of the laboratory. But sometime he must set about the opus himself, for, as the alchemists emphasize, nobody else can do it for him. Like this apprentice, the modern man begins with an unseemly prima materia which presents itself in unexpected form – a contemptible fantasy which, like the stone that the builders rejected, is 'flung into the street' and is so 'cheap' that people do not even look at it. He will observe it from day to day and note its alterations until his eyes are opened or, as the alchemists say, until the fish's eyes, or the sparks, shine in the dark solution. For the eyes of the fish are always open and therefore must always see, which is why the alchemists used them as a symbol of perpetual attention.

753   The light that gradually dawns on him consists in his understanding that his fantasy is a real psychic process which is happening to him personally. Although, to a certain extent, he looks on from outside, impartially, he is also an acting and suffering figure in the drama of the psyche. This recognition is absolutely necessary and marks an important advance. So long as he simply looks at the pictures he is like the foolish Parsifal, who forgot to ask the vital question because he was not aware of his own participation in the action. Then, if the flow of images ceases, next to nothing has happened even though the process is repeated a thousand times. But if you recognize your own involvement you yourself must enter into the process with your personal reactions, just as if you were one of the fantasy figures, or rather, as if the drama being enacted before your eyes were real. It is a psychic fact that this fantasy is happening, and it is as real as you – as a psychic entity – are real. If this crucial operation is not carried out, all the changes are left to the flow of images, and you yourself remain unchanged. As Dorn says, you will never make the One unless you become one yourself. It is, however, possible that if you have a dramatic fantasy you will enter the interior world of images as a *fictitious personality* and thereby prevent any real participation; it may even endanger consciousness because you then become the victim of your own fantasy and succumb to the powers of the unconscious, whose dangers the analyst knows all too well. But if you place yourself in the drama as you really are, not only does it gain in actuality but you also create, by your criticism of the fantasy, an effective counterbalance to its tendency to get out of hand. For what is now happening is the decisive rapprochement with the unconscious. This is where insight, the *unio mentalis*, begins to become real. What you are now creating is the beginning of individuation, whose immediate goal is the experience and production of the symbol of totality.

754   It not infrequently happens that the patient simply continues to observe his images without considering what they mean to him. He can and he should understand their meaning, but this is of practical value only so long as he is not sufficiently convinced that the unconscious can give him valuable insights. But once he has recognized this fact, he should also know that he then has in his hands an opportunity to win, by his knowledge, independence of the analyst. This conclusion is one which he does not like to draw, with the result that he frequently stops short at mere observation of his images. The analyst, if he has not tried out the procedure on himself, cannot help him over this stile – assuming, of course, that there are compelling reasons why the procedure should be continued. In these cases there is no medical or ethical imperative but only a command of fate, which is why patients who by no means lack the necessary acumen often come to a standstill at this point. As this experience is not uncommon I can only conclude that the transition from a merely perceptive, i.e., *aesthetic*, attitude to one of *judgment* is far from easy. Indeed, modern psychotherapy has just reached this point and is beginning to recognize the usefulness of perceiving and giving shape to the images, whether by pencil and brush or by modelling. A musical configuration might also be possible provided that it were really composed and written down. Though I have never met a case of this kind, Bach's *Art of Fugue* would seem to offer an example, just as the representation of the archetypes is a basic feature of Wagner's music. (These phenomena, however, arise less from personal necessity than from the unconscious compensations produced by the *Zeitgeist*, though I cannot discuss this here.)

755   The step beyond a merely aesthetic attitude may be unfamiliar to most of my readers. I myself have said little about it and have contented myself with hints.[223] It is not a matter that can be taken lightly. I tried it out on myself and others thirty years ago and must admit that although it is feasible and leads to satisfactory results it is also very difficult. It can be recommended without misgiving if a patient has reached the stage of knowledge described above. If he finds the task too difficult he will usually fail right at the beginning and never get through the dangerous impasse. The danger inherent in analysis is that, in a psychopathically disposed patient, it will unleash a psychosis. This very unpleasant possibility generally presents itself at the beginning of the treatment, when, for instance, dream-analysis has activated the unconscious. But if it has got so far that the patient can do active imagination and shape out his fantasies, and there are no suspicious incidents, then there is as a rule no longer any serious danger. One naturally asks oneself what fear – if fear it is – prevents him from taking the next step, the transition to an attitude of judgment. (The judgment of course should be morally and intellectually binding.) There are sufficient reasons for fear and uncertainty because voluntary participation in the fantasy is alarming to a naïve mind and amounts to an anticipated psychosis.

756   Naturally there is an enormous difference between an anticipated psychosis and a real one, but the difference is not always clearly perceived and this gives rise to uncertainty or even a fit of panic. Unlike a real psychosis, which comes on you and inundates you with uncontrollable fantasies irrupting from the unconscious, the judging attitude implies a voluntary involvement in those fantasy-processes which compensate the individual and – in particular – the collective situation of consciousness. The avowed purpose of this involvement is to integrate the statements of the unconscious, to assimilate their compensatory content, and thereby produce a whole meaning which alone makes life worth living and, for not a few people, possible at all. The reason why the involvement looks very like a psychosis is that the patient is integrating the same fantasy-material to which the insane person falls victim because he cannot integrate it but is swallowed up by it. In myths the hero is the one who conquers the dragon, not the one who is devoured by it. And yet both have to deal with the same dragon. Also, he is no hero who never met the dragon, or who, if he once saw it, declared afterwards that he saw nothing. Equally, only one who has risked the fight with the dragon and is not overcome by it wins the hoard, the 'treasure hard to attain.' He alone has a genuine claim to self-confidence, for he has faced the dark ground of his self and thereby has gained himself. This experience gives him faith and trust, the *pistis* in the ability of the self to sustain him, for everything that menaced him from inside he has made his own. He has acquired the right to believe that he will be able to overcome all future threats by the same means. He has arrived at an inner certainty which makes him capable of self-reliance, and attained what the alchemists called the *unio mentalis*.

NOTES

*   * [The *caelum* is the sought-for heavenly substance, the natural sweetness of life, joy. – J.C.]
126 A σύμβολον is a 'throwing together.'
127 Cf. 'Relations between the Ego and the Unconscious,' pars. 341ff (see above, pp. 61–72).
128 [Cf. *Lexicon*, p. 226 [Martin Ruland (1622) *Lexicon*, Frankfurt am Main; English translation, London, 1892.]
129 Cf. *Aion*, pars. 70ff in CW9.II.
130 In Chinese alchemy this is *chên-yên*, the true man (τέλειος ανθρωπος). 'True man is the extreme of excellence. He is and he is not. He resembles a vast pool of water, suddenly sinking and suddenly floating. . . . When first gathered, it may be classified as white. Treat it and it turns red. . . . The white lives inside like a virgin. The squareness, the roundness, the diameter and the dimensions mix and restrain one another. Having been in existence before the beginning of the heavens and the earth: lordly, lordly, high and revered.' (Wei Po-yang, pp. 237f.) [. . .]
222 'Omne quo indiget' is frequently said of the lapis.
223 Cf. 'The Transcendent Function,' pars. 166ff (see above, pp. 53–60).

12 Foreword to van Helsdingen: *Beelden uit het Onbewuste*[1]

From: *The Symbolic Life* (CW 18), pars. 1252–5

1252 Dr R. J. van Helsdingen has asked me to write a foreword to his book. I am happy to comply with his request for a particular reason: the case that is discussed and commented on was one that I treated many years ago, as can now be said publicly with the kind permission of my former patient. Such liberality is not encountered everywhere, because many one-time patients are understandably shy about exposing their intimate, tormenting, pathogenic problems to the eye of the public. And indeed one must admit that their drawings or paintings do not as a rule have anything that would recommend them to the aesthetic needs of the public at large. If only for technical reasons the pictures are usually unpleasant to look at and, lacking artistic power, have little expressive value for outsiders. These short-comings are happily absent in the present case: the pictures are artistic compositions in the positive sense and are uncommonly expressive. They communicate their frightening, daemonic content to the beholder and convince him of the terrors of a fantastic underworld.

1253 While it was the patient's own mother country that produced the great masters of the monstrous, Hieronymus Bosch and others, who opened the flood-gates of creative fantasy, the pictures in this book show us imaginative activity unleashed in another form: the Indomalaysian phantasmagoria of pullulating vegetation and of fear-haunted, stifling tropical nights. Environment and inner disposition conspired to produce this series of pictures which give expression to an infantile-archaic fear. Partly it is the fear of a child who, deprived of her partents, is defencelessly exposed to the unconscious and its menacing, phantasmal figures; partly the fear of a European who can find no other attitude to everything that the East conjures up in her save that of rejection and repression. Because the European does not know his own unconscious, he does not understand the East and projects into it everything he fears and despises in himself.

1254 For a sensitive child it is a veritable catastrophe to be removed from her parents and sent to Europe after the unconscious influence of the Oriental world had moulded her relation to the instincts, and then, at the critical period of puberty, to be transported back to the East, when this development had been interrupted by Western education and crippled by neglect.[2]

The pictures not only illustrate the phase of treatment that brought the contents of her neurosis to consciousness, they were also an instrument of treatment, as they reduced the half conscious or unconscious images floating about in her mind to a common denominator and fixated them. Once an expression of this kind has been found, it proves its 'magical' efficacy by putting a spell, as it were, on the content so represented and making it relatively innocuous. The more complex this content is, the more pictures are needed to depotentiate it. The therapeutic effect of this technique consists in inducing the conscious mind to collaborate with the unconscious, the latter being integrated in the process. In this way the neurotic dissociation is gradually remedied.

1255   The author is to be congratulated on having edited this valuable and unusual material. Although only the initial stages of the analysis are presented here, some of the pictures indicate possibilities of a further development. Even with these limitations, however, the case offers a considerable enrichment of the literature on the subject, which is still very meagre.

May 1954

NOTES

1 [Arnhem (Netherlands), 1957. ('Pictures from the Unconscious.') Foreword in German.]
2 [This case is not to be confused with the similar case – the patients were in fact sisters – discussed in 'The Realities of Practical Psychotherapy,' appendix to *The Practice of Psychotherapy* (*CW*, vol. 16, 2nd edn.).]

Afterword

Post-Jungian contributions

Many Jungian analysts and authors have been inspired to take up different facets of active imagination. Case studies of active imagination in the context of analysis are presented by Kirsch (1955), Adler (1961), Singer (1972/94), Hannah (1981), and Edinger (1990). Essays and books that offer an overview of the topic include Hannah (1953), Humbert (1971), Weaver (1973), Dieckmann (1979), von Franz (1980), Dallett (1982), Johnson (1986), Kast (1988), and Cwik (1995). Effective variations of Jung's active imagination have been developed by Fry (1974), Middlekoop (1985), Mindell (1985) and Allan (1988; 1992). Rosen (1993) looks at the treatment of depression and the healing powers of the arts.

A number of biographies and biographical memoirs include experiences with active imagination (Jaffe 1971/72; von Franz 1972; Van der Post 1975; Hannah 1976; Keller 1982; Wehr 1988, 1989; Douglas 1993). *C.G. Jung: Word and Image* (edited by Jaffe, 1979) is an illustrated biography with reproductions of Jung's paintings and stone carvings. Tilly (1982) describes a memorable visit with Jung in 1956 when she played for him and they discussed music therapy. Stevens (1986) contributes a memoir about Withymead, a therapeutic community in England where the arts were a central part of the treatment program.

Dehing (1992) and Sandner (1992) offer a fine overview and stimulating discussion of the transcendent function. Hull (1971) presents a bibliographical review of Jung's works on active imagination. Watkins (1976) looks at many approaches to imaginal experience and places active imagination in a broad historical context.

Lockhart (1982, 1983) seems to embody the symbolic perspective as he considers the inner and outer worlds. Durand (1971) and Casey (1974) explore their questions and express their passion for the imaginal realm.

Hillman's brief chapter in *Healing Fiction* (1983, pp. 78–81) begins with a reminder of what active imagination is *not*; he then turns to its ultimate value, *Know Thyself*. In *Emotion*, he recognizes the healing power of the expressive therapies: 'Since art therapy activates imagination and allows it to materialize – that is, enter the world via the emotions of the patient – therapy by means of the arts must take precedence over all other kinds'

(1960/92, p. xiv). The compelling power of Hillman surely has at its source his ongoing, continuous engagement with the imagination and the emotions.

In an early paper, Fordham (1956) tries to differentiate between active imagination and imaginative activity. In contrast to Jung's understanding of play as an integrative function of the Self, Fordham sees the value of play in terms of ego development. His contribution to active imagination may be best described by August Cwik: 'The important point for Fordham is not the presence of the creative imagination *per se*, but is to allow and "hold" the patient in developing his or her own capacity to play' (Cwik 1995, p. 164).

In his important scholarly work *Jung and the Post-Jungians* (1985), Samuels identifies three schools of analytical psychology that have developed since Jung's death in 1961: Developmental, Classical, and Archetypal. He points out that in the practice of analysis, the developmental school gives special attention to the interaction between analyst and patient, while the classical and archetypal schools focus more on the healing power of the symbol. A larger perspective on active imagination may include the therapeutic interaction as well as the symbol, providing a way to 'bridge the divide that has grown up between the classical-symbolic-synthetic approach and that of interactional dialectic' (p. 204). In addition to Samuels, Davidson (1966), Schwartz-Salant (1982) and Powell (1985) are among those who understand that work with the transference can be a form of active imagination.

Stewart (1987b) proposes the terms Ritual, Rhythm, Reason, and Relationship as a kind of mnemonic device to remember something of the dynamic expressive quality of each of the fourfold categories of the imagination. Ritual is the expressive aspect of ceremony, the religious imagination; Rhythm is the expressive quality that inspires and transforms the arts; Reason is the dynamic expression of the philosophic, scientific, scholarly imagination; Relationship is the essence of kinship and human society. Stewart's contribution offers a new perspective on active imagination as Ritual (rites of entry and exit, meditation, dialogue and exchange with the gods), Rhythm (giving it form through the expressive arts), Reason (scholarly elucidation, symbolic amplification) and Relationship (the empathic imagination, fantasies that individuals have about each other). These are not presented as stages of active imagination, rather they are the intrinsic forms of the imagination itself. Naturally, everything depends on developing the central, self-reflective, symbolic attitude.

A beautiful book by Adamson (1990) shows page after page of intense, colorful images, deeply moving paintings, pottery, sculptures and wood carvings made by hospitalized psychiatric patients. Keyes (1983) offers a fine practical guide for therapists who wish to offer art materials in their work. In *Art as Medicine* Mcniff (1992) follows Jung's example by using his own pictures and inner experience to elucidate his methods.

Whitmont (1972) and Greene (1983) explore the links between body experience and psychological awareness. Fay (1977, 1996), Chodorow (1978, 1991), Whitehouse (1979), Keller (1972), Woodman (1982), McNeely

(1987), Wyman (1991), Oppikofer (1991), and Adorisio (1995) take up dance as a form of active imagination. Hall (1977), Bosnack (1986), Whitmont and Perera (1989), and Signell (1990) are among those who invite fantasy and enactment in their work with dreams.

In addition to Kalff (1980, see above p. 8), the Jungian literature on Sandplay includes Aite (1978), Bradway (1979, in press), Bradway et al. (1981), Stewart (1982), Weinribb (1983), Amman (1991), Ryce-Menuhin (1992), Mitchell and Friedman (1994).

Classic works that recognize the essential role of the arts in education include Read (1943) and Ashton-Warner (1971). A beautifully written study by Igoa (1995) is filled with the spirit of active imagination; she describes her work as a teacher in *The Inner World of the Immigrant Child*.

In closing, I am reminded that humans have always turned to the basic elements to express the imagination. In Jung's words: 'I had no choice but to return [...] and take up once more that child's life with his childish games' (Jung 1961, p. 174).

Joan Chodorow

Bibliography

Achterberg, J. (1985) *Imagery in Healing: Shamanism and modern medicine* (Boston and London: Shambhala).

Adamson, E. (1990) *Art as Healing* (Boston: Sigo Press).

Adler, G. (1961) *The Living Symbol: A case study in the process of individuation* (New York: Bollingen Foundation).

Adler, J. (1973) 'Integrity of body and psyche: Some notes on work in process,' in *What is Dance Therapy, Really?* ed. B. Govine and J. Chodorow (Columbia, Maryland: American Dance Therapy Association) 42–53.

—— (1995) *Arching Backward – The mystical initiation of a contemporary woman* (Rochester, VT.: Inner Traditions).

Adorisio, A. (1995) 'Il corpo e l'immaginazione attiva,' *Rivista di Psicologia Analitica* fascicolo n. 51: anno 26°, April, 161–80.

Aite, P. (1978) 'Ego and Image: Some observations on the theme of Sandplay,' *Journal of Analytical Psychology*, 23, 332–8.

Allan, J. (1988) *Inscapes of the Child's World* (Dallas: Spring Publications).

—— (1992) *Written Paths to Healing* (Dallas: Spring Publications).

Amman, R. (1991) *Healing and Transformation in Sandplay* (La Salle, Il.: Open Court).

Ashton-Warner, S. (1971) *Teacher* (New York: Bantham Books).

Assagioli, R. (1965) *Psychosynthesis* (New York: Viking Press).

Bosnak, R. (1986) *A Little Course in Dreams* (Boston: Shambhala, 1991).

Bradway, K. (1979) 'Sandplay in psychotherapy,' *Art Psychotherapy* 6, 85–93.

Bradway, K. (in press) *Sandplay: Silent Workshop of the Psyche* (London and New York: Routledge).

Bradway, K., Signell, K.A., Spare, G.H., Stewart, C.T., Stewart L.H. and Thompson C. (1981) *Sandplay Studies: Origins, theory, practice* (San Francisco: C. G. Jung Institute).

Casey, E. (1974) 'Toward an archetypal imagination,' *Spring*, 1–32.

Chodorow, J. (1978) 'Dance therapy and the transcendent function,' *American Journal of Dance Therapy* 2/1, 16–23.

—— (1982) 'Dance/movement and body experience in analysis,' in *Jungian Analysis*, ed. M. Stein. (Peru, Ill.: Open Court, second edition, 1995) 391–404.

—— (1991) *Dance Therapy and Depth Psychology – the moving imagination* (London/New York: Routledge).

Cwik, A. (1995) 'Active imagination: Synthesis in analysis,' in *Jungian Analysis*, ed. M. Stein (Peru, Ill.: Open Court, second edition, 1995) 137–69.

Dallett, J. (1982) 'Active imagination in practice,' in *Jungian Analysis* ed. M. Stein (La Salle: Open Court) 173–91.

Davidson, D. (1966) 'Transference as a form of active imagination,' *Journal of Analytical Psychology* 11/2, 135–46.

Dehing, J. (1992) 'The transcendent function: a critical re-evaluation,' in *Proceedings of the Twelfth International Congress for Analytical Psychology* ed. M. A. Mattoon (Einsiedeln, Switzerland: Daimon Verlag) 15–30.

Desoille, R. (1966) *The Directed Daydream* (New York: Psychosynthesis Research Foundation).

Dieckmann, H. (1979) 'Active imagination,' in *Methods in Analytical Psychology* (Wilmette, Ill.: Chiron Publications, 1991) 183–91.

Douglas, C. (1993) *Translate this Darkness: The life of Christiana Morgan* (New York: Simon & Schuster).

—— (1995) Personal communication.

Durand, G. (1971) 'Exploration of the imaginal,' *Spring*, 84–100.

Edinger, E. (1990) *The Living Psyche: A Jungian analysis in pictures* (Wilmette, Il.: Chiron Publications).

Erikson, E. (1963) *Childhood and Society* (New York: W. W. Norton & Co.).

Fay, C. G. (1977) 'Movement and Fantasy: A dance therapy model based on the psychology of Carl G. Jung,' Master's thesis, Goddard College, Plainfield, Vt.

—— (1996) 'At the threshold: A journey to the sacred through the integration of the psychology of C.G. Jung and the expressive arts, with Carolyn Grant Fay,' videotape (Boston: Bushy Theater, Inc.).

Fordham, M. (1956) 'Active imagination and imaginative activity,' *Journal of Analytical Psychology* 1/2, 207–8.

—— (1967) 'Active imagination – deintegration or disintegration?' *Journal of Analytical Psychology* 12/1, 51–65.

Franz, M.-L. von (1972) 'The journey to the beyond,' in *C. G. Jung: His myth in our time*, trans. W. H. Kennedy (New York: G. P. Putnam's Sons, 1975).

—— (1980) 'On active imagination,' in *Inward Journey: art as therapy* (La Salle and London: Open Court, 1983) 125–33.

Fry, R. T. (1974) 'Teaching active imagination meditation,' Doctoral dissertation, Laurence University, Goleta, Calif.

Greene, A. (1983) 'Giving the body its due', in *Quadrant*, 17/2, 9–24, 1984.

Hall, J. (1977) *Clinical use of Dreams: Jungian interpretations and enactments* (New York: Grune & Stratton).

Hannah, B. (1953) 'Some remarks on active imagination,' *Spring*, 38–58.

—— (1976) *Jung, his Life and Work: A biographical memoir* (New York: G. P. Putnam's Sons).

—— (1981) *Encounters with the Soul: Active imagination* (Santa Monica: Sigo Press).

Henderson, J. L. (1984) *Cultural Attitudes in Psychological Perspective* (Toronto: Inner City Books).

Hendricks, G. and Hendricks, K. (1993) *At the Speed of Life – a new approach to personal change through body centered therapy* (New York: Bantam Books).

Hillman, J. (1960) *Emotion: A comprehensive phenomenology of theories and their meanings for therapy* (Evanston: Northwestern University Press, 1972; first paperback edition, 1992).

—— (1983) *Healing Fiction* (Barrytown, New York: Station Hill Press).

Hull, R. F. C. (1971) 'Bibliographical notes on active imagination in the works of C. G. Jung,' *Spring*, 115–20.

Humbert, E. (1971) 'Active imagination: Theory and practice,' *Spring*, 101–14.

Igoa, C. (1995) *The Inner World of the Immigrant Child* (New York: St Martin's Press).

Jaffe, A. (1971/72) 'The creative phases in Jung's life,' in *Jung's Last Years and Other Essays* (Dallas, TX: Spring Publications, 1984).

—— (ed.) (1979) *C. G. Jung: Word and image* (Princeton: Princeton University Press).

Johnson, R. A. (1986) *Inner Work: Using dreams and active imagination for personal growth* (San Francisco: Harper & Row).

Jung, C. G. (1916) 'The structure of the unconscious' [on creative fantasies], *Collected Works*, vol. 7 (Princeton: Princeton University Press, 1953/1966; third printing, 1975) pars 490–91.

—— (1916/25) 'The seven sermons to the dead' [example of Jung's active imagination], in *Memories, Dreams, Reflections* (New York: Random House–Vintage Books, 1965) Appendix V.

—— (1916/58) 'The transcendent function,' *Collected Works*, vol. 8 (Princeton: Princeton University Press, 1975) 'Prefatory Note' and pars. 131–93.

—— (1917) 'The synthetic or constructive method' [transcendent function], *Collected works*, vol. 7 (Princeton: Princeton University Press, 1953/1966; third printing, 1975) par. 121.

—— (1921) *Psychological Types: Collected Works*, vol. 6 (Princeton: Princeton University Press, 1971, second printing, 1974) [Definition of fantasy, pars. 711–22; transcendent function, par. 184; symbol, pars. 827–28].

—— (1925) *Analytical Psychology: Notes on the seminar given in 1925*, ed. W. McGuire (Princeton: Princeton University Press, 1989) [Jung tells his experiences with active imagination].

—— (1928a) 'Anima and animus,' *Collected Works*, vol. 7 (Princeton: Princeton University Press, 1953/1966, third printing, 1975) 188–211 [Dialogue with anima, pars. 321–3].

—— (1928b) 'The technique of differentiation between the ego and the figures of the unconscious,' *Collected Works*, vol. 7 (Princeton: Princeton University Press, 1953/1966; third printing, 1975) pars. 341–73.

—— (1928–30) *Dream Analysis – notes of the seminar*, ed. Wm. McGuire (Princeton: Princeton University Press, 1984) [Patient danced her mandala painting for Jung, p. 304].

—— (1929) 'Commentary on *The Secret of the Golden Flower*', *Collected Works*, vol. 13 (Princeton: Princeton University Press, 1976) pars. 17–45.

—— (1930–34a) *Interpretation of Visions*, privately mimeographed seminar notes of Mary Foote, 1941.

—— (1930–34b) *The Visions Seminars*, from the complete notes of Mary Foote: Books One and Two (Zurich: Spring Publications, 1976).

—— (1930–34c) *The Visions Seminars*, ed. Claire Douglas (Princeton: Princeton University Press, forthcoming).

—— (1931) 'The aims of psychotherapy,' *Collected Works*, vol. 16 (Princeton: Princeton University Press, 1954/1966; third printing, 1975) pars. 66–113.

—— (1933/50) 'A study in the process of individuation,' *Collected Works*, vol. 9. 1 (Princeton: Princeton University Press, second edition, 1968) pars. 525–626.

—— (1934) 'A review of the complex theory,' *Collected Works*, vol. 8 (Princeton: Princeton University Press, 1975) 92–104.

—— (1934–39) *Nietzche's Zarathustra – Notes of the seminar*, ed. J. Jarrett, 2 vols (Princeton: Princeton University Press, 1988).

—— (1935) 'The Tavistock Lectures: On the theory and practice of analytical psychology,' *Collected Works*, vol. 18 (Princeton: Princeton University Press, 1976) [Active imagination, par. 4 and pars. 390–415].

—— (1935/59) 'Modern psychology: Notes on lectures given at the Eidgenössische Technische Hochschule, Zurich,' unpublished lecture notes [Active imagination: Lecture II, 10 May 1935, p. 207 (1959 edition); Lecture III, 17 May 1935, p. 208; Lecture V, 31 May 1935].

—— (1935/36) 'Individual dream symbolism in relation to alchemy,' *Psychology and Alchemy, Part II, Collected Works*, vol. 12 (Princeton: Princeton University

Press). [Jung amplifies a series of dreams and visions, pars. 44–331. Also see healing function of mandala, par. 123; alchemy and active imagination, pars. 37, 357, 448; Meditation and Imagination, pars. 390–96].

—— (1936a) 'The concept of the collective unconscious,' *Collected Works*, vol. 9. 1 (Princeton: Princeton University Press, second edition, 1968) [Active imagination, pars. 101, 110].

—— (1936b) 'Yoga and the west,' *Collected Works*, vol. 11 (Princeton: Princeton University Press, 1975) [Value of active imagination, par. 875].

—— (1937) 'On the "Rosarium Philosophorum",' *Collected Works*, vol. 18 (Princeton: Princeton University Press, 1976) 799–800 [par. 1787 and par. 1789].

—— (1938/54) 'The texts introducing the visions of Zosimos,' *Collected Works*, vol. 13 (Princeton: Princeton University Press, 1976) pars. 85–7.

—— (1940) 'The psychological aspects of the Kore,' *Collected Works*, vol. 9. 1 (Princeton: Princeton University Press, 1959/1969; fourth printing, 1975) [Example of a series of visions, pars. 319–34].

—— (1947) 'On the nature of the psyche,' *Collected Works*, vol. 8 (Princeton: Princeton University Press) [Active imagination, pars. 397–404].

—— (1950) 'Concerning mandala symbolism,' *Collected Works*, vol. 9. 1 (Princeton: Princeton University Press, 1959/1969; fourth printing, 1975).

—— (1951) *Aion, Collected Works*, vol. 9. 2 (Princeton: Princeton University Press, 1968).

—— (1955) *Mysterium Coniunctionis, Collected Works*, vol. 14 (Princeton: Princeton University Press, 1974).

—— (1957) 'Foreword' to Van Helsdingen, *Pictures from the Unconscious, Collected Works*, vol. 18, 530–31.

—— (1961) *Memories, Dreams, Reflections* (New York: Random House–Vintage Books, 1965).

—— (1906–50) *Letters*, vol. 1 (Princeton: Princeton University Press, 1973).

—— (1951–61) *Letters*, vol. 2 (Princeton: Princeton University Press, 1975).

Kalff, D. (1980) *Sandplay* (Santa Monica: Sigo Press).

Kast, V. (1988) *Imagination as Space of Freedom* (New York: Fromm International Publishing Co., 1993).

Keller, T. (1972) *Wege inneren Wachstums: Aus meinen erinnerungen an C. G. Jung* (Bircher-Benner Verlag: Erlenbach ZH und Bad Homburg vdH).

—— (1973) *Wege inneren Wachstums: Das Ja zu sich selber* (Bircher-Benner Verlag: Erlenbach ZH und Bad Homburg vdH).

—— (1974/75) *Wege inneren Wachstums: Persönliche Stellungnahme* (Bircher-Benner Verlag: Erlenbach ZH und Bad Homburg vdH).

—— (1977) *Wege inneren Wachstums: Ich möchte mich selbst werden* (Bircher-Benner Verlag: Erlenbach ZH und Bad Homburg vdH).

—— (1982) 'Beginnings of active imagination – analysis with C. G. Jung and Toni Wolff, 1915–1928,' *Spring*, 279–94.

Keyes, M. F. (1983) *Inward Journey – Art as therapy* (La Salle and London: Open Court).

Kirsch, J. (1955) '"Journey to the Moon": A study in active imagination,' in *Studien zur analytichen psychologie C. G. Jung*, vol. 1. (Zurich: Rascher).

Levy, F.J. (ed.) (1995) *Dance and Other Expressive Art Therapies* (London and New York: Routledge).

Lewis, P. (1993) *Creative Transformation: The healing power of the arts* (Wilmette, Ill.: Chiron Publications).

Lockhart, R. (1982) *Psyche Speaks* (Wilmette, Il.: Chiron Publications).

—— (1983) *Words as Eggs* (Dallas: Spring Publications).

McNeely, D.A. (1987) *Touching: Body therapy and depth psychology* (Toronto: Inner City Books).

McNiff, S. (1992) *Art as Medicine* (Boston and London: Shambhala).

Mahlendorf, U. (1973) 'Art therapy,' in *Man for Man* (Springfield, Ill.: Charles C. Thomas) 311–28.

Middlekoop, P. (1985) *The Wise Old Man: Healing through inner images* (Boston: Shambhala, 1988).

Mindell, A. (1985) *Working with the Dreambody* (Boston: Routledge & Kegan Paul).

Mitchell, R. R. and Friedman, H. S. (1994) *Sandplay: Past, present, and future* (London and New York: Routledge).

Oppikofer, R. (1991) 'Vom erleben der emotionen: Emotion und körperarbeit im therapeutischen prozess,' Diplomthesis am C.G. Jung Institute, Zurich.

Perera, S. B. (1981) *Descent to the Goddess* (Toronto: Inner City Books).

Powell, S. (1985) 'A bridge to understanding: The transcendent function in the analyst,' *Journal of Analytical Psychology* 30, 29–45.

Read, H. (1943) *Education through Art* (New York: Pantheon Books, 1956).

Rilke, R. M. (1903–8/1984) *Letters to a Young Poet*, trans. Stephen Mitchell (New York: Vintage Books, 1986).

Roberts, J. and Sutton-Smith, B. (1970) 'The cross-cultural and psychological study of games,' in *The Cross-Cultural Analysis of Games*, ed. G. Luschen (Champaign, Ill.: Stipes).

Rosen, D. (1993) *Transforming Depression: A Jungian approach using the creative arts* (New York and Los Angeles: Jeremy P. Tarcher and G. P. Putnam).

Ryce-Menuhin, J. (1992) *Jungian Sandplay: The wonderful therapy* (London and New York: Routledge).

Samuels, A. (1985) *Jung and the Post-Jungians* (London/New York: Routledge).

Sandner, D. (1992) 'The transcendent function – response to Jef Dehing,' in *Proceedings of the Twelfth International Congress for Analytical Psychology*, ed. M. A. Mattoon (Einsiedeln, Switzerland: Daimon Verlag) 31–7.

Schwartz-Salant, N. (1982) *Narcissism and Character Transformation* (Toronto: Inner City Books).

Signell, K.A. (1990) *Wisdom of the Heart* (New York: Bantam Books).

Singer, J. (1972) 'Dreaming the dream onward: Active imagination,' in *Boundaries of the Soul* (Garden City, NY: Doubleday & Co., Inc., second edition, 1994).

Stein, M. (1984) 'Power, shamanism, and maieutics in the countertransference,' in *Transference/countertransference*, ed. N. Schwartz-Salant and M. Stein (Wilmette, Ill.: Chiron Publications) 67–87.

Stevens, A. (1986) *Withymead: A Jungian community for the healing arts* (London: Coventure).

Stewart, C. T. (1981) 'Developmental psychology of sandplay,' in *Sandplay Studies: Origins, theory and practice*, ed. G. Hill (San Francisco: C. G. Jung Institute of San Francisco) 39–92.

Stewart, L. H. (1982) 'Sandplay and Jungian analysis,' in *Jungian Analysis*, ed. M. Stein (La Salle: Open Court Publishing Co., second edition, 1995) 372–90.

—— (1986) 'Work in progress: Affect and archetype,' in *The Body in Analysis,* ed. N. Schwartz-Salant and Stein, M. (Wilmette, Ill.: Chiron Publications) 183–203.

—— (1987a) 'A brief report: Affect and archetype,' *Journal of Analytical Psychology* 32/1, 35–46.

—— (1987b) 'Affect and archetype in analysis,' in *Archetypal Processes in Psychotherapy*, ed. N. Schwartz-Salant and M. Stein (Wilmette: Ill.: Chiron Publications) 131–62.

—— (1992) *Changemakers: A Jungian perspective on sibling position and the family atmosphere* (London and New York: Routledge, Chapman & Hall).

Tilly, M. (1982) 'Margaret Tilly,' in *C. G. Jung, Emma Jung and Toni Wolff: A collection of remembrances*, ed. F. Jensen (San Francisco: The Analytical Psychology Club).

Van der Post, L. (1975) *Jung and the Story of our Time* (New York: Vintage Books).

Watkins, M. (1976) *Waking Dreams* (New York: Harper & Row, 1977).

—— (1981) 'Six approaches to the image in art therapy,' *Spring* 107–25.

Weaver, R. (1973) *The Old Wise Woman: A study of active imagination* (Boston: Shambhala, 1991).

Wehr, G. (1988) *Jung: A biography*, trans. D. M. Weeks (Boston: Shambhala).

—— (1989) *An Illustrated Biography of C. G. Jung* (Boston: Shambhala).

Weinribb, E. (1983) *Images of the Self* (Boston: Sigo Press).

Whitehouse, M. (1968) 'Reflections on a metamorphosis,' in *A Well of Living Waters – Festschrift for Hilda Kirsch*, ed. R. Head, et al. (Los Angeles: C. G. Jung Institute, 1977) 272–7.

—— (1979) 'C. G. Jung and dance therapy,' in *Eight Theoretical Approaches in Dance-Movement Therapy,* ed. P. Lewis Bernstein (Dubuque: Kendall/Hunt) 51–70.

Whitmont, E. (1972) 'Body experience and psychological awareness,' *Quadrant* 12, 5–16.

Whitmont, E. C. and Perera, S. B. (1989) *Dreams: A portal to the source* (London and New York: Routledge).

Winnicott, D. W. (1971) *Playing and Reality* (New York: Basic Books).

Woodman, M. (1982) *Addiction to Perfection* (Toronto: Inner City Books).

Wyman, W. (1991) 'The body as a manifestation of unconscious experience,' Unpublished.

Zeller, M. (1982) 'Max Zeller,' in *C. G. Jung, Emma Jung and Toni Wolff: A collection of remembrances*, ed. F. Jensen (San Francisco: The Analytical Psychology Club) 108–10.

List of fantasies and visions

in order of presentation

FROM INTRODUCTION

Jung's building game, placing the alter stone inside the miniature church, p. 2

Jung's voluntary descents, p. 2

Woman squeezes and kneads clay until the figures arise of child and mother, pp. 7–8

Woman sculpts an open, stretched out figure, interweaving movement and sculpture, p. 9

Rilke's description of dialogue with inner critic, p. 11

Jung's patient (Miss X) painted her fantasy of being stuck in a block of rock and then painted the act of liberation, pp. 13–14

Country girl's spirit returns through singing and dancing with Jung, p. 15

Woman patient drew a mandala and then danced it; Jung is analyst-witness, p. 16

Woman discovered she could dance a feeling that had no words; Toni Wolff is analyst-witness, p. 16

FROM CHAPTER 1

Jung's fantasies: Something is dead, but also still alive, pp. 22–23

Jung's building game, pp. 23–25

Jung's vision: Flood covers Europe, pp. 24–25

Jung's fantasy: Fountain of blood in cave, p. 27

Jung's fantasies: Steep descents, Elijah, Salome and the snake, pp. 28–29

Jung painted his dream of old man with keys, horns, and wings, pp. 29–30

Jung's continuing inner dialogues with Philemon and Ka, pp. 30–31

Jung's fantasy: Voice of a woman saying his writing is art, pp. 31–33

Jung's Black Book and Red Book, p. 33

Jung's "Seven Sermons," conversations with the dead, pp. 34–36

"The Picture of a Fisherman" a drawing by Jung's nine year old son, pp. 34–35

Jung's soul flies away, p. 35

Mandala drawings, pp. 38–39

FROM CHAPTER 3

Man watches fiancée drown, p. 62, par. 343
Woman ascends in blue flame, p. 69, par. 366

FROM CHAPTER 4

Mandala drawings, pp. 77–79, pars. 31, 36
Mandala dance, p. 78, par. 32
Vision of light reported by Edward Maitland, pp. 80–81, par. 40
Vision of light reported by Hildegard of Bingen, pp. 81–82, par. 42

FROM CHAPTER 6

Fantasy images in 19 paintings by Miss X (many mandala drawings), pp.
    97–142, pars. 525–626
Lightning strikes, sketch, p. 110

FROM CHAPTER 7

Artist has fantasy about poster, p. 143–144, pars. 392–395
Jung as child: Concentrated on picture of grandfather, p. 145, par. 397
Man wrote down 1300 dreams and visions and began to draw them, pp. 146–
    148, pars. 402–406. (Also see Part II of *Psychology and Alchemy*, CW 12)
Drawings of containers with breaking lines, pp. 148–152 pars. 407–412

FROM CHAPTER 8

Vision: White bird lights on blue-clad mother figure, p. 155, par. 321
Painted mother figure, p. 155, par 322
Vision: Maiden on white bull; ritual with child, p. 155, par. 323
Vision: Dances, descent, rape, p. 155, par. 325
Vision: Youth dances and sinks into lap of mother figure, p. 156. par. 327
Vision: Sacrifice of sheep, p. 156, par. 329
Vision: X enters den of snakes, p. 156, par. 330
Vision: Earth Mother kisses X and hands her to many men, p. 156, par. 331
Vision: X emerges from depths, illumination, p. 156, par. 333

FROM CHAPTER 10

Mr O's vision of Beatrice, p. 165

FROM CHAPTER 12

Series of pictures of pullulating vegetation and fear-haunted tropical nights,
    p. 175, par. 1253

Subject index

abstract images *see* symbols
accoustic emotional expression 159; *see also* music *and* verbal
action 10, 126
active fantasy *see* active imagination *and* fantasy
active imagination 6, 42, 54, 135, 154: advantages of 146; application of 164; and consciousness 10; dangers of 12, 155, 173 (*see also* psychosis); definition 145, 178; in diagnosis 14, 153; discovery of 1; dreams and 4, 7, 16, 17, 161, 179; form of 2–4, 7–11; healing and 14, 18, 147–8, 153, 155, 160, 177, 178; methods of 5, 7, 8, 10, 11, 143, 144 (*see also* specific methods); as natural process 3, 13; reinvention of 147; role of analyst 13–17, 163; stages of 10–11; transference as 15, 178; and unconscious 10; *see also* fantasy *and* imagination
adaptation, social *see* personality adjustment
adjustment *see* personality adjustment
aesthetic 12, 16, 40, 42, 76, 98, 130, 173; formulation 12, 55–8
affects *see* emotions
air, symbolism of 108, 113
alchemy, philosophical 19, 31, 34, 67, 69, 70, 77, 104, 106–7, 117, 123, 168, 170, 174
amplification, symbolic 12, 14, 18, 161, 178; *see also* reason
analysis *see* psychotherapy
analyst: liberation from 13; as mediator 14–16; role in active imagination 13–17, 163; as witness 16–17

ancestors, role in unconscious 35–6
anger 37, 136, 147
anima/animus 29, 32, 33, 61, 66, 70, 97, 98, 105, 108, 111, 118, 152, 156, 165
anthropos 101, 107–8
anticlockwise *see* leftward
application, of insight 10–11, 43, 164; *see also* moral obligation *and* self knowledge *and* understanding
approval 167
archeology *see* history
archetypes 3, 23, 26, 35, 120, 127, 135, 136, 146, 148, 150, 154, 178; dream 106, 136, 147–8, 154; interpretation 161; *see also* fantasy
art: fantasy as 31–3, 38; therapy 1, 93–4, 177–8; *see also* drawing *and* painting
artistic: emotional expression 1, 2, 4, 7–9, 15–17, 19, 54, 57, 78, 92–4, 98, 122, 135, 146–7, 155, 159, 173, 177, 179; formulation *see* aesthetic formulation
assertion, self 85
assimilation *see* transcendent function
association 164; dream 90; free 42, 53, 56, 92; word 143
astrology, symbolism of 152
attitude *see* personality development
audio-verbal *see* verbal
auseinandersetzung 10, 11, 58, 59, 163, 167
awareness: psychological 178; unconscious 11

balance: aesthetic/scientific 12; conscious/unconscious 4, 10, 14, 33,

44–5, 47, 51, 56, 57, 60, 63, 166, 168, 174; symbolism of 104, 126, 151; *see also* one-sidedness
ball, symbolism of 155–6; *see also* sphere
beauty 12, 16, 40; *see also* aesthetic
behaviour patterns 158–9, 162
being, inner *see* self
betrachten see looking
bible 28–9; *see also* God *and* religion
'big' *see* archetype
bird, symbolism of 118
black *see* darkness; *see also* depression
blue, symbolism of 108, 113, 115, 119; *see also* colour
body: movement *see* movement; and psychological awareness 178
breaking lines 149–50, 152
breath, symbolism of 108
brown, symbolism of 119
Buddhism 42, 78, 112, 117, 119, 121–3, 150, 152

caelum 19, 166, 174
Cancer *see* astrology *and* crab
carving *see* sculpting
caution 125
censorship *see* repression
centre 39, 40, 95, 126, 151, 160 nb spelling varies from Amer/Eng on different pages
ceremony *see* ritual
changeability 136, 137
changes, attitude *see* personality adjustment *and* individuation
chaos 160, 168
child sacrifice 155; *see also* ritual
childhood 1, 179; psychological 93; *see also* fantasy *and* play
childlessness 118
Chinese 18, 19, 38, 76, 124
Christian symbolism 120, 122, 123
chthonic principle 111, 114, 118, 119, 125, 156
circle, symbolism of 114, 150, 151, 160; *see also* mandala *and* sphere
circulation 80
clay *see* modelling
climax, life 106, 126
clockwise *see* rightward
collective: psyche 84; unconscious 71,

82, 95, 104
colour: unconscious symbolism of 101–2, 104–5, 107–9, 112–19, 127; use of 13, 95, 100, 114; *see also* specific colours
compensation 167
complete *see* wholeness; *see also* spiritual man
complexes 12, 42; emotional 3, 4; transformation of 61; *see also* neurosis
comprehension *see* understanding
concentration 7, 145, 169; *see also* meditation
concretization, of fantasy 65
confidence 134; self 174
conflict: conscious/unconscious 166–7 (*see also* opposites); emotional 4, 15, 46, 71, 123; pathology of 74; *see also* personality adjustment
conscious: intention 145; way 77; *see also* meditation
consciousness 2, 33, 80; and active-imagination 10; complementing unconsciousness 4, 6, 10, 14, 33, 43–5, 47, 51, 56, 57, 60, 63, 66, 166, 168, 174 (*see also* transcendent function); differentiation of 112–13, 119–20, 126; directedness of 43; and fantasy 74–5, 154; freeing of 115; functions of 103, 113, 119; and instinct 159; intention 145; and life 77, 79; light of 115; multiple 130; over-valuing 4, 94; and psyche 158; realization of 106; relativism of 158; structure of 43; switching off 75; threshold of 43, 44, 47, 56; waking 155; weakening of 43, 135, 155; widening of 60, 66, 73, 82, 112, 118; *see also* ego
constructive method 12, 48
container *see* vessel
contemplation *see* meditation
continuity *see* directedness
contradictions, of psyche 108, 123, 158, 167
cortices *see* skin
counter-position *see* opposites *and* unconscious
crab, symbolism of 125
creative: formulation 12, 55–8; imagination 6, 17, 91
creativity 5; and fantasy 91
crisis, emotions of 6, 19; *see also* fear

and anger *and* sadness *and* disgust *and* humiliation
critical faculties *see* reason
cross, symbolism of 116, 120
cultural symbols *see* symbols
cure, analysis as *see* healing *and* personality adjustment
cynicism 166

dance, as emotional expression 7, 8, 15, 16, 78, 122, 146, 159, 179
darkness 39, 40, 79; fear of 121; of spirit *see* depression; symbolism of 102, 107, 109, 112, 115–20, 152, 160; *see also* unconscious
dead *see* ancestors; *see also* resurrection
death, obsession with 2, 22–3, 27, 35; and unconscious 35
defense *see* skin
definiteness *see* directedness
depression 7, 53, 62, 63, 64, 66, 109, 110, 114, 168; *see also* neurosis *and* psychosis
descent 2, 28; *see also* active imagination *and* unconscious
desperation 66
development, psychic *see* individuation
devil *see* evil
diagnosis: active imagination as 14, 153; painting as 14, 149–50
dialectical method *see* active imagination
dialogue, conscious/unconscious 167, 172; *see also* transcendent function
differentiation 61–72; of consciousness 112–13, 119–20, 126; *see also* active imagination
directedness 43–5, 51
disgust 28
disorientation 21, 23
divinity *see* God
division *see* differentiation
dominants *see* regulators
dragon, symbolism of 107–8, 174
drama, as emotional expression 1, 4, 5–6, 8, 10, 15, 16, 159
drawing, as emotional expression 2, 7–9, 57, 92, 146–7, 155, 159, 173
dreams: and active imagination 4, 7, 16, 17, 161, 179; analysis 143, 147; archetypal 106, 136, 147–8, 154; association 90; and fantasy 155; function of 159; image 159; interpretation 21, 28, 45, 49, 148;

and mythology 89–90; and psychotherapy 88–9; terrifying 2; and unconscious 21, 22, 25, 45, 49,
dropping down *see* descent
duality *see* opposites
duplication 126

earth, symbolism of 98, 106–8, 127; *see also* sphere
earth mother 156; *see also* maternal
East 175
eggs, symbolism of 100, 104; *see also* sphere
ego 3, 12, 103, 158; relinquishing 111–12; role of 112; and self 94, 106; strengthening 135; and unconscious 57, 58, 59, 95, 135; universality of 111; *see also* consciousness
emotionally toned complex *see* complex
emotions 3; artistic expression of 1, 2, 4, 7–9, 15–17, 19, 54, 57, 78, 92–4, 98, 122, 135, 146–7, 155, 159, 173, 177, 179; conflicting 4, 15, 46, 123; experiencing 119; and images 2, 7, 26; and imagination 178; of life-enhancement 19; as object 73; unconscious 56–8; emotional dysfunction 4, 177; *see also* crisis
empathic imagination *see* relationship
enantiodromia 130, 132
energy: disposable 158; divine 150; law of 63; psychic 4, 6, 53, 168; tension 49, 50, 168
enthusiasm 122
erotic, in mythology 29
ethics *see* morals
ethnology *see* history *and* mythology
European 175
evaluation, critical 6, 10, 11, 26–7, 33, 74–5; symbolic 48; *see also* reason *and* understanding
evil, principle of 114
exercises *see* active imagination
experiment, with unconscious 26–8
expression: artistic 2; emotional 2; form of 2, 3, 4, 7–10; symbolic 2
eyes, symbolism of 101, 103, 110, 111, 120, 130, 172

faith 174; *see also* religion
fantasy 2, 5–6, 24–5, 62, 69, 81, 91, 135, 154; as art 31–3, 38; audio-verbal 8, 54, 155; biblical 28–9;

concretization of 65; and creativity
91; critical evaluation of 6, 26, 27,
74, 75; definition of 144–5; and
dreaming 155; fear of 65;
hypnagogic 144; image 98; and
instinct 91; light in 79–82; passive 6;
sexual 118; objective observation of
74, 154; repression of 74–5, 154;
symbolic 79, 80, 81; transformation
of 98–132, 149–52, 167, 170, 172
(*see also* individuation); unconscious
10, 61, 63–6, 70, 79, 100, 154;
uncontrollable 173–4; use of 13–14,
50, 53, 144; *see also* active
imagination *and* archetype *and*
imagination
father *see* paternal
fear 2, 26–8, 30, 34–5, 37, 173, 175;
of darkness 121; of fantasy 65
feeling, as function of consciousness:
113, 119
feminine 125, 152
fire, symbolism of 110, 130
firmament 174
flash *see* lightening
foresight 125
form, imagination 2–4, 7–11;
unconscious 56–7
free association 42, 53, 56, 92
freeing *see* releasing
fright *see* fear

games *see* play
ghosts *see* haunting
globe *see* sphere
goat, symbolism of 122, 125
God 104, 136, 137, 144; four spirits of
120; image 166, 169; symbols of
120, 137, 150; *see also* religion *and*
Tao
gold, symbolism of 101, 102, 104, 105,
107, 108, 109, 116, 127
Golden Flower 10, 39, 73–83, 135
green, symbolism of 114
growth: psychic *see* individuation; and
play 178
guru 30, 31

hallucination *see* fantasy
harmony 152
haunting 34–5
healing: and active imagination 14, 18,
147–8, 153, 155, 160, 176–8;
through art 1, 93–4, 177–8; through

dream interpretation 88–9; through
music 177; non-directive 13; through
play 5–6; of psychic pain 6; self 1, 4,
150; and symbols 178; through
transcendent function 176
heaven 71; inner 174; light of 77, 78;
see also religion
history, and unconscious symbolism 14,
90, 95, 146, 158, 160; *see also*
mythology
holy *see* religion
horoscope *see* astrology
human nature 80
humiliation 23, 32
hypnagogic fantasies 144

I Ching 122–4
identification, unconscious 2, 135
archetypal 135
ideogram, unconscious 135
idols 152 *see also* God *and* religion
illumination *see* light
illusion 95, 96
image: and emotion 2, 7, 26; and form
8; of instinct 158–9; mythological
14, 21, 60, 156; obscene 118; of soul
101–2, 121, 124; unconscious 21–36,
108, 135
imagination 5–6; creative 6, 17, 91;
empathic 178; motor 8; religious
178; *see also* active
imagination *and* fantasy
imaginative activity 6, 178
impersonal 101, 103
imprisonment 98; *see also* releasing
independence, psychological 94
indicium 87
individuation: process of 4, 17, 18, 39,
71, 73–4, 77, 82, 91, 106, 111, 114,
123, 132–4, 136, 137, 146, 148, 159,
164, 166, 172; role of symbols 82; as
transformation 100; *see also* self
knowledge *and* transformation *and*
wholeness
inferior function 103
inferiority, sense of 85
inside 115
insight *see* understanding
instinct 103, 158, 161–2; and fantasy
91; image of 158–9; loss of 51, 52,
59, 134; relation to 175
integration, conscious/unconscious *see*
transcendent function *and* wholeness
intention, conscious 145

interest 6
interference, unconscious 50, 51
interpretation *see* understanding
introspection *see* active imagination
    and fantasy *and* meditation
introversion *see* active imagination
intuition, as function of consciousness
    103, 113, 119
irrationality 91, 95; *see also* reason

joy 6, 19, 136
judgement, attitude of 173–4; *see also*
    understanding

kinship *see* relationship 178
knowledge 134; representation in myth
    29; self 17, 45, 60, 169, 174, 177

lamp *see* light
leftward movement 112–14, 119, 126
'letting go' 111, 112
liberation *see* releasing; *see also*
    imprisonment
libido 3, 63, 66; loss of 88
life: devotion to 79;-enhancement 19;
    meaning of 93
light: of heaven 77–8; inner 117;
    symbolism of 103, 106, 112, 116,
    119, 120, 121, 126, 160; vision of
    79, 80, 81, 82; *see also* light
lightening, symbolism of 101–5, 109
linguistic *see* verbal
living *see* application
logic *see* reason
loneliness 117, 147, 148
looking, psychological 7, 10, 145; *see also*
    meditation
lotus, symbolism of 117

magic, as projection of psyche 79, 152,
    176; symbolism of 98–9, 101, 107,
    112, 150–51
magician 99, 101, 102, 107
maiden, symbolism of 155
mandala 8, 14, 18, 33, 38, 39, 78–9, 82,
    110, 111, 114, 117, 119, 120, 122–7,
    136, 150; inner processes of 135; as
    symbol of God 137, 150; as symbol
    of self 104, 130, 174
marriage, symbolism of 130
masculine *see* animus
materialistic attitude 87
maternal principle 99, 118, 155
matter, in relation to spirit 108

maturity, psychological 94, 146;
    see also individuation *and*
    wholeness
meaning, of life 93; *see also*
    understanding
meditation 2, 4, 77, 111, 164, 168, 169;
    see also active imagination *and*
    looking *and* unconscious
medium *see* form
melancholia *see* depression
mental picture *see* fantasy *and*
    imagination
mercury *see* Mercury *and* quicksilver
metaphysics, unconscious 89–90; *see
    also* philosophy
microcosm 174
mid-point, of personality 68–9
mind 108
mirroring 12, 14, 17
modelling 9, 54, 57, 146, 155, 159,
    173; *see also* sculpting
mood, visualized 7, 53, 54, 64,
    167
moon, symbolism of 104, 124, 125,
    127, 152
moral, obligation 10, 11, 36, 43, 56, 95;
    see also application
mother *see* maternal
motor imagination 8
movement: as emotional expression 4,
    8, 9, 17, 54; leftward 112–14, 119,
    126; rightward 112–16, 151; *see also*
    circulation *and* dance
multiplicity, chaotic 160
music: as emotional expression 4, 8, 15,
    122, 173; therapy 1, 177
mythology: in dreams 89, 90; erotic
    representation 29; images of 14, 21,
    60, 156; recognition of 171;
    symbolism 29, 89–90, 100; and
    unconscious 21, 160; *see also* history

narcissism 169
nature, as maternal principle 118
negative: feelings 63; of unconscious
    see opposites
neuroses 58, 61, 66, 84, 86, 92, 153,
    166, 170; brought to consciousness
    176; *see also* depression
night *see* darkness
nightmares *see* dreams
nodal points 106
normalization, of personality *see*
    healing *and* personality

nous *see* mind *and* reason

objectivity 30, 74, 154
obscene, images 118
one *see* wholeness
one-sidedness 59, 63, 66, 88, 146, 147;
    see also balance
opening, to unconscious 11
opposites: conflict of 81, 166–7; uniting
    see transcendent function
order 160
other 68, 167; denial of 58
outgrowing *see* individuation
outside 115

pain: of unconscious content 56; *see
    also* healing
painting; as diagnosis 14; as emotional
    expression 2, 7, 8, 19, 57, 92–4, 98,
    135, 146, 147, 155, 159, 173, 177
paradox *see* contradictions
paternal principle 97, 118
path *see* way
pathology: of conflict 74; psychic *see*
    neurosis *and* psychosis; *see also*
    healing
Persona 3
personality: adjustment 45–6, 61, 94,
    147; creation of 17; development *see*
    individuation; enrichment 75; mid-
    point of 68; synthesis of 166, 169;
    transformation of 58, 66–9, 112; true
    106; *see also* self *and* transcendent
    function *and* wholeness
personification, of unconscious 32, 70,
    152, 165
phallus *see* sexual symbolism
phantasmagoria 12, 42, 175
philosophic *see* reason
philosophy, medieval 147; *see also*
    alchemy
picture method *see* active imagination;
    see also painting *and* drawing
pink, symbolism of 119
play 5–6, 179; dramatic 5; and ego
    development 178; healing power of
    5, 6; humanity and 91; Jung and
    23–4; and repression 5; symbolic 1,
    2, 4, 5, 6
pneumatic symbol 108, 111, 113, 130
points, symbolism of 104; *see also*
    pushing upwards
polarity *see* opposites
polyopthalmia *see* eyes

possession, unconscious 70
pride 164
primitive, psychology 90; *see also*
    history
projection 147, 169, 175
providence *see* Tao
psyche: collective 84; and
    consciousness 158; energy 4, 6, 53,
    168; and evolutionary history 158;
    nature of 158
psychoanalysis *see* psychotherapy
psychodrama *see* drama
psychology: analytical 3, 178;
    archetypal 178; classical 178;
    developmental 178; primitive 90
psychosis 25, 26, 33, 43, 44, 57, 70, 75,
    134–5, 149–50, 153, 169, 174; latent
    155, 173;. and unconscious 25, 33
psychotherapy: dream 88–9; getting
    stuck 88, 98; non-directive 13; and
    unconscious 61; *see also* healing
pushing upwards 104, 123

quaternity 113, 114, 119, 120, 127, 130,
    136, 160
quicksilver, symbolism of 105, 107,
    108, 110, 111, 127

rainbow *see* colour
Rainmaker 19–20
rationality *see* reason
readjustment *see* personality adjustment
reality 65, 66, 167
reason 12, 14, 95, 103, 105, 108, 167,
    178; conscious 113, 119; failure of
    166; limitations of 92; suspension of
    6, 10, 54; symbolism 100; inability
    to 143
receptacle *see* vessel
red, symbolism of 108, 114, 115, 118
redeeming 103
reductive method 12
regression 133
regulators, unconscious 160–61
rejection 175
relationship 178; empathic 178;
    personal 101, 103, 123
releasing 98, 100, 102–3
reliability *see* directedness
religion 2; importance to psyche 92,
    134, 153, 168; and imagination 178;
    symbolism 14, 90, 95, 120, 122–3,
    134, 137, 150; *see also* bible *and* God
repression 86, 175; conscious 43, 154,

155; of fantasy 74–5, 154; and play 5; unconscious 44–5, 56, 103, 166, 169

resentment 166–7

resurrection, of dead 136

reversal, process of 77

rhythm 178

rightward movement 112, 114, 115, 116, 151

ritual 8, 11, 155, 178

rock *see* stone

rotundum *see* sphere

'round and square' 104, 107; *see also* sphere

round form *see* circle *and* sphere

sacred 152

sadness: and grief 28, 136; *see also* depression

sandplay, as emotional expression 1, 8, 17, 179

schizophrenia *see* psychosis

scholarly elucidation *see* reason

scientific *see* reason

sculpting 4, 7, 8, 9, 177; *see also* modelling

Secret of the Golden Flower *see* Golden Flower

self 3, 5, 39, 94, 103; confidence 174; development *see* individuation; expression 125; as God 169; -healing 1, 4, 150; influence of 120; knowledge 17, 45, 60, 169, 174, 177; nature of *see* personality; -pity 118; -reflection 9, 10, 12, 15, 168, 178 (*see also* meditation); restraint 122; symbolism of 104, 108, 130, 174; totality of *see* wholeness; *see also* ego

sensation, as function of consciousness: 113, 119; type 103

sexual: attitudes 84, 118; fantasy 118; symbolism 99, 109–11, 117, 118, 127

shadow, unconscious 3, 166–8; *see* darkness *and* evil; *see also* opposites

shape *see* form

silver *see* quicksilver

skin, symbolism of 117, 120, 121

snake, symbolism of 29, 105–11, 114, 116, 118, 125, 127, 130, 152, 156

society *see* relationship

songs *see* music

soul 32, 35, 71; images of 101–2, 121, 124; union with spirit 168

spermatozoa *see* sexual symbolism 127

sphere: division of 112; symbolism of 101, 102, 104, 106–8, 110, 112, 152, 160; *see also* mandala

spirit: identification with 118; as paternal principle 118; in relation to matter 108; symbolism of 118; union with soul 168

spiritual: attitude 87; man 100; relation to unconscious 59, 111

stability, of psyche 44

stone, symbolism of 102, 103, 108

'stuck, getting' in psychotherapy 88, 98

substantia coelestis see transcendent 170

suffering 116, 126

suggestion 90

sun, symbolism of 125, 127

sunshine *see* light

suppression *see* repression

swastika, symbolism of 112, 114, 116

symbolic: amplification 12, 14, 18, 161, 178; enactment 8; expression *see* form; evaluation 48; interpretation 14, 96, 147; perspective 15, 177; play 1, 2, 4–6

symbolism: of air 108, 113; of astrology 125, 152; of balance 104, 126, 151; of ball 155–6; of bird 118; of breath 108; of circle 114, 150, 151, 160; of colour 101–2, 104–5, 107–9, 112–19, 127; of cross 116, 120; of darkness 102, 107, 109, 112, 115–20, 152, 160; of dragon 107–8, 174; of earth 98, 106–8, 127; of eggs 100, 104; erotic 29; of eyes 101, 103, 110, 111, 120, 130, 172; of fire 110, 130; of goat 122, 125; historical 14, 90, 95, 146, 158, 160; of knowledge 29; of light 103, 106, 112, 116, 119–21, 126, 160; of lightening 101–5, 109; of lotus 117; of magic 98–9, 101, 107, 112, 150–51; of maiden 155; of marriage 130; of moon 104, 124–5, 127, 152; mythological 29, 89–90; of play 1, 2, 4–6; pneumatic 108, 111, 113, 130; of points 104; primitive 95; of pushing upward 104, 123; of reason 100; religious 14, 90, 95, 120, 122–3, 134, 137, 150; of self 104, 108, 130, 174; of skin 117, 120, 121; of snake 29, 105–11, 114, 116, 118, 125, 127, 130, 152, 156; of sphere 101–2, 104, 106–8, 110, 112, 152,

160; of spirit 118; of stone 102–3, 108; of sun 125, 127; of swastika 112, 114, 116; of symmetry 152; of tree 115, 118, 120; of vessel 149–52; of water 114, 125; of wind 108
symbols: abstract 14, 18, 77–8, 82; cultural 14; and fantasy 79, 80, 81; healing power of 178; and individuation 82
symmetry, symbolism of 152
synthesis *see* transcendent function *and* wholeness
Syzygy 3, 156; *see also* anima/animus

Tao, concept of 18, 68, 76, 77, 78, 79, 80, 122, 123, 126
tension, emotional 4, 25, 49, 50, 168; of opposites 81, 166–7; resolution of 28, 168, (*see also* transcendent function)
terror *see* fear
therapy *see* healing
thinking *see* reason; *see also* understanding
threshold conscious/unconscious 43, 44, 47, 56
totality *see* wholeness
tradition *see* history *and* mythology
trancing *see* active imagination *and* fantasy
transcendent function 2, 4–5, 10, 11, 14–16, 18, 43, 47–50, 53, 56, 57, 59, 60, 66–7, 69, 70, 73–7, 95–6, 112–13, 115, 122–6, 133–6, 158, 160, 162, 165–70, 172, 174, 176–7; *see also* active imagination *and* wholeness
transference 4, 15, 47, 61, 86, 130, 171; as active imagination 15, 178
transformation 61, 100: fantasy 98–132, 148–52, 167, 170, 172; *see also* individuation *and* personality adjustment
transience 123
tree, symbolism of 115, 118, 120
true *see* wholeness
trust 134, 174
truth 60, 125, 166

unconscious: acceptance 10, 11, 42, 58, 59, 70; analysis 61; archaic vestiges 4, 21, 35, 36, 158, 160–61, (*see also* history *and* mythology); collective 4, 71, 82, 95, 104; complementing

consciousness 4, 6, 10, 14, 33, 43–5, 47, 51, 56–8, 60, 63, 77, 166, 168, 174, (*see also* transcendent function); confronting 4, 6, 10–12, 17, 18, 21–41, 50, 58, 61, 65, 100, 143, 152, 168; and death 35; defensiveness of 133; descent 2, 28; dreams 21, 22, 25, 45, 49; emotions 56–8; experiment with 26–8; fantasy 10, 21–36 61, 63–6, 70, 79, 100, 108, 135, 154; form 56–7; identification 2, 135; impulses 23; interference 50, 51; metaphysics 89–90; as multiple consciousness 130; negative aspects of 56, 70; over-valuing 55; personification of 32, 70, 152, 165; power of 12, 45, 61, 63–4, 66, 70, 98–100, 151, 160; projection 147, 169; and psychosis 25, 33; regulating influence of 50, 51, 52, 53, 57, 160, 161; releasing 98, 100, 102–3; repression 44–5, 56, 103, 166, 169; shadow 3, 166–8; and spirit 59, 111; structure 43, 143; symbolism *see* symbolism; synthesis 2, 67, 69, 70, 96, 112, 113, 133–5, 158, 162, 166–7, 172, 174, 176; under-valuing 4, 43, 55, 63, 175; unfolding 98–132, 148–52, 167, 170, 172; as underworld 152, 175; as unknown 42
understanding 10–12, 14, 33, 36, 55–7, 58, 61–3, 95, 132, 134–5, 146, 147, 148, 160, 161, 164, 172; application of 10–11, 43, 164; of archetypes 161; crude 111; dreams 21, 28, 45, 49, 148; and formulation 12; representation in myth 30; symbolic 14, 96, 147; *see also* reason *and* self knowledge *and* transcendent function
underworld 152, 175
unio mentalis see self knowledge
union, of spirit and soul 168
unity *see* transcendent function *and* wholeness
universality, of experience 91; *see also* collective unconscious
unknown, unconscious as 42
usefulness, social 94

verbal/non-verbal medium 8, 9; fantasy 8, 54, 155
vessel, symbolism of 149–52
visioning *see* active imagination
visions *see* fantasy

water, symbolism of 114, 125
way, conscious 77; of Tao 76, 126; *see also* individuation
weaving, as emotional expression 8, 146
wholeness, psychic 5, 59, 79, 82, 103–4, 106–7, 134, 137, 156, 164, 168, 172; *see also* individuation *and* transcendent function
will power 145; *see also* ego
wind, symbolism of 108
wood *see* sculpting

word association method 143
world *see* earth
writing, as emotional expression 2, 4, 7, 8, 54, 146
wu wei 10, 18, 74

yang and yin 80, 124
yellow, symbolism of 119
yoga 25–6, 111

Zen *see* Buddhism
zodiac *see* astrology

I am empty
I do not exist

Do I exist by doing or being
I am nothing

Doing or Being, I am loneliness, Thought,
which prefers and manufacture
I sit in nothing being nothing
but every activity motion

Name index

Adamson, E. 178
Adler, A. 18, 85, 86
Adler, G. 177
Adler, J. 180
Adorisio, A. 179
Agni x
Aite, P. 179
Allan, J. 5, 177
Amman, R. 179
Ashton-Warner, S. 179

Bach, J.S. 173
Bennet, Dr. 18, 148
Böhme, J. 78, 117, 120, 123
Bosch, H. 175
Bosnack, R. 179
Bradway, K. 179
Buddha see Buddhism

Casey, E. 177
Chodorow, J. 178
Coleridge, S.T. 85, 96
Confucius 122
Cwik, A. 177, 178

Dallett, J. 11, 177
Davidson, D. 15, 178
Dehing, J. 177
Denmark 98
Dieckmann, H. 177
Dorn, G. 169, 170, 172
Douglas, C. 9, 177
Durand, G. 177

Ebreo, L. 109
Edinger, E. 177
Elijah 28–9
Ellis, H. 84

Erikson, E. 5

Fay, C. 178
Fordham, M. 178
Forel, A. 84
Franz, M.L. von 8, 11, 177
Freud, S. 1, 12, 13, 18, 21, 23, 40, 42,
    45, 56, 58, 84, 85, 86, 92, 158
Friedman, H.S. 179
Fry, R.T. ix, 4, 177

Goethe, J.W. 33
Greene, A. 178

Hadfield, Dr J.A. 18, 143
Hall, J. 179
Hall, S. 146
Hannah, B. 5, 177
Helen 29
Henderson, J.L. 17
Hermes see Mercury
Hildegard of Bingen 18, 81, 82
Hillman, J. 177, 178
Hölderlin, J.C.F. 25
Hull, R.F.C. 177
Humbert, E. 177

Igoa, C. 179

Jaffe, A. 177
Johnson, R.A. 11, 177
Jung, C.G. 1; and active imagination
    3–19, 21–41, 143–53, 177; building
    game 23–4; contradictions 3; dreams
    and fantasies 26–41, 186–7; family
    34; inner development 1, 2, 17, 37;
    Institute 42; psychoanalytic style 13;
    and play 23–4; and religion 2; split

with Freud 1, 12, 13, 21, 40; works of 17–19
Ka 31
Kalff, D. 8, 179
Kast, V. 177
Keller, T. 3, 16, 177, 178
Kerényi, C. 156
Keyes, M.F. 178
Kingsford, A. 80
Kirsch, J. 177
Kubin, A. 62

Lao-tzu 68, 97, 137
Liverpool 39–40
Lockhart, R. 177
Lü-tsu, Master 74

McNeely, D.A. 178
McNiff, S. 178
Magus, S. 29
Mahlendorf, U. 9, 10
Maitland, E. 18, 80
Mercurius 104–5, 107–8, 168, 170
Mercury, wings of 105, 107–9, 114, 116, 119; *see also* Mercurius
Middlekoo, P. 177
Mindell, A. 177
Mitchell, R.R. 179
Morgan, C. 9
Multatuli 125
Mysterium Coniunctionis 19, 166–74

Nietzsche, F.W. 25, 34, 52, 159

O. Mr 163–5
Oppikofer, R. ix, x, 16, 178

Perera, S.B. 179
Philemon 29–31, 34
Powell, S. 178
Pragâpati x

Read, H. 179
Rilke, R.M. 11
Roberts, J. 5
Rosen, D. 177
Ryce-Menuhin, J. 179

Salome 29
Samuels, A. ix, 5, 178
Sandner, D. 177
Satapatha Brâhmana x
Schiller, J.C.F. 5, 91
Schwartz-Salant, N. 178
Septem Sermones 35, 38
Siegfried 27, 28
Signell, K. 179
Silberer, H. 67
Singer, J. 177
Stevens, A. 177
Stewart, C.T. 5
Stewart, L.H. x, 5, 6, 17, 19, 178–9
Sutton-Smith, B. 5

Tavistock Lectures 3, 18, 143–52
Tilly, M. 177

Van der Post, L. 15, 177
Van Helsingen, R.J. 175

Wagner, W.R. 173
Watkins, M. 177
Weaver, R. 177
Wehr, G. 177
Weinribb, E. 179
Whitehouse, M. 178
Whitmont, E.C. 178, 179
Wilhelm, R. 39, 76
Winnicott, D.W. 5
Withymead 177
Wolff, T. x, 16
Woodman, M. 178
Wyman, W. 178

The experience of Autumn 2001 was related to structure of psyche that was built layer by layer in objects/ills, systems, etc. Under exhaustion and illness, the whole process of sub-cons. come onto the stage. The sadistic fantasies, murderous impulses, anxiety attacks and overpowering feelings of losing control were full blown expressions of what had been suppressed. There is in my dreams to associations have been # d. orientation and the process has been "Once understood, the detrimental affective associations are neutralized."